CORNUCOPIA

Essays on *Architecture, Sculpture* and
Decorative *Arts* in Honour of
Terry Friedman (1940–2013)

CORNUCOPIA

Essays on Architecture, Sculpture and
Decorative Arts in Honour of
Terry Friedman (1940–2013)

EDITORS
James Lomax, Evelyn Silber
and Christopher Webster

Leeds Art Fund 2015

Published by the Leeds Art Fund
www.leedsartfund.org

ISBN:978 0 9547979 3 5

Text © 2015 the contributors
Illustrations © 2015 as credited in captions

FRONT COVER: James Tissot, *London Visitors*, 1874 (detail), Toledo Museum
of Art. Purchased with funds from the Libbey Endowment, Gift of
Edward, Drummond Libbey
BACK COVER: Terry Friedman at the installation of the Epstein
exhibition 1987. Photo: Evelyn Silber
TITLE PAGE: Terry Friedman in his garden, c. 2005.
Photo: Evelyn Silber

Produced in the UK by Oblong Creative Ltd,
416B Thorp Arch Estate, Wetherby LS23 7FG

Preface

Terry Friedman was one of an increasingly rare breed, a scholar curator working in a regional museum, an outstanding art historian, educator and collector. American-born and raised he spent most of his life in Britain. Between 1969 and 1993, as Keeper of Decorative Art Studies at Temple Newsam, Leeds, and later, as Principal Keeper at Leeds City Art Gallery where he was largely responsible for setting up the Henry Moore Centre for the Study of Sculpture, he made a major but largely unsung contribution to the life of the city. Both the contemporary and historic collections benefited from his acquisitions: he masterminded a decade of memorable exhibitions; at the Study Centre, by linking exhibition curatorship and research he established a unique, powerful identity for Leeds' partnership with the Henry Moore Foundation within the context of their UK-wide philanthropic activity. He fostered the talent of many young art historian and artists in his various roles as teacher, collector and curator. One of the finest art historians of his generation and the leading authority on eighteenth century ecclesiastical architecture, he was a prolific writer and the author of two classics — *James Gibbs* (Yale 1984) and the magisterial *The Eighteenth Century Church in Britain* (Yale 2011) for which he won the Berger Prize in 2012.

The Leeds Art Fund is therefore delighted to publish this collection of essays written by a number of his friends and colleagues and dedicated to his memory. They represent Terry's wide range of interests and their very diversity is a testimony to his unique personality and his legacy both to Leeds and to the world of scholarship. Terry was always happy to support the Leeds Art Fund and led many of our visits and events. This book is a small gesture of thanks.

James Lomax
Chairman, Leeds Art Fund

The Leeds Art Fund is grateful for financial assistance towards this publication from:

The Paul Mellon Centre for the Study of British Art
The Henry Moore Foundation
The Leeds Philosophical and Literary Society
Tomasso Brothers Fine Art
Jacob Simon

and the following subscribers:

Ann and Neill Alexander
Martin Arnold
Olav Arnold
Ronnie Duncan
Jim Fox
Andy Goldsworthy
John and Anne Harris
Mary Herbert
Peter Hirschman
Jane Ingham
Lisa Le Feuvre
James Lomax
Karen and David Lynch
Elizabeth Minkin
Simon and Jane Mitchell

Sarah Nichols
Elizabeth Osborne
Margaret Pearson
Jacki Proctor
Margaret Pullan
Benedict Read
Jeffrey and Ruth Sherwin
Celia Tempest
John Thorp
Terry Thorp
Keith Wark
Christopher Webster
Brian Welch
Kathleen Wenban
Stephen Wood

The editors would like to thank all those who have helped in the preparation of this book particularly Marjorie Trusted, Philippa Glanville and Geoffrey Brandwood who generously acted as readers; the Friedman family and colleagues and friends who have shared their memories; the staff of the Henry Moore Institute particularly Jon Wood and Jackie Howson; Tony Mills at the Leeds Art Fund; Ruth Baumberg who kindly acted as Picture Editor for a number of chapters; and Derek Brown and Jackie Maidment at Oblong.

The Henry Moore Foundation

TOMASSO BROTHERS
FINE ART

Contents

Contributors

Rosamond Allwood

Studied Fine Art at Leeds University, with three years at Temple Newsam House, where Terry was her tutor in the history of decorative art and encouraged her interest in the late nineteenth century at a time when it was not highly regarded. From Leeds she won a two-year post-graduate studentship to the V & A, moving to Wolverhampton Art Gallery, and then the Geffrye Museum, where she was Deputy Director. From 1987 she worked freelance, organising exhibitions including *Arts & Crafts to Avant-Garde* at the Royal Festival Hall, and *Foundations for the Future*, on the treasures of Cambridge University, at Christie's. She is currently Cultural Services Manager for North Hertfordshire District Council, where she is overseeing a major new museum, opening in Hitchin in 2015. She has published widely, particularly on nineteenth-century furniture, and the Camden Town artist William Ratcliffe.

Dr Penelope Curtis

Studied History, and then History of Art, mainly in Paris, where she worked in the archives of the Musée Bourdelle, the Musée Rodin and the nascent Musée d'Orsay. She worked in Leeds for nearly seventeen years, succeeding Terry Friedman as Head of the Henry Moore Centre for Sculpture Studies which she later amalgamated into the Henry Moore Institute, and which she curated for ten years from 1999. In 2010 she was appointed Director of Tate Britain.

Katharine Eustace

Has degrees in Medieval History from the University of St Andrews and the History of Art from the Courtauld Institute of Art, and is a Fellow of the Society of Antiquaries of London. After training at the Victoria and Albert Museum, she worked at Bristol City Museum and Art Gallery, the Ashmolean Museum of Art and Archaeology, Oxford, and the National Portrait Gallery, London, where she was Curator of Twentieth Century Collections from 2001 to 2004. She was the founder-curator of the Mead Gallery at the University of Warwick from 1982 to 1992. She has just stepped down after ten years as Editor of the *Sculpture Journal*, published by the Public Monuments and Sculpture Association and Liverpool University Press.

Embarking, as a fledgling fine art curator at the Bristol City Museum and Art Gallery in 1980, on an exhibition devoted to the sculptor Michael Rysbrack (1694–1770), she was advised to seek the advice of Dr Terry Friedman, already a legend: his advice was invaluable, his generosity proverbial. Subsequently, Terry and she climbed ladders together, and peered into dim sacristies in pursuit of his architectural interests. She was proud to see him receive the Berger Prize for British Art History in 2012, of which she had been a juror, for his great work *The Eighteenth Century Church in Britain* (Yale, 2011), just a few months before he died. She owes him much in her career in sculpture studies. At a personal level the debt is, if possible, even greater, for Terry introduced her to her husband, James Hamilton, and he remained a mentor and a friend.

Dr Patrick Eyres

Is editor-publisher of the *New Arcadian Journal*, which engages with the cultural politics of landscape gardens and specializes in Georgian Britain. Thirty two editions have been published since 1981. He has also published in numerous books and other journals. He was editor of *Wentworth Castle and Georgian Political Gardening* (2012), co-editor of *Sculpture and The Garden* (2006) and co-editor with James Lomax of *Diplomats, Goldsmiths and Baroque Court Culture* (2014). He is a member of the boards of the Wentworth Castle Heritage Trust, the Little Sparta Trust, the Garden History Society and the Leeds Arts Fund.

Martha Friedman

Was born in 1975 in Detroit, Michigan and lives and works in Brooklyn. She holds a BFA from the School of the Art Institute of Chicago (1998) and an MFA from Yale University School of Art (2003). Solo exhibitions include the Museum of Contemporary Art, Detroit, MI (2010); DeCordova Museum and Sculpture Park, Lincoln, MA (2010); Shane Campbell Gallery, Chicago (2010); Wallspace, New York (2007, 2009, 2012).

Andy Goldsworthy

Was born in 1956 in Cheshire, England; he grew up on the Harrogate side of Leeds, West Yorkshire, and has lived and worked in Dumfriesshire, Scotland since the mid-1980s. He studied fine art at Bradford College of Art (1974–75) and at Preston Polytechnic (now the University of Central Lancashire; 1975–78). He was A. D. White Professor-at-Large at Cornell University in Ithaca, New York (2000–2008). Goldsworthy explores the tension of working outdoors, where he finds his materials, making temporal works rooted in the particular conditions or material encountered. From the outset he had a profound feeling for the character and natural cycles of nature and for the sculptural potential of natural materials such as wood, leaves, ice and stone. 'For me, looking, touching, material, place and form are all inseparable from the resulting work.' His work is now widely known internationally; he has produced work in environments as diverse as the Arctic, the rainforest of Queensland, Australia, the cities of Rio or New York, the terrains of New Mexico in the US, Haute-Provence in France and central Spain, or the fells of Cumbria and Dumfriesshire. His work has been exhibited in contexts as varied as the Egyptian galleries of the British Museum, the early Scottish collections at the National Museum of Scotland, the Yorkshire Sculpture Park and the Palacio di Cristal in Madrid.

Terry co-curated Goldsworthy's first major one-man show and first publication, *Rain sun snow hail mist calm* in 1985, for Leeds City Art Gallery and Sunderland's Northern Centre for Contemporary Art. This exhibition toured, bringing Andy's work to a wider audience and playing a significant part in establishing his national reputation. In 1990 Terry organised a large retrospective *Hand to Earth: Andy Goldsworthy Sculpture, 1976–1990* and subsequently contributed an introduction to *Wood* (1996) and a chronology for *Earth* (2000). Leeds holds a significant collection of his work and pieces Terry purchased for his own collection he subsequently presented to public collections in Glasgow (Hunterian Art Gallery) and Middlesborough

Melanie Hall

Is Associate Professor and Director of Museum Studies in the Department of the History of Art and Architecture, at Boston University. She studied the History of Fine and Decorative Arts at Leeds University, taught in conjunction with Temple Newsam House. She was the first Research Assistant at the Henry Moore Centre for the Study of Sculpture where, under Terry's guidance, she compiled an archive of material related to public sculpture in Leeds. This resulted in her guide to *Leeds Statues* (Leeds Civic Trust, 1995). Terry fired her interest in architectural history and she subsequently worked for English Heritage on the Listed Buildings Re-survey. Her recent publications include the edited volume, *Towards World Heritage: International Origins of the Preservation Movement 1870–1930* (2011). Her current research focuses on the origins and early years of the National Trust.

James Hamilton

Began his career as an art curator at Portsmouth City Museums (1972–74) and Wakefield City Art Gallery (1974–76). He was Keeper of the Mappin Art Gallery, Sheffield (1976–84), and Director of the Yorkshire Contemporary Art Group, Leeds (1984–89), where he worked with Antony Gormley on the *Brickman* project. Subsequently he was University Curator at the University of Birmingham (1992–2013), and Senior Research Fellow in History of Art. He was the Alistair Horne Fellow at St Antony's College, Oxford, 1998–99.

He is the author of *Turner – A Life* (1997), *Faraday – The Life* (2002), *London Lights: The Minds that Moved the City that Shook the World 1805–51* (2007) and *A Strange Business: Making Art and Money in Nineteenth Century Britain* (2014). He has curated exhibitions including *Turner and the Scientists* at the Tate Gallery (1998), *Turner's Britain* (Gas Hall, Birmingham, 2003–04), *Turner and Italy* (Ferrara, Edinburgh and Budapest, 2008–09), and *Making Painting: Helen Frankenthaler and J. M. W. Turner* (Turner Contemporary, Margate, 2014). His other books include the biographies *Arthur Rackham* (1990) and *William Heath Robinson* (1992), *Wood Engraving and the Woodcut in Britain c. 1890–1990* (1994), *The Sculpture of Austin Wright* (1994) *Hughie O'Donoghue – Painting, Memory, Myth* (2003) and *Volcano: Nature and Culture* (2012).

Terry visited James in Sheffield in the early 1980s and became a friend as well as colleague. He encouraged James's unorthodox leap from relatively secure local authority curatorship to the more entrepreneurial, high risk role of leading a con-temporary art organisation in Leeds, a move that culminated in the *Brickman* project and proved life-changing. Terry was an unfailing source of advice, friendship and inspiration.

Richard Hewlings

Is an Historian at English Heritage, and has edited the *Georgian Group Journal* (from 1995 to 2007) and *English Heritage Historical Review* (from 2004). He first met Terry Friedman when re-surveying the list of Historic Buildings for Huddersfield in 1974–76, and, after the usual preliminary verbal spat, grew to like him very much. He edited many of Terry's meticulous church articles for the *Georgian Group Journal*, of which he was very appreciative. He misses the many conversations and telephone calls from Wensley Drive which conveyed Terry's imaginative and thoughtful ideas about eighteenth-century Britain.

Charles Hind

Is the Chief Curator and H. J. Heinz Curator of Drawings at the Royal Institute of British Architects, where he has been since 1996. Previously he has worked at the British Library, Sotheby's and the publisher Macmillan. Charles is an architectural historian with a particular interest in the work of Andrea Palladio and Anglo-Palladianism. He has published widely on architecture and architectural history as well as curating various exhibitions for the RIBA since 1998, most notably *Palladio and his Legacy: a Transatlantic Journey*, which travelled in the United States 2010–11. Charles is a Fellow of the Society of Antiquaries of London. He met Terry Friedman through Terry's great friend, Derek Linstrum, in about 2003 and shared enthusiasms led to a lasting friendship. Terry's library was bequeathed to the RIBA's Drawings & Archives Collections to join Derek's as a lasting memorial to two remarkable architectural historians.

Professor Derek Linstrum

Was an architect, conservationist, architectural historian, and lecturer; in all these fields he had an international reputation. As Director of the post-graduate Architectural Conservation course at York he travelled the world speaking at conferences and acting as a consultant, although he was always happy to return to his home in Leeds, the house where he lived for most of his life. His real passion was nineteenth-century architecture and he was an early champion of the Victorian period. His books included: *Sir Jeffrey Wyatville* (1972), *West Yorkshire Architects and Architecture* (1978) and *Cuthbert Brodrick* (1999). Terry must have sought him out soon after arriving in Leeds and thereafter they enjoyed a number of collaborative projects and an unshakable friendship. Derek died in 2009.

James Lomax

Trained as a curator under the benign eye of Terry Friedman at Temple Newsam in the late 1970s. It was as a result of one of Terry's frequent brainstorming sessions that the idea of his first major exhibition was born, *John Singer Sargent and the Edwardian Age*, on which he collaborated with Richard Ormond 1979–80 and which showed at Lotherton Hall, the National Portrait Gallery, London, and in Terry's home town at the Detroit Institute of Arts. From 1980 to 1985 he worked at Manchester City Art Galleries, responsible for Heaton Hall and the silver and furniture collections, but returned to become Keeper of Temple Newsam in 1985. He continued the great tradition of publishing catalogues of the permanent collection with his *British Silver at Temple Newsam and Lotherton Hall* (1992). He has curated numerous exhibitions, lectured and written extensively on the decorative arts including the catalogue *Country House Silver from Dunham Massey* with James Rothwell (2006). He was one of the small team who saw the extraordinary expansion of the Temple Newsam collections over some twenty-five years. He is President of the Silver Society, Chairman of the Leeds Art Fund, past Hon Editor of the Furniture History Society, Hon Curator of the Chippendale Society and President of Leeds NADFAS.

George Meyrick

Studied at St Martin's School of Art, Brighton Polytechnic and Chelsea School of Art in the 1970s and was a part-time lecturer in the sculpture department at Chelsea until becoming a full-time teacher of art and photography in 1990. He has exhibited widely in the UK and Europe and in addition to the Henry Moore

Institute his work is held in a number of public collections including the British Council and Arts Council England. He lives in Cornwall and his most recent solo show was at The Exchange in Penzance in 2012.

Peter Randall-Page

Studied sculpture at Bath Academy of Art from 1973–77. He has undertaken numerous large-scale commissions and exhibited widely and his work is held in public and private collections. A selection of his public sculptures can be found in many urban and rural locations throughout the UK. His practice has always been informed and inspired by the study of natural phenomena and its subjective impact on our emotions. In recent years his work has become increasingly concerned with the underlying principles determining growth and the forms it produces. In his words 'geometry is the theme on which nature plays her infinite variations, and can be seen as a kind of pattern book on which the most complex and sophisticated structures are based.'

Ryan Riddington

Grew up in various locations in England and West Germany due to his army upbringing. A keen drawer he later became fascinated with using found objects, leading to an undergraduate degree in Fine Art Sculpture at Loughborough University School of Art and Design. After teaching English and exhibiting with the British Council in St Petersburg he moved to Leeds in 2002 and worked as an invigilator at the Henry Moore Institute. This exposed him to many varying approaches to sculpture and its reception. In 2008 he attended Slade School of Art, London taking an MFA in Sculpture. He has exhibited at the Henry Moore Institute, Leeds Art Gallery, Clifford Chance, Charlie Smith, Fred and Mori + Stein and his work has featured in Granta, Chroma and SuperMassiveBlackHole. He lives in London.

Daru Rooke

Studied History of the Fine and Decorative Arts at Leeds University. Under Terry Friedman's tutorship he discovered the merits of syncopated columns, the sublime creativity of James Gibbs and the scientific marvels of ice cream — soda combinations at the Lyons Corner House in London.

After postgraduate study at Manchester University, Daru returned to Leeds to become Research Assistant at the recently established Henry Moore Centre for the Study of Sculpture. Working directly with Terry Friedman the post opened up new vistas of modernity including direct interactions with sculptors such as Eduardo Paolozzi and Andy Goldsworthy and mammoth tasks such as the transcription of the celebrated Hamo Thorneycroft archive. He also discovered that when Terry said 'No, no, no' in a particular tone of voice, projects usually had to be re-done very smartly.

Subsequent curatorial posts have included the care of an Edwardian country house, a Cistercian abbey, a Regency textile mill and latterly a Victorian industrialist's fantasy mansion in Keighley. Other activities have included historical advisor roles to National Theatre productions and Hollywood films and TV presentation. These occasional forays into consultancy and broadcasting have kept alive Terry's own inspiring spirit of delight in the new and respect for the old.

Evelyn Silber

Is an Honorary Professorial Research Fellow in the History of Art at the University of Glasgow. She was curator and Assistant Director of Birmingham Museums and Art Gallery (1979-95), Director of Leeds Museums and Galleries (1995–2001) and Director of the Hunterian, University of Glasgow (2001–2006). She is the author of *The Sculpture of Epstein* (Phaidon, 1986) and of *Gaudier-Brzeska. Life and Art* (Thames & Hudson, 1996). In 1986–87 she co-curated the exhibition *Jacob Epstein. Sculpture and Drawings* for Leeds Art Gallery and the Whitechapel Art Gallery, London and, in 1987, was curatorial adviser on *Rebel Angel*, a film on Epstein for Central Television's 'Contrasts', made partly in Leeds Art Gallery and nationally networked during the exhibition.

Terry and Evelyn met during the latter stages of the research for her book on Epstein. He seized the opportunity to suggest an exhibition of Jacob Epstein's work and they jointly curated the exhibition and catalogue. One of the most ambitious sculpture shows held in Leeds, it was the first major exhibition of Epstein's work since the Memorial show in Edinburgh in 1960. Terry secured the support of the Henry Moore Foundation and negotiated with the Director, Nick Serota, a London showing at the Whitechapel Art Gallery. The collaboration led to a lifelong friendship and important acquisitions of Epstein material for the collection. During Evelyn's time as Director of Leeds Museums and Galleries Terry, who had by then left the Art Gallery to work on his architectural *magnum opus*, remained a supportive, stimulating and generous friend.

Karin Walton

Has been a Curator in the Applied Art section of Bristol Museum and Art Gallery for over forty years. She has taken a particular interest in Bristol's two period house museums, the Elizabethan Red Lodge and the Georgian House, and has lectured and written widely, particularly on ceramics and textiles.

From 1971 to 1973 she was one of the first postgraduate students at Temple Newsam House, Leeds, researching for her M.Phil. on eighteenth-century upholstery. Although Terry was not officially her supervisor, he encouraged and took a close interest in her work, frequently supplying references from his own architecture studies which she might not otherwise have come across and chasing off any researcher he suspected of seeking to plunder her work before it was completed. Terry's dry but incisive humour came to the fore when he was in relaxed mood and she remembers with especial fondness the after-work suppers at Whitelocks.

Dr Christopher Webster

Was taught by Terry on the Temple Newsam course. Although always interested in architecture, it was Terry who gave him his love of the Georgian period and thereafter they remained firm friends, often meeting to discuss the other's current research. After Leeds, most of his career was spent at Staffordshire University. He has published widely on late-Georgian architecture including *R.D Chantrell and the Architecture of a Lost Generation* (2010) and he edited *Building a Great Victorian City: Leeds Architects and Architecture, 1790–1914* (2011) and *Episodes in the Gothic Revival* (2011); the last two included essays by Terry. Currently he is working on the English parish church, 1790–1840, planning to produce for a book to follow on from where Terry's most recent one finished.

Anthony Wells-Cole

Was briefly Curator of the Print Room at Leeds City Art Gallery before becoming Assistant Keeper at Temple Newsam. Here, with other curators, he helped Terry teach the Decorative Arts on the course run jointly with the Fine Art Department of Leeds University from 1969 onwards. When he assumed responsibility for restoring the interiors and fabric of Temple Newsam from 1983, devising and contributing to a series of Country House Studies exhibitions to help inform the process, Terry kept feeding relevant information even though he had by then moved to the City Art Gallery. While writing his spare-time book, *Art and Decoration in Elizabethan and Jacobean England 1558–1625* (Yale University Press, 1997), Terry's knowledge of architectural pattern books — albeit of a later period — meant that he maintained a sympathetic interest in the work. The restoration of Temple Newsam occupied him for twenty-five years whilst Principal Keeper of Leeds City Art Galleries and Senior Curator of Temple Newsam, and he wrote up his discoveries made during the process in numerous articles in the *Leeds Arts Calendar*, to which he had already contributed on a range of subjects and subsequently edited.

He has regularly been a specialist advisor to the committees considering Allocations in Lieu and the Export of Works of Art and Objects of Cultural Interest. He has also been for many years a member of the Arts Panel of the National Trust. In retirement he is an independent scholar, lecturing widely in Europe, Scandinavia and North America. He is writing a book on two lost masterpieces, the windows installed at Lambeth by William Laud when Archbishop of Canterbury, and the Japanese lacquer bedrail commissioned by Princess Amalia van Solms of the Netherlands in the 1630s.

Adam White

Worked under Terry Friedman as Research Assistant at the Henry Moore Centre for the Study of Sculpture at Leeds City Art Gallery from 1982–87. He recalls this as an exciting, if not always easy start to his career. Since 1994 he has worked as Curator of Lotherton Hall, Leeds Museums and Galleries.

Dr Jon Wood

Is Research Curator at the Henry Moore Institute in Leeds where he coordinates the academic research programme and curates exhibitions. He specialises in twentieth-century and contemporary sculpture and has a particular research interest in the artist's studio. His studio writings have been recently reprinted in *The Studio Reader* (University of Chicago Press, 2010), *The Fall of the Studio* (Valiz, 2010) and *The Studio* (MIT/Whitechapel, 2012). He is the HMI editor of the 'Subject/Object' series and one of the editors of *Sculpture in Twentieth-Century Britain* (2003) and the new co-editor of the *Sculpture Journal*. Recent publications include: *Modern Sculpture Reader* (with Alex Potts and David Hulks) (HMI 2007, and Getty 2012), *1913: The Shape of Time* (2012), *United Enemies: The Problem of Sculpture in Britain in the 1960s and 1970s* (2011), a new edition of Ede's *Savage Messiah* (with Barassi and Silber) (2011) and *Articulate Objects: Voice, Sculpture, and Performance* (with Aura Satz) (2009).

Terry Friedman (1940–2013) — Appreciations

Evelyn Silber

Born in Detroit, Michigan, the second of three academically high achieving brothers, Terry early developed an interest in art influenced by his home surroundings; his parents ran a paint manufacturing company and, latterly, an interiors and antiques business specialising in eighteenth-century English furniture. After attending Cass Technical High School, Detroit, and the University of Michigan he moved to London in 1964 for postgraduate study at the Courtauld Institute of Art where his doctorate on James Gibbs (1971), best known as the architect of St Martin-in-the-Fields, London, set the direction of his subsequent studies in eighteenth-century architecture.

In 1969 he moved to Leeds, his home for the rest of his life, to run the BA programme in the History of Decorative Arts and Museum Studies. This recently established course was an enlightened and, at that time, unique partnership

1. Terry at Culzean, 2002 (photo: Evelyn Silber).

between university and museum, initiated by Professor Quentin Bell of Leeds University, and the Director of the Art Galleries, Robert Rowe, himself an expert on silver. Based at Temple Newsam House, harnessing the expertise of curators, including Christopher Gilbert, Peter Walton, Anthony Wells Cole, James Lomax and Adam White, and exploiting the exceptional wealth of its collections, the course nurtured a number of able students who went on to study for higher degrees and to heritage, curatorial and academic careers. Several are represented in this publication (Daru Rooke, Karin Walton, Melanie Hall, Rosamond Allwood and Christopher Webster).

During these years Terry's enthusiasm and desire to bring out the best in his students resulted in some excellently researched dissertations, many of them based on the Leeds collections. He fostered and undertook considerable new work on the Gascoignes of Parlington and Lotherton; he edited the *Leeds Arts Calendar* for many years and made some remarkable acquisitions of historic sculpture, with works by Joseph Gott, Peter Turnerelli, Richard James Wyatt, Samuel Joseph and Joseph Nollekens. Under the indulgent and benign directorship of Robert Rowe Terry was able to spread his wings: his exhibitions were curated with flair and style within the practical restraints of the times: *Joseph Gott* (1972), *Benjamin Henry Latrobe* (1976) and *John Cheere, the Man at Hyde Park Corner* (with Timothy Clifford, 1974) were real trail blazers.

In 1982 the Henry Moore Sculpture Galleries extension to Leeds City Art Gallery was completed. This development necessitated the redecoration and re-display of the entire Art Gallery and marked the beginning of the Henry Moore Centre for the Study of Sculpture (which in 1993 became the Henry Moore Institute). Terry moved to the Art Gallery to set this up, the remit of the undergraduate course being broadened as the History of Fine and Decorative Arts. He rapidly made his mark, in part through his commitment to contemporary design; the blanket-covered Magistretti sofas added both comfort and a distinctive style to the art galleries; he played a strong supporting role in the establishment of the Craft and Design Gallery beneath the Art Gallery as a place to see and buy work by leading craftspeople. He set a standard of excellence in the research and supporting programme that accompanied the inaugural gallery exhibition, *Henry Moore's Early Carvings 1920–1940*. The development of archival and sculpture collections to embrace the processes of making sculpture as well as the finished product became an important element in the collecting and exhibition policy. Terry's comprehension of sculpture as including hitherto overlooked areas, such as casts, garden and architectural sculpture, coins and medals, sketches, archival material, studio photographs and personalia, was ahead of its time and set the tone for the research, symposia, exhibitions and artist's projects embracing the historic and contemporary, subsequently pursued by the Institute with the support of the Henry Moore Foundation and the Leeds Art Collections Fund. Gifts and bequests of sculptors' papers and studio archives began to be offered to Leeds, notably the papers of the leading Victorian sculptor, Sir Hamo Thornycroft.

In 1984 he became Principal Keeper at Leeds City Art Gallery. In this new role he and his colleagues brought about a decade of important and memorably beautiful exhibitions accompanied by well researched, handsomely designed and illustrated catalogues. The Foundation's financial support, partnered for a period by the Arts

2. Terry in action on a walking tour during the Epstein exhibition, 1987 (photo: Evelyn Silber).

Council's 'Glory of the Garden' funding, gave the exhibition programme greater impetus.

Under the curatorship of Terry, Miranda Strickland-Constable, Alex Robertson and, later, Corinne Miller and Nigel Walsh, Leeds City Art Gallery ran an exhibition programme of national calibre. Young curators found Terry a facilitator who encouraged their projects as keenly as he pursued his own. The re-assessment of British Surrealism in the 1930s, brought about by the 1986 exhibition, was something of a landmark. George Meyrick (1884), Andy Goldsworthy (1985 and 1990) and Peter Randall-Page (1992) are sculptors for whom Terry's early championship of their work through exhibitions also resulted in valuable additions to the collection and archive. The catalogue of the second Goldsworthy show, *Hand to Earth* (1990) which also toured, has been several times reprinted; Terry also contributed, at the artist's invitation, to *Wood* (1996) and *Time* (2000).

Jacob Epstein, long an undervalued figure in twentieth-century sculpture, received a major exhibition which went on from Leeds to the Whitechapel Art Gallery in 1987. Several remarkable acquisitions were collateral benefits of the show; the great Indian-inspired carving, *Maternity* (1910) was brought back from the USA; a hitherto unknown album of watercolours for *Rima*, the W. H. Hudson memorial in Hyde Park, 1924–25, led to an exhibition and a substantial study by Terry; more

EVELYN SILBER   3

archival gifts and acquisitions followed. One of his most ambitious shows, *A Bottle of Notes and Some Voyages*, brought the work of the major American sculptor, Claes Oldenburg and his wife and collaborator, Coosje van Bruggen, unseen in Britain since a Tate exhibition in 1970, to the attention of British audiences (1988). The exhibition of the hugely influential author and critic, *Herbert Read* (1993), was a pioneering show examining aspects of twentieth-century art through the critical discourse it engendered. His championship of the nineteenth-century Leeds sculptor, Joseph Gott, several of whose works he identified and purchased for very modest sums, resulted in important re-appraisals of his work (1972 and 2010).

In 1993 Terry took early retirement from Leeds, facilitated in part by his family's support, to dedicate himself to the massive research project on which he had already been working for several years in his spare time — a study of the architecture of eighteenth-century British churches, a huge but somewhat neglected field demanding exhaustive researches in vestries, archives and county record offices, the excavation of plans and prints from rarely visited recesses, to say nothing of trawling contemporary sources for evidence about liturgical practice, modes of musical performance and literary and social references. Projects of this scope are more usually undertaken these days by teams of university-based researchers supported by Research Council grants but Terry took this on as an independent, self-funded scholar. Tales are often told of Nikolaus Pevsner's peregrinations in the course of his epic *Buildings of England* series. Terry's were no less assiduous and perhaps more idiosyncratic. Meticulously prepared for each field trip with contacts established and appointments made, a package of neatly pencil-written file cards, references, photocopies, photos and plans, camera and film at the ready, he would establish himself at a local b&b. He would then ensconce himself in the regional record office or archive, interspersing these labours with forays to important local churches and sites. For these he would negotiate the hire of a car and driver (a Motown native he abandoned any effort to learn to drive after an unfortunate early encounter with a tree). Thus, he and his gear were chauffeured from one rural church and vicarage appointment to another, enabling him for focus on the scenery and on visits ahead. No doubt he gladdened (and occasionally worried) many a cleric and archivist with his intense interest in and appreciation of the material in their care and the information and advice he would impart.

A stream of articles and two more substantial works, *Church Architecture in Leeds 1700–99* (Thoresby Society, 1996) and *The Georgian Parish Church: 'Monuments to Posterity'* (2004) preceded his authoritative study, *The Eighteenth-Century Church in Britain* (Yale, 2011), the culmination of twenty-five years' work, for which he was awarded the Berger Prize for British Art History in 2012.

The diagnosis of a brain tumour and consequent surgery in 2004 could have brought to a premature end both his career as a scholar and his 'grand projet' which had not yet reached draft stage. Fortunately, the tumour was benign and he survived surgery with his mental faculties unimpaired, though in the long term his health was affected. It was entirely characteristic of his generosity and on-going commitment to helping the Gallery and his former colleagues that, while still convalescing in hospital, he assisted Corinne Miller with the preparations for *Drawing from the Past; William Weddell and the Transformation of Newby Hall* (2004–05), an exhibition of architectural drawings the importance of which he himself had first

3. Terry's living room
(photo: Evelyn Silber).

recognised years before and whose study he encouraged through the doctoral research of his student, Jill Lowe.

He was able to bring his great study to completion (all 790 pages plus CD appendices!) in 2011, thanks in no small measure to the support of the Paul Mellon Centre and Yale University Press. The scholarly recognition evident in the book's shortlisting for the Hitchcock Medallion of the Society of Architectural Historians of Great Britain and award of the Berger Prize in 2012 gave him the greatest pleasure. Though his health was in decline and he could no longer manage much travel, he was pressing forward with a new book on the architectural drawings for St Martin-in-the-Fields and had just received Yale's acceptance of his book proposal at the time of his death.

He made numerous outstanding acquisitions for the Leeds collections as well as collecting eclectically in a private capacity to create a quirky personal and often changing environment in his spacious apartment in Chapel Allerton. To visit him was to experience what must have been one of the richest and most unusual interiors in the city, an aesthetic feast for the privileged visitor.

His tastes were catholic but discriminating, embracing contemporary art and design as well as furniture, architectural drawings, sculpture, Asian and Oceanic textiles and artefacts, and — on a lighter note — entertaining constructions and old toys. His encyclopaedic knowledge and keen eye led him to unrecognised treasures and the work of promising young artists. Recognising a Robert Adam drawing of the Nostell estate's Huntwick Lodge, wrongly attributed by a dealer, he bought it and at once presented it to Nostell Priory ('Rare work of art restored to Yorkshire stately home', *Yorkshire Post*, 16.5.2005)

From 2004 onwards he made a number of gifts to public collections — to Leeds, Glasgow, and Middlesbrough Institute of Contemporary Art, where he was keen to support the young collection and the ambition of its architecture and programming, and the RIBA drawings collection to which he and his good friend, the late Professor Derek Linstrum (see Chapter 9), jointly bequeathed their architectural books as the Linstrum and Friedman Library.

Terry was a paradoxical personality in many ways — single-minded in achieving his goals, provocatively dogmatic in some of his opinions, yet creative, outgoing and inspirational in working with colleagues and students. A steadfast, generous friend to a few, he did not suffer fools gladly and was quick to take offence. He could be appallingly rude. Uncomfortable with the show-off bonhomie and networking of professional and academic conferences, he stayed away, which contributed to a certain academic isolation and less recognition than his scholarship merited.

Happily solitary, he took pleasure in music, American TV and the companionship of a small circle of close friends and colleagues. Over a meal at a favourite local Italian or Thai restaurant, he would delight companions with his wicked and sometimes barbed humour, often at the expense of politicians — American and British. He was immensely supportive and generous to young artists and scholars whose confidence grew through his confidence in them. He would buy the work of young artists and made a point of attending their shows. He took especial pride in the developing sculpture career of his niece Martha who had spent a year in Leeds, latterly working as an assistant to Andy Goldsworthy. The splendid collection and exhibition catalogues he masterminded were invariably sold at or even below cost price to ensure they were within the reach of the student pocket. Art had been his raison d'être and he delighted in sharing the joy and the knowledge.

T. F. and the letter to Le Corbusier

Art nouveau, specifically the work of Hector Guimard, was an early enthusiasm and Terry considered his work as a possible PhD subject. Visiting Paris in 1960 he noted a similarity between a metal and glass canopy over the entrance of Guimard's Place Dauphine metro station and an element of Le Corbusier's Ronchamp Chapel. He had the chutzpah to write to Le Corbusier and ask him whether he had in fact looked at Guimard's work. He received a courteous reply in which Corbu denied Guimard as a source, explaining he was in strong reaction against him, but was happy to defend that kind of work because the rest of mainstream architecture was so extremely academic. (This letter, recently returned by a serendipitous route to the Friedman family, is transcribed, fig. 4.)

My thanks to James Lomax, Corinne Miller and others who have contributed to this Appreciation.

Paris 16th.December 1960.

Mr.Jerry (for Terry) FRIEDMAN
25,Rodborough Road,
Golders Green,
LONDON

Dear Sir,

        I have your letter of 12th.December.1960. I never knew Guimard. I felt a quite natural reaction against his architectural mannerisms but I defended very forcibly his kind of genius, for architecture was academic to such a degree (le Grand Palais, la Gare d/Orsay, le Petit Palais) that I maintained that Guimard's Metro Station entrances were among the few good works to choose from and worth keeping.

        I must have written to that effect quite a few times and I must admit that I have discovered that some of my Press articles did a little good, for nowadays they are piously preserving the few remnants left in Paris.

        At that period I was wedded to reinforced concrete - the concrete cast, at that date, between deal boards - as a result reinforced concrete, by its very nature, eliminated from my architecture the sensitive curves of the 'Modern Style'. That is all I can usefully say.

        I have youthful recollections of Mackintosh, who you mention, and Gaudi, whom I discovered in Barcelona and whose work I have praised - to the great astonishment of the young fans of 'Father Corb.' As for Victor Horta, he has foresaken with age all the vitality of his youth.

        With best wishes..

        signed.. LE CORBUSIER

35,Rue de Sevres. Paris 6
Telephone LITTRE 99-62

4. Terry's transcript of le Corbusier's letter, 16. 12. 60 (courtesy of Richard Friedman).

Martha Friedman

5.   Installation of the exhibition, *Caught*, Wallspace Gallery, New York, September 7 – October 20, 2012. The pieces are:
Mechanical Disadvantage I, 2012, steel, concrete, silicone rubber, pigment, 118.5 × 60 × 60 in
Mechanical Disadvantage II, 2012, steel, concrete, 121 × 60 × 60 in
Mechanical Disadvantage III, 2012, steel, concrete, silicone rubber, pigment, 121 × 105 × 60 in
Hairball, 2012, synthetic hair, wood, plastic, paint, 63 × 34 × 34 in

The following is taken from a recent message from Terry's niece, Martha Friedman, who has also contributed this letter, so characteristic of his meticulous approach to exhibition planning and the relation between sculpture and space.

'... I am also working hard on some very large steel and rubber weavings in my studio that I deeply wish I could share with Terry. I think he and I would have a great conversation about textiles, the history/semiotics of British men's suiting cloth, monumentality, tactility, ... and such ... I would have learned so much. I think I may have started this body of work in part because of his collection of textiles.

The image shows the installation of my exhibition which was titled *Caught* and it took place at Wallspace Gallery, New York, in the Fall of 2012. The pieces are called *Mechanical Disadvantage I*, *Mechanical Disadvantage II*, *Mechanical Disadvantage III* and *Hairball*.'

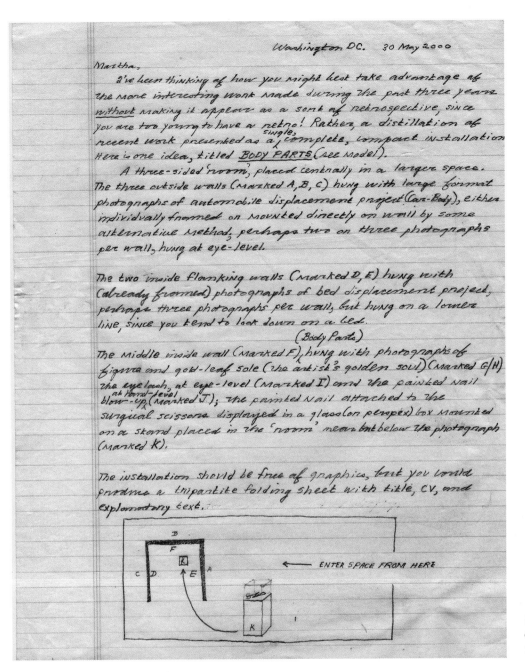

Washington DC.   30 May 2000

Martha,

I've been thinking of how you might best take advantage of the more interesting work made during the past three years without making it appear as a sort of retrospective, since you are too young to have a retro! Rather, a distillation of recent work presented as a single, complete, compact installation. Here is one idea, titled BODY PARTS (see model).

A three-sided 'room', placed centrally in a larger space. The three outside walls (marked A, B, C) hung with large format photographs of automobile displacement project (Car-Body), either individually framed or mounted directly on wall by some alternative method; perhaps two or three photographs per wall, hung at eye-level.

The two inside flanking walls (marked D, E) hung with (already framed) photographs of bed displacement project, perhaps three photographs per wall, but hung on a lower line, since you tend to look down on a bed.

(Body Parts)

The middle inside wall (marked F), hung with photographs of figure and gold-leaf sole (the artist's golden soul) (marked G/H) the eyelash, at eye-level (marked I) and the painted nail blow-up at hand-level (marked J); the painted nail attached to the surgical scissors displayed in a glass (or perspex) box mounted on a stand placed in the 'room' near but below the photograph (marked K).

The installation should be free of graphics, but you could produce a tripartite folding sheet with title, CV, and explanatory text.

ENTER SPACE FROM HERE

6. Terry to Martha with exhibition plan, 30 May 2000.

'...I never made that little exhibition that Terry so generously suggested/curated in that letter. The letter included a small folded and stapled model made out of index cards that I keep on my desk at home and I often have thought about it so I am sure it has influenced me countless times.'

MARTHA FRIEDMAN   9

Andy Goldsworthy

Figs 7, 8, 9.   Andy Goldsworthy, *Three snowballs. For Terry Friedman*, 13 February, 17 and 19 March 2013.

'The three snowballs were made around the time of Terry's death. These particular snowballs are reminiscent of those made during in my early years in Yorkshire — the black mud-covered snowball on a frozen white pond, the white snowball in a warm, snowless wood are works that Terry loved. Snowballs, for me, have always addressed the idea of loss. Indeed this new group was provoked by the tree upon which they were made being partly cut up and removed for fire wood. I had made many works on and about the tree since it fell in 2007. Despite the removal of the so many limbs I have continued to work with the tree. I often think of Terry when I am at the tree.'

George Meyrick

'I first met Terry in 1982, at the opening of a group show at the St Paul's Gallery in Leeds. I had just spotted the red dot next to my work which he had purchased that afternoon; it was a perfect introduction.

The following day he took several of us across to the site that would become The Henry Moore Centre for the Study of Sculpture and walked us through the spaces. Every detail had been planned; I remember that he was particularly pleased with the chairs and sofas that would be used and it was clearly going to be a rather special place.

He had first seen my work in a previous exhibition at St Paul's in 1978 and remained a strong supporter. The last time that we met, over lunch, he reminded us that the show *Six Sculptures* in 1984 was actually the first in the Study Centre gallery. He was thoughtful, careful and extremely fastidious with detail, which made the time spent on preparing the catalogue and exhibition both lengthy and very illuminating.

Terry had an extraordinary range of interests and specialisms and whether discussing Nicholas Hawksmoor, Joseph Beuys, Claus Oldenburg or Andy Goldsworthy he had his personal take on all. His courtesy, warmth and interest in people made him very inclusive; he would ensure that you met, were introduced and had the opportunity to connect.

However it wasn't just the art world that could energise him. I vividly remember his 'cancel everything' reaction at the thought of missing the last episode of *Jewel in the Crown* on the television, but that was Terry; always a great enthusiast.'

10. Installation at Leeds Art Gallery.

Peter Randall-Page

'Terry Friedman was a rare phenomenon; a free spirit and maverick curator with faith in his own judgement.

He organised a touring retrospective of my work in 1992 and purchased a number of works for the Henry Moore Centre in Leeds.

Setting up the show with Terry was a great pleasure and the respect he showed for my work was hugely flattering.

He will be greatly missed.'

11. *Red Fruit*, red marble, 1987 65 × 42 × 40 cm. Bought from the artist by the Centre for the Study of Sculpture, 1989.

Ryan Riddington

'I met Terry Friedman in late 2004. That summer I exhibited collage, drawing and photographic works and a welded sculpture at the Brahm Gallery, Leeds. Denise Raine, Librarian at the Henry Moore Institute, then set me the challenge of showing sculpture there. This spurred me on to reconstruct a weld-mesh and steel rod work that had been languishing in pieces in a cardboard box since I rescued them from the garage of the Andover café owners, to whom I had entrusted it whilst living in St Petersburg in 2000–01. Moving to Leeds in 2002 and becoming an invigilator at the Institute started my re-engagement and further education in sculpture. Without the resurrection of the work and the subsequent display, *Correspondence* (fig. 12) I may never have met Terry. He said he wanted to meet the artist who had made the 'drawing' that turned out a compact wall-based sculpture. He was less interested in the accompanying photograph of the object's re-oriented silhouette but was happy to accept it as long as he acquired the sculpture.

Terry kindly lent *Correspondence* to the exhibition *Beauty Of Shapes* at Leeds Art Gallery before it was installed above the doorway of his incredible living room. I saw it there many times and was thrilled to be among the varied artists and artisans that he had collected over the years. He said he enjoyed observing the structure in the different lights that altered the attending shadow on the wall.

I will always be grateful that he sought me out because of it.

Terry attended the opening of my debut London solo exhibition in 2012 and it was very reassuring to hear him praise my new work. When I see interesting exhibitions I often think of him. I miss his wry humour, forthright opinions and generous support.'

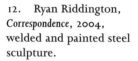

12. Ryan Riddington, *Correspondence*, 2004, welded and painted steel sculpture.

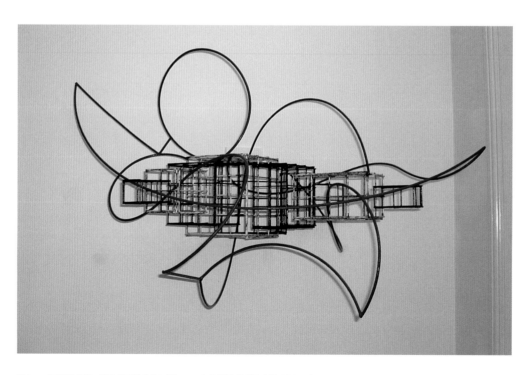

Silver as Architecture and Sculpture 1578–1776: some recent acquisitions at Temple Newsam[1]

James Lomax

The connection between architecture, sculpture and goldsmiths' work might seem so obvious as not to be worth mentioning or labouring. From time immemorial craftsmen in precious metals have relied on architectural principles including mathematics, geometry and proportion not to mention the use of decorative motifs from Classical and Gothic styles. Similarly they have used many of the same methods and techniques employed by sculptors: modelling, casting — in lost wax or sand cast — chasing, embossing, hammering and soldering. These connections are sometimes overlooked by scholars of the different disciplines[2] but recent acquisitions at Temple Newsam usefully demonstrate how some of the principles and practices which underpin these three plastic arts are so closely related.

From the earliest days of antiquity goldsmiths are recorded creating sculptural, even architectural ensembles. Thus for example Bezalel, perhaps the earliest known named goldsmith in history, was summoned by Moses to make the Ark of the Covenant to be 'overlaid with gold and made with a gold moulding to go round it'; the Seat of Mercy which surmounted the Ark 'was modelled with two great winged creatures of beaten gold…'.[3] By the Middle Ages goldsmiths, working with expensive materials for an elite clientele, had become highly valued and educated craftsmen for whom knowledge of mathematics and Euclidian geometry was essential. The use of geometric shapes, such as polygons, trefoils, hexafoils and ogees, was widespread, echoing architectural shapes and forms. Sets of dividers and callipers were to be found among the tools in goldsmiths' workshops, instruments as essential for these craftsmen as much as for masons, architects or sculptors. Decorative details such as crocketting and shafted columns have scaled-up counterparts in Gothic architecture and decorative sculpture.

In the great age of Renaissance goldsmiths there was little distinction between these artistic roles: Brunelleschi considered himself equally an architect, a sculptor and a goldsmith; while Ghiberti and Cellini considered themselves as much sculptors as goldsmiths, and Juan de Arfe regarded his great silver *custodias* to be works of architecture.

With the Renaissance came a deeper fascination with the place of geometry in art and space and the re-discovery of the harmonic proportions of Vitruvian Classicism. Early and High Renaissance works of art are characterised by a harmonious balance between the different parts which make the whole so

1 This paper was first delivered as a lecture to the Silver Society at a meeting at Temple Newsam on 12 May 2014.

2 A notable exception being Jennifer Montagu: see *Roman Baroque Sculpture, The Industry of Art*, New Haven and London, 1989; *Gold, Silver and Bronze, Metal Sculpture of the Roman Baroque*, New Haven and London, 1996; 'The Practice of Roman Baroque Silver Sculpture', *Silver Society Journal*, 12, Autumn 2000, pp. 18–25.

3 Exodus 37: 1–16.

completely satisfying. In northern Europe, Durer's *Unterweisung der Messung* (1525) showed his profound understanding of perspective and proportion; while Wenzel Jamnitzer's *Perspectiva Corporum Regularium* (1568) explored complex geometric shapes further: his famous portrait shows him with callipers, a calibrating instrument as well as a drawing and a finely cast figure.[4]

In England the publication of two books within seven years was to prove highly significant for the course of architecture and its associated arts: John Shute's *First and Chief Grounds of Architecture*, much influenced by Serlio, came out in 1563, the first book illustrating the classical orders; John Dee's translation of Euclid in 1570, provided, as E. G. R. Taylor pointed out, 'a magnificent exposition of the relationship and application of mathematics, especially arithmetic and geometry, to the practice of various skilled arts and crafts'.[5] Knowledge of these treatises and their successors well into the eighteenth century became part and parcel of the education of accomplished gentlemen and of the training for apprentices in the leading mechanical trades.[6] As the century advanced forms and decoration in architecture, sculpture and goldsmiths' work became profoundly imbued with the exaggerated and complex language of Northern Mannerism.

Perhaps it was in Spain that the direct connection between High Renaissance architectural principles and goldsmiths' work was most graphically demonstrated. Juan de Arfe's *De Varia Commensuracion* (1585) was closely concerned with geometry and the proportions of the human body, while the fourth book dealt with classical architecture and the relationship of ratios and proportions to the main types of ecclesiastical goldsmiths' work: chalices, processional crosses and above all the *custodias* with which he and his family were so associated. He claimed that these fantastical monstrances were really architecture in miniature.[7]

The Hurst Cup [8] (fig. 1a–d)

The silver-gilt cup and cover of 1578/9 was purchased in 2013 from the heirs of the great American collector J. Pierpont Morgan. Its maker's mark, a bird, has since 1988 been attributed to Affabel Partridge (fl. c. 1550–80), a royal goldsmith.[9] Much of its attraction derives from its scale and ideal proportions: its height is almost exactly 10 in., while the three elements, foot and stem, bowl, and cover, all measure 3⅓ in. each. Indeed this feature of divisions into thirds continues elsewhere on this cup: for example the bowl has three horizontal bands dividing it into divisions of 1 in., 1½ in., and 1¾ in.; the diameter of the bowl is 3⅔ in., while the diameter of the foot is 3 in. The masks, which are such a feature of this piece (and of this goldsmith's work elsewhere), are found three times on the foot, on the stem, on the bowl and on the cover.

Is there an identifiable iconography behind this? Threes are symbolic of many things, notably the Trinity and the Theological Virtues, yet there is absolutely no suggestion that this cup has a sacred purpose. Can it just be that this is merely a pleasing proportion which works well and satisfactorily for this object? It is curious that the same feature of divisions into thirds also occurs on the Drapers' Company Cup, also by Partridge from 1578/89 and with which it shares other affinities also, including fine engraving.[10] Clearly the principles of ratio and proportion have been successfully brought to bear on these objects. In addition the cup has the underlying aesthetic of Renaissance design of a balanced tension between vertical

4 In the Musée d'Art et d'Histoire, Geneva. J. F. Hayward, *Virtuoso Goldsmiths 1540–1620*, London, 1976, pp. 64–65.

5 Christopher Hartop, *Geometry and the Silversmith: the Domcha Collection*, Cambridge, 2008, p. 16.

6 See R. Campbell, *The London Tradesmen* (1747), Whitefish, Montana (Kessinger reprint, 2009), pp. 141–47.

7 C. C. Oman, *The Golden Age of Hispanic Silver 1400–1665*, London, 1968, p. xx, note 1.

8 Named after Lt. Col. Henry and Mrs Patricia Hurst whose generous bequest enabled the cup to be bought for Temple Newsam in 2013. The cup was exhibited at the V&A Museum in the 1860s and 70s when it was owned by William Maskell (1814–90); it was sold from the collection of T. W. Waller, Christie's, 7 June 1910; bought by J. Pierpont Morgan and retained by his family until 2010.

9 Timothy Schroder, *The Gilbert Collection of Gold and Silver*, London, 1988, pp. 48–53.

10 Philippa Glanville, *Silver in Tudor and early Stuart England*, London, 1990, pp. 254–55, fig. 145. She suggests (p. 163) that the engraved fish-tailed figures are derived from Etienne Delaune's *Grottescho* (1574).

and horizontal elements, and a clear sense of structure. They also have a remarkably controlled rhythm of ornament with a careful alternation of flat and relief surfaces, so very different to the *horror vacui* of most surviving later Elizabethan silver.

Affabel Partridge, the maker of this cup, was a remarkable craftsman, one of Queen Elizabeth's goldsmiths and a Prime Warden of the Goldsmiths Company with premises on Cheapside, where Lady Jane Grey lodged prior to being proclaimed Queen in 1553.[11] To date some twenty works with his mark have been identified and these include some of the most celebrated English plate from the third quarter of the sixteenth century.[12] Although his surviving work is quite diverse it is characterised not only by a sense of proportion and scale, fine engraving by independent masters based on grotesque and narrative sources, but also by a remarkably sophisticated use of sculptural ornament including cast masks. In at least two additional cases, the Vintners' Company Salt (1569/70),[13] and 'Queen Elizabeth's Salt' among the Regalia of the Tower of London (1572/73),[14] he incorporates chased figurative panels taken directly from plaquettes carved in boxwood or honestone or modelled as lead patterns by the Augsburg sculptor and designer Pieter Flötner (1485–1546). For the Vintners' Salt they represent the four Cardinal Virtues: Justice, Fortitude, Temperance and Chastity, and for 'Queen Elizabeth's Salt' the three Theological Virtues, Faith, Hope and Charity.

This suggests that the goldsmith must have had a close association with the Continent, possibly employing journeymen from centres of fine craftsmanship in France, Germany or the Low Countries, or importing significant plate which may have influenced his workshop style.[15] The number of alien goldsmiths working in London in Queen Elizabeth's reign was considerable: it has been estimated that there were at least 500 active between 1558 and 1598.[16] In addition, the custom for foreign goldsmiths to gain experience through their *wanderjahre* encouraged many from the Protestant centres to come to London for varied periods. The wars in the Netherlands were producing religious and economic refugees bringing with them new ideas in design and technical accomplishment. At the same time there was a thriving market for sophisticated 'Almain' plate imported from Germany, Flanders and France.[17]

In the case of the Hurst Cup at Temple Newsam one of the most distinctive features is the use of cast grotesque masks, male and female, bearded and clean shaven, human and mythological, applied sequentially on the foot, stem, bowl and cover (figs 1a–d). Very similar but not identical masks appear on a number of Partridge's objects (and also possibly on other pieces apparently marked by different makers). In this case they are contained within consistent chased strapwork cartouches on the foot and cover, engraved roundels on the bowl and further strapwork cartouches on the stem. If they are indeed unique it would follow that each mask would have been individually modelled in wax, and then cast by *cire-perdue* and without the use of an intermediary mould.[18] In other words because the masks are so small and not difficult to model, and because no more than one was ever going to be required, they were probably cast directly from the unique wax model which would have been destroyed in the process. The cast masks on the bowl, in particular, are exceptionally well modelled, ultimately deriving from Renaissance grotesques. In this case there are some affinities with designs by Erasmus Hornick (d. 1583) or Matthias Zundt (1498–1586), both associated with the workshops of Wenzel Jamnitzer (1507–1585).

11 Sir W. S. Prideaux, *Memorials of the Goldsmiths' Company*, London, 1896, p. 70; British Library, Harleian MSS, no. 194.
12 For a list of his known works see Appendix.
13 Sophia Lee, *The Worshipful Company of Vintners: a Catalogue of Plate*, London, 1996, pp. 24–25.
14 Arthur Grimwade, 'The Plate Catalogue', in Claude Blair (ed.), *The Crown Jewels*, London, c. 1998, pp. 283–93.
15 Glanville, as at note 10, p. 163.
16 Lien Bich Luu, 'Aliens and their impact on the goldsmiths' craft in London in the sixteenth century', in David Mitchell (ed.), *Goldsmiths, Silversmiths and Bankers: innovation and the transfer of skill 1550 to 1750*, London University, Centre for Metropolitan History Working Papers Series, no. 2, 1995, pp. 43–52, esp. p. 45.
17 Christopher Hartop, 'German Silver in England', in Patrick Eyres and James Lomax (eds), *Diplomats, Goldsmiths and Baroque Court Culture: Lord Raby in Berlin, The Hague and Wentworth Castle*, Barnsley, 2014, pp. 159–71.
18 C. R. Ashbee (trans), *The Treatises of Benvenuto Cellini on Goldsmithing and Sculpture*, London,

1a. The Hurst Cup, silver gilt (photo Norman Taylor © Leeds Museums and Galleries).

18   SILVER AS ARCHITECTURE AND SCULPTURE

1b–d.   The Hurst Cup, details, silver gilt, maker's mark attributed to Affabel Partridge, London, 1578/79. Bought by Leeds Museums and Galleries 2013 from the bequest of Colonel Henry and Mrs Patricia Hurst. Height 9¾ in. (photo Norman Taylor © Leeds Museums and Galleries).

1888 (Kessinger Reprint, 2006), ch. XXII, pp. 87–88.

19 See C. C. Oman, *English Engraved Silver 1150–1900*, London, 1978; Ellenor Alcorn, *English Silver in the Museum of Fine Arts Boston*, vol 1, 1993, pp. 48–52.

20 Charles Oman, 'Nicaise Roussel and the Mostyn Flagons', *Leeds Arts Calendar*, no 83 (1978), pp. 4–8. Recent opinion has discounted some of Oman's attributions on the basis of considerable differences in style and handling among the different examples (Glanville, as at note 10, p. 166).

21 Glanville, as at note 10, fig. 159, p. 272.

22 Timothy Schroder, *Renaissance Silver from the Schroder Collection*, London, 2007, no. 13, p. 77.

23 Hayward, as at note 4, pp. 304–05.

24 Alcorn, as at note 19, pp. 58–60. I am grateful to Tom Michie for inspecting and photographing the masks. Similar small-scale masks, perhaps from the same modeller, are found on other fine plate not marked by Partridge: for example the Waterbeach Cup at Manchester Art Gallery (1557) with maker's mark W over a crescent. They should be distinguished from the large number of fine masks of a different scale and character which become ubiquitous on later Elizabethan plate.

The exquisite and subtly delicate engraving on this cup is equally remarkable. It consists of an interweaving rhythm of shaded and hatched scrolls, recalling the moresques or arabesques engraved by Thomas Geminus (1510–1562), and Peter Flötner (1485–1546) but with additional exotic chimeras, winged horses, birds and insects more akin to the grotesques of Etienne Delaune (1518–1595). Since Flötner's plaquettes were evidently circulating in Partridge's workshop in the 1560s and 70s it can be assumed his engraved designs could also have been found there. The same engraver may well have worked under Partridge to decorate the Drapers' Cup for it shows the same delicate use of the burin. Partridge also used the highly skilled but still unidentified foreign engraver known by his initials P over M signed on three of the twelve plates depicting the *Labours of Hercules* in the Fowler Collection (1567) (based on prints by Heinrich Aldegrever).[19]

The identity of the many foreign craftsmen, including modeller-sculptors and engravers, working in London at this time is almost impossible to establish. Nicaise Roussel, a migrant craftsman from Bruges from at least 1573, whose grotesque designs were published as late as 1623, has been credited both as the source and as the artist responsible for a number of engraved pieces, including the Mostyn Flagon at Temple Newsam, on the basis of his distinctive style, but it would be hazardous to make an attribution to him in this case.[20] Clearly there is a distinct and individual hand at work on a number of pieces such as the Magdalen Cup at Manchester Art Gallery[21] and the tankard in the Schroder Collection,[22] but it was not the same engraver working on the Hurst or the Drapers' Cups. It is remarkable that this delicate engraving style, often entirely enveloping a silver object, is without parallel elsewhere in Europe at this time when three dimensional chased or cast decoration was ubiquitous.[23]

The cast masks on the bowl appear to represent a devilish he-goat, a serene goddess-like female head with bunched earpieces and ringlets, and an aggressive 'wild man', or satyr (figs 1a–c). On the cover there are three human masks of indeterminate but perhaps feminine gender; one with a slender face; the second with a fuller, more middle-aged face; and the third with a balding head with pouched cheeks and pouting lips (fig. 1d). On the foot one of the heads is a naïf young male; the second a hirsute half man-half lion; and the third an elderly male with a double forked beard, somewhat resembling a pagan river god.

Is there a secular or pagan iconography behind this imagery? Is it too fanciful to suggest a coded anti-Dionysiac tract, describing the effects of excessive wine? If this is the correct interpretation, the serene mask on the bowl might represent the human spirit before drinking; the lion mask might suggest the aggression which comes from excessive alcohol; and the devilish he-goat the hellish addiction into which a drinker finally lapses. On the cover the three degrees of drunkenness in women might be discerned in the increasing bloated masks. On the foot there are again three 'deteriorating' male heads: from the androgynous youth, to the hirsute wildman to the devilish pagan figure. On the stem the three skull–like masks appear to be grimacing in horror at the metamorphosis occurring above and below them.

The only other object marked by Partridge, which is similarly clad with masks with which it is possible to make a comparison at this present time, is the 1577/78 salt at the Museum of Fine Arts, Boston.[24] Here a figure of Venus holding a wreath and accompanied by two putti are enclosed in a rock crystal cylinder. She is protected by four female caryatid figures, while on the foot are four mask heads again; and another four on the cover. Although they appear to correspond in type, they are all different and individually modelled. Hence there are two bearded males, one crowned and one bare-headed, and two females, one with a wimple, the other bare-headed. They appear to display different emotions: some are happy, even laughing, and others sad. Are they commenting on the scene of Venus entrapped within her rock crystal cage? At all events they appear to be different models from those seen on the Temple Newsam cup.

This might suggest that there were a number of freelance modellers and craftsmen perhaps working primarily for one master goldsmith, but also sometimes for others, providing either cast masks, or at least models, and other sculptural elements which may also have included figures and caryatids, even 'apostles' for spoon terminals, as required. If so, their names and their working methods are unknown although some of their source material can be surmised. For larger scale work, and if following Continental working practices, they would have used lead casting patterns or carved wood plaquettes for sand casting or even for hammering from sheet silver. These survive in considerable quantities in Europe but must surely have been used in England too.[25]

There are other cast elements which appear to be repeated on Partridge's work and that of other fine goldsmiths, not least elements of the stem and foot. The concave fluting and overhanging lobes in the Hurst Cup are found again on Partridge's Glynne Cup (1579/80) (V&A Museum), and his Goodricke Cup (1563/64) (British Museum), and a variation of it is found on a communion cup at St Michael-le-Belfry, York, from 1558/59 (maker's mark indecipherable).[26] The possibility that a Continental journeyman craftsman may be responsible for these and other elements such as the bulbous stems has been suggested by the very similar features which appear on pieces as diverse as a mounted serpentine cup from Frankfurt c. 1580 (Schroder Collection) and a gilt cup from Strasbourg c. 1555 (Toledo Museum of Art).[27]

Turning from the questions of style and authorship it is interesting to speculate on the possible early provenance of this piece. Partridge was one of the royal goldsmiths, supplying plate to the Jewel House and its Keeper, John Astley, from at least 1560 when he and another goldsmith Robert Brandon received 4,000 ounces of old and unserviceable plate explicitly for making into New Year or diplomatic gifts over the next few years.[28] The complexities of this transaction are difficult to follow but it is clear that both Brandon and Partridge had ceased to be royal goldsmiths by July 1579 and that all the bullion from the 1560 transfer had been used, perhaps much of it in the previous three years.[29] The documents are entirely between Brandon and the Jewel House, perhaps implying that Partridge was in retirement by this date. Partridge is referred to elsewhere in the Jewel House records: his delivery of three gilt salts 'of French making' in 1575/76 indicates he also dealt in high quality imported plate.[30]

It would be tempting to conjecture that the Hurst Cup might have been a royal New Year's gift to a courtier but unfortunately the records do not substantiate this. Assuming that the date letter A found here came into effect when the new Goldsmiths' Company wardens were elected on 19 May 1578 (St Dunstan's Day) and remained in force for the following twelve months one might attempt to find a gift of a cup weighing 16 oz during that period. The descriptions of the New Year

25 Hayward, as at note 4, pp. 59–61.
26 T. M. Fallow and H. B. McCall, Yorkshire Church Plate, Leeds, 1912, 1, pl. VII.
27 Schroder, as at note 9, pp. 48–53; as at note 10, p. 139; also ibid, 'Sixteenth-century English Silver: some problems of attribution', Proceedings of the Silver Society, III, 1 and 2 (Spring 1983), pp. 42–46.
28 British Library Add. MS 5751.A.f.206. Cited by A. J. Collins, The Jewels and Plate of Queen Elizabeth I; the inventory of 1574, London, 1955, p. 60.
29 Collins, as at note 28, pp. 160–61, 549–50.
30 Collins, as at note 28, p. 553.

gifts for 1578 are generally unspecific, merely recording quantities 'in guilt plate', sometimes 'from our store'. Many of them state 'Brandon' implying they had been made by the other royal goldsmith, and there is no mention of Partridge. In August the Queen went on a progress to Norfolk when she would have expected to receive gifts, and in return bestow knighthoods rather than gifts of plate. In total she distributed 5,738 oz of plate during the course of this year.[31] The relative lightness of the cup would not make it conspicuous among the lists of plate, but its high quality might have been indicated as being for example a 'fair cup' or 'finely wrought'. Sometimes indeed highly personal plate was small but exquisite: 'my Ladies Cup' belonging to Bess of Hardwick in 1601 weighed just 13 oz.[32]

Lord Raby's Silver Cistern (fig. 2a–b)

This celebrated object, part of the ambassadorial plate given to Thomas Wentworth Lord Raby (later Earl of Strafford) (1672–1739) from the Jewel House in 1705–06 for his embassy to Berlin, was acquired for Temple Newsam in 2011 after an Export Licence deferral and a major appeal, and has been much published.[33] Marked by Phillip Rollos senior (c. 1650–1711), the construction of such a massive piece marks it out as a remarkable work of sculpture: the raising of the basin from a single sheet of silver, ensuring the pressure was kept even throughout, was a truly remarkable feat. Indeed it seems likely that this part of its construction was in part due to coppersmiths whose heavier tools and hammers would be more capable to raise the metal. Henry Jernegan and his silversmith Charles Kandler had to resort to them when supervising the making of the vast Jernegan cistern in 1734, weighing over 9,000 oz, 'the largest and finest ever made', since 'the Silversmiths Hamers not having weight sufficient to make any Impression on it'.[34] John Culme has suggested there were coppersmiths operating in Wandsworth, Surrey, where the elder Philip Rollos was living by 1711,[35] including one Adolphus Rachon, possibly a fellow German expatriate.

The other sculptural elements of this object are its lion head handles; magnificent feats of sand casting from moulds taken from sculptured models giving a lively naturalistic effect. Interestingly they do not represent Raby's heraldic supporters which are a wyvern and a lion rampant (Wentworth) for here the lions are 'salient' or apparently 'leaping' with their forelegs together. However, among other armigerous families, lions' salient are the heraldic supporters of the Pierreponts, Dukes of Kingston. In this role they are the principal sculptural feature on the cistern made for the second Duke of Kingston by Philip Rollos in 1699 now in the Hermitage. The mane and facial expressions appear to be identical on the Raby Cistern, although the Kingston lions have garlands of oak leaves in their mouths. As the Kingston cistern pre-dates Lord Raby's by five years it seems highly probable that the original moulds were made for the Duke and were re-used by Rollos for his work for Lord Raby at the Jewel House. Lions are symbolic not only of strength, giving the impression that they are lifting the cistern, but also of royalty, being the kings of the animal world, and so very suitable for an object intended to represent the power of the British monarchy through Queen Anne's ambassador. This symbolism is echoed by King of Denmark's three lions guarding the throne at Rosenborg, in its turn evoking King Solomon's in Jerusalem.[36]

It is difficult to find examples of such ambitious three-dimensional casting of silver heraldic figures in England before this date: the massive gilt leopards from

31 J. Nichols, *Progresses and Public Processions of Queen Elizabeth*, 2nd edition, London, 1821–23, vol. 1, pp. xix, xxxvi; vol. 2, pp. 137–78, 264–85.

32 Lindsay Boynton (ed), *The Hardwick Hall Inventories of 1601*, London, 1971, p. 35.

33 John Culme's masterly sale catalogue footnote for *Treasures: aristocratic heirlooms*, Sotheby's, 6 July 2010, lot VIII, pp. 70–83; Eyres and Lomax as at note 17, pp. 68–74, 149–51 and passim.

34 Peter Cameron, 'Henry Jernegan, the Kandlers and the client who changed his mind', *Silver Society Journal*, 8 (1996), p. 488.

35 Unpublished presentation at 2012 Wentworth Castle Conference.

36 Jorgen Hein, 'Au chateau de Rosenborg', in Catherine Arminjon (ed), *Quand Versailles etait meuble d'argent* (exh. cat.), Versailles, 2007–08, pp. 100–23. I Kings 10:19–21 'The throne had six steps, a back with a rounded top, and arms on each side of the seat; two lions stood beside the arms, and twelve lions stood on each side of the six steps'.

2a–b. Lord Raby's Silver Cistern, and detail, Philip Rollos senior, London 1705/06. Bought by Leeds Museums and Galleries 2011 after an Export Licence Deferral and a major public appeal with contributions from the Heritage Memorial Fund, the Art Fund, the Monument Trust, the Leeds Art Fund and many others. Width across the handles 51 in. (photo: Norman Taylor © Leeds Museums and Galleries).

1600 (maker's mark a triangle and two crosses), now in the Kremlin, are exceptional. Elements such as massive lion paw feet only enter the repertoire of English goldsmiths' work at about this time: they appear in Marot's engravings, and heraldic lions are found on the Osterley cistern of 1695.[37] The huge pair of cisterns weighing over 10,000 oz and sent by William III from his Jewel Office to Frederick I of Prussia in 1694 (melted down in 1745) were replete with cast lion paw feet, masks and heraldic shields. Tellingly though, the more three-dimensional fountains, which accompanied them and which sported the Prussian eagle as finials, were apparently made in Holland perhaps by more sculpturally-aware goldsmiths, and sent to Berlin separately.[38] Lord Raby's cistern was intended in part to

37 Timothy Schroder, 'The Silver at Osterley', Apollo, CXLI, no. 398 (NS), April 1995, pp. 24–25.
38 Alfred Hagemann and Matthew Winterbottom, 'New Discoveries concerning the Berlin silver buffet', Silver Studies, no 22, 2007, pp. 116–22.

JAMES LOMAX   **23**

39 Culme, as at note 33, pp. 79–80.

40 James Lomax and James Rothwell, *Country House Silver at Dunham Massey*, London, 2006, pp. 58–60.

41 Cameron, as at note 34, passim.

42 Marina Lopato, 'Notes on some celebrated pieces of English silver in the Hermitage Collection', *Silver Studies*, no. 28, 2012, pp. 34–42.

43 The sculptor Caius Gabriel Cibber (1630–1700) not only worked extensively for the Crown (and therefore potentially for the Jewel House) but also on ornamental sculpture for the Duke of Kingston at Thoresby 1685–87, suggesting a potential link with the Duke's cistern and its heraldic lions. Cibber was also active in the German Lutheran Church in London where the family of Philip Rollos was associated. Alternatively, Grinling Gibbons (1648–1721) is recorded as making a 'model for a marble bathing cistern with wainscot border, with copper water pipes'. John Nost the elder (d. 1710) also worked for the Crown (including a clay model for a fountain) and for the Duke of Kingston in 1686 (Ingrid Roscoe, *A Biographical Dictionary of Sculptors in Britain, 1660–1851*, New Haven and London, 2009, passim).

44 Terry Friedman was interested in the architectural settings of massive cisterns. See his articles, 'The English Appreciation of Italian Decorations', *Burlington Magazine*, December 1975, pp. 84–85 and 'Foggini's Statue of Queen Anne', in *Kunst des Barock in der Toscana: Studien zur Kunst unter der letzten Medici* (Munich, 1976).

45 James Lomax, 'The Ambassador's Plate Revisited', in Eyres and Lomax as at note 17, pp. 65–87.

46 The crest is that of Jodrell, probably for Gilbert Jodrell (c. 1714–72) of Duffield, Derbyshire, lawyers with city interests. They were keen buyers of rococo silver: examples of their plate are found in the Metropolitan Museum of Art, New York, the Art Institute of Chicago, and the Philadelphia Museum of Art. Sarah Jodrell (1742–93) daughter of Gilbert Jodrell of Ankerwyke, Bucks, married Robert Child of Osterley in 1763 and a set of dinner plates by George Hindmarsh, 1740, re-engraved with their arms is at Osterley (*National Trust Historic Houses & Collections Annual* 2014, published in association with *Apollo Magazine*, July 2014, p. 65).

show off the skill of the English craftsmen to the Berlin courtiers who were well acquainted with the highly sculptural Augsburg silver of the Rittersaal or Throne Room. It seems ironic therefore that Philip Rollos may originally have come from Berlin.[39]

All the cast elements on the Raby cistern including the stylised shells, the gadrooned border and even the lobes are repeated again on a smaller scale on the 1701 small cistern 'to wash glasses in' at Dunham Massey.[40] Clearly there was a master modeller at work providing Rollos with moulds from which casts could be made. The fact that he may have been a leading sculptor is suggested by the evidence given at the trial *Henry Jernegan v. Littleton Poyntz Meynell* in 1738.[41] Here the patron 'commissioned several curious Draftsmen and consulted with them and others in order to procure Drafts of proper subjects…' and then 'applied to one of the best statuaries to make a model in clay and wax.' This turned out to be John Michael Rysbrack (1694–1770) from whom Jernegan was involved 'at very great Expense in procuring proper Moulds for casting the many and varied figures'. Thereafter 'he employ'd many curious hands in making and finishing ye said cistern', referring to the craftsmen employed in the casting and chasing processes. At one point a major disaster occurred when a mould which was not properly dry had burst endangering the lives of several people.

The spectacular sculptural character of the Jernegan Cistern (now in the Hermitage) has many affinities with Paul de Lamerie's cistern for Lord Scarsdale of 1726 (also in the Hermitage) by which it was inspired and which was probably also modelled by Rysbrack.[42] But these examples belong to the next generation of silver cisterns. The question still remains, who was the sculptor capable of making models for the Rollos workshop in 1705?[43]

Whoever he was, he was certainly a pioneer: by the time the Burghley Cistern (Burghley House, Lincs) came to be made, just a few years later, by Philip Rollos junior, there is no hesitancy in the modelling or casting: the massive scrolling feet with their wyvern terminals are *tours de force* of near-abstract sculpture, and the lion supporters are full grown and fully salient now. There is an assurance and skill which has reached maturity.

All these massive cisterns have architectural qualities too.[44] They were always intended to be static and in the nature of a fixture or fitting. The proposed location of Lord Raby's at Wentworth Castle is indicated in a detail of Jan de Bodt's famous sectional elevation, at the base of a great pyramid of plate (V&A Museum). Likewise, the architectural quality of silver furniture (including cisterns) intended to be placed in a particular location in a state room, is found again with Raby's silver 'triad' of table, mirror and two candlestands which he acquired in Holland when he was ambassador at the time of the Peace of Utrecht (1713). Originally this was placed in the pier of the State Bedroom in his London house but was re-located to Wentworth Castle in 1748 when it was placed in the pier of the Yellow Bedroom until its sale in 1919.[45]

A Shell Basket, by Phillips Garden, 1754[46] (fig. 3a–b)

The shell basket from 1754/55 whose obscured mark is attributed to Phillips Garden (fl. 1730–after 1773) is a brilliant and witty object representing a uniquely English contribution to rococo silver design. The shell form prompted P. A. S. Philips to write 'Nothing more successful as table ornaments ever emanated from the goldsmith's workshop'.[47] All the different elements which make up these objects had been used before this date by London goldsmiths: escallop shells as sugar boxes and as ornaments on flagons and standing cups from the early seventeenth century; dolphins on salts by Johan Lutma in the mid-seventeenth century; and mermaid handles which had come into vogue on ewers at the turn of the century.[48] But their combination here, together with the decorative piercing, is entirely rococo.

Shells and crustaceous forms are the very essence of the rococo style, appearing in some of the earliest fully rococo designs for silver salts by Meissonier from the 1730s[49] and in the silver dinner service provided for the King of Portugal by Thomas Germain. They are entirely appropriate for dining.[50] As Christopher Hartop has pointed these 'Venus' baskets, complete with mermaid handles, dolphin feet and borders of encrusted shells, seaweed and sea foam, illustrate the Latin poet Terence's line 'Sine Cerere et Tempero friget Venus' (Without grain or grape love withers).[51] Although no doubt they could have been used for bread or fruit, they would surely have been used most appropriately when filled with oysters — an aphrodisiac being offered, from the emblem of the goddess of Love herself.

The cast borders of shells, seaweed and foam strongly recall the same features on the shell-shaped sauce boats and stands, some of which are marked by Nicolas Sprimont, c. 1746–47, made for the 1st Marquess of Rockingham of Wentworth Woodhouse, and now in Boston Museum of Fine Art (Hartman Collection).[52] At first glance one might be forgiven for thinking that they were part of the same dinner service. Not surprisingly such baskets were popular in ceramics, at Sprimont's Chelsea, at Bow and elsewhere. Merfolk handles on the other hand are

47 P. A. S. Phillips, Paul de Lamerie, Citizen and Goldsmith of London. A Study of his Life and Work 1688–1751, London, 1935, p. 109.
48 Rococo Art and Design in Hogarth's England (exh. cat.), London, 1984, pp. 115–16.
49 Peter Fuhring, Juste-Aurele Meissonier, Turin and London, 1999, p. 346.
50 Leonor d'Orey, 'L'histoire des services d'orfevrerie franciase a la cour de Portugal', in Versailles et les tables royals en Europe (exh. cat.), Versailles, 1993–94, pp. 165–170.
51 Christopher Hartop, The Huguenot Legacy: English Silver 1680–1760 from the Alan and Simone Hartman Collection, London, 1996, pp. 234–35.
52 Hartop, as at note 51, pp. 216–19.

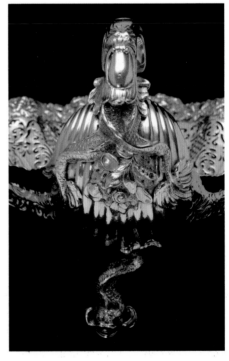

3a–b.   Shell Basket, silver, Phillips Garden, London, 1754/55. Bought by Leeds Museums and Galleries 2013 with grants from the V&A Purchase Grant Fund, the Art Fund and the Colonel Henry and Mrs Patricia Hurst Bequest Fund. Width 14 in. (photo: Norman Taylor © Leeds Museums and Galleries).

much less easy to model for ceramics and are rarely found. Dolphins are of course another staple of the rococo style and can be seen carved in furniture and modelled in creamware.

Silver shell baskets of this design are associated with Paul de Lamerie's workshop from about 1743 and they may well have originated in his circle, although a drawn or engraved source has not been found.[53] They very clearly post-date the years when Lamerie's master modeller and chaser known as the Maynard Master was working for him. Very similar models are found by other makers, particularly, as here, by Phillips Garden.[54] A theory once circulated that the moulds for these baskets were acquired by Phillips Garden after Lamerie's death but as Timothy Schroder has pointed out, this should now be discounted, not least because several have come to light which were made by Garden before Lamerie's death. There are considerable differences between the Lamerie and Garden models: in this instance the rocaille borders contrast with the plain gadrooning on the Lamerie pair in the Ashmolean. Not surprisingly the patterns of the piercing, perhaps imitating lace, are very different. It has also been noted that the piercing on the Ashmolean baskets is similar to the painted diaper border of a Meissen escallop dish from about 1728, and Philippa Glanville has suggested there may have existed a French version.[55] When looking at Garden's well known trade card it might even be possible to identify a group of them on the middle shelves of the press slightly to the left of the lady's head.[56]

A Chinoiserie Epergne, Thomas Pitts, 1759/60 [57] (fig. 4)

The chinoiserie epergne of 1759/60 probably comes closest to a piece of architecture, albeit an ephemeral and fantastical 'structure'. With its canopied pagoda and entwined columns from which spring the baskets and small dishes it evokes a 'Chinese house' or garden pavilion or gazebo. Such buildings became highly fashionable as part of the move towards informal landscape design and the cult of 'sharawadgi' or beautiful disorder which travellers such as Fr Jean Attiret reported from the East. Possibly the first of these was erected at Stowe in 1738 and often they were built in ponds or lakes where they evoked the buildings seen on imported coromandel screens.[58] As well as being decorative eye-catchers in the landscape, they would have been used in the same tradition of 'banqueting houses', as places for informal retirement, where desserts and wine might be served after dinner.

There were innumerable designs in the rococo architectural manuals of the mid-century of which William Halfpenny's *New Designs for Chinese temples, triumphal arches, garden seats, palings etc* of 1750 can serve as an example. Even the pierced work of the baskets and canopy can suggest Chinese lattice work to be found in windows, doors and balustrades. These prints equally served as inspiration for furniture designers such as Chippendale who devoted many plates to Chinese style beds, china cases and shelves of an architectural character.

From here it is but a short transposition to silver (or indeed porcelain) epergnes as centrepieces for the dining table. Generally their appearance evokes a garden arbour, with a trellised canopy supported by flower entwined columns. An extremely rare gilt bronze example signed by Denis Réné Gastecloux and dated 1768 appeared on the art market in 2013 which was a true architectural model of a fantastical building, such as might have been made for an elaborate national festival,

53 Timothy Schroder, *British and Continental Gold and Silver in the Ashmolean Museum*, Oxford, 2009, vol. 2, pp. 690–93.
54 Schroder, as at note 53, where a list is supplied.
55 *Rococo* as at note 48, pp. 115–16.
56 Illustrated (ia) Helen Clifford, *Silver in London: the Parker and Wakelin Partnership 1760–1776*, New York, New Haven and London, 2004, front cover.
57 Formerly in the collection of the celebrated hostess the Hon. Mrs Daisy Fellowes (1890–1962).
58 Patrick Conner, 'Chinese Themes in 18th century Gardens', in David Beevers (ed), *Chinese Whispers: chinoiserie in Britain 1650–1930* (exh. cat.), Brighton & Hove, 2008, pp. 55–64.

complete with domes, balconies, balustrades and flights of steps.[59] It echoes the examples seen in the caterer Negri and Wettin's trade card, which also included a Chinese centrepiece in the background. Possibly the lack of an engraved coat of arms on the Temple Newsam example is explained by the fact that it may originally have belonged to a caterer who hired it out to clients.

For all its rococo frivolity the epergne is most carefully considered. Its proportions are those of a double cube; while many of its features are repeated in rhythms of fours: it rests on four feet, with four columns which support the canopy of sixteen upturned eaves and eight bells. There are four baskets with twelve ogee points each, four dishes with eight ogee points each and the large basket at the bottom with sixteen similar points. Finally the whole ensemble is united with beading which runs down the creases in the canopy, around the borders of the baskets and dishes, all the way to the tips of the feet.

A Pair of Ewers, makers' marks for Matthew Boulton and John Fothergill, Birmingham, 1776 (fig. 5)

In 1768 James Wyatt (1746–1813) returned from Italy and almost immediately threatened the pre-eminence of Robert Adam (1728–1792) as the most fashionable

4.   Chinoiserie Epergne, silver, Thomas Pitts, London, 1759/60. Bought by Leeds Museums and Galleries 2011 with grants from the V&A Purchase Grant Fund and the Heritage Lottery Fund (photo: Norman Taylor © Leeds Museums and Galleries).

59 Christie's London, 4 July 2013, lot 4.

5. Pair of Ewers, silver, Matthew Boulton and John Fothergill, Birmingham, 1776. Bought Leeds Museums and Galleries 2010 in memory of Robert Rowe with grants from the Art Fund, the V&A Purchase Grant Fund and a number of well wishers. Height 14½ in. (photo: Norman Taylor © Leeds Museums and Galleries).

60 John Martin Robinson, *James Wyatt, Architect to George III*, New Haven and London, 2011, pp. 131–34.
61 Frances Fergusson, 'Wyatt Silver', *Burlington Magazine*, 116 (December 1974), pp. 751–56; Nicholas Goodison, *Matthew Boulton: Ormolu*, London, c. 2002, passim; 'The Context of Neo Classicism', in Shena Mason (ed), *Matthew Boulton: selling what all the world desires* (exh. cat), New Haven and London, 2009, pp. 39–40; Kenneth Quickenden, 'Boulton and Fothergill Silver: an epergne designed by James Wyatt', *Burlington Magazine*, 128 (June 1986), pp. 417–21.
62 Interestingly, James Wyatt's client, Sir Thomas Egerton of Heaton Hall, Lancs, bought silver including candlesticks from Boulton in 1775 '16 March 1775 To Messrs Boulton & Co for some candlesticks £4-15-0d' (Greater Manchester Record Office, Earl of Wilton's archives, E4/99, Accounts, vols 1–4).
63 Robinson, as at note 60, p. 137. For the Nuttall plasterwork see *Country Life*, 28 April 1923, p. 573, fig. 9.

architect in town. His Oxford Street Pantheon, the main assembly rooms for London, opened in 1772, was a brilliant conflation of the Pantheon in Rome with Santa Sophia in Istanbul, and — in the tradition of neo-Classical architects — Wyatt designed many of its internal fittings: furniture, stoves, candelabra. All this can be seen in Hodges' and Pars' famous painting at Temple Newsam.

It was not surprising that the precocious and versatile young architect should team up with the most adventurous entrepreneur of the day, Matthew Boulton (1728–1809) in Birmingham, not least because the Wyatt family's connections with the Boulton firm were already close.[60] Many of Wyatt's original designs for Boulton are found in the 'Noailles sketchbook', for which certain examples were replicated in the Boulton Pattern Books now at Birmingham Reference Library.[61]

The drawings and the finished objects, such as the pair of ewers from 1776, bought in memory of the late Robert Rowe, Director of Leeds Art Galleries 1958–1983 and a renowned silver scholar, display much the same architectural vocabulary as Adam but avoid his over-elaboration and deliberate 'learnedness'. Possibly under Boulton's supervision Wyatt showed a respect for the intrinsic qualities of the material for which he designed, whereas Adam appears to ignore the fact that too much relief ornament can cause visual confusion on an object made from a reflective material like silver. Wyatt was able to contrast plain and decorated surfaces in a perfect balance which Boulton well understood his clients wanted.

A Wyatt interior such as the dining room at Heaton Hall, with its subtle shapes and proportions, decorated sparsely but elegantly with plasterwork grotesques, shares much the same refined aesthetic as the ewers.[62] The integration of architecture, sculpture and the decorative arts at this moment is almost total. John Martin Robinson has pointed out that the design of these ewers is identical to examples in stucco seen at Wyatt's Crichel and Nuttall.[63]

Boulton's success lay in taking generic motifs or features from the Wyatt drawings and reassembling them as he saw fit. In these examples the alternating flutings and plain surfaces of the jugs are found on designs for ewers, while the guilloche pattern on the foot emanates from a candlestick design. The tall sweeping handles and the use of beading are all characteristic of Wyatt's vocabulary of ornament of which Boulton made use depending on his clients' requirements and ability to pay for the additional 'fashion'.

As a coda it is pleasing to recall that Lord Irwin employed James Wyatt to build a new neo-Classical staircase at Temple Newsam in the 1770s, using the architect's favourite Imperial design rising in a single flight, returning in two. Although this was replaced by C. E. Kempe's new antiquarian Oak Staircase in the 1890s, Wyatt's wrought iron balustrade, an elegant grotesque design of three reducing ovals containing paterae and anthemia, supplied by the whitesmith Maurice Tobin of Leeds, was saved and installed in the North West staircase.

Appendix: Affable Partridge

Manuscript notes of Gerald Taylor and T. F. Reddaway at Goldsmiths' Hall reveal his apprenticeships in 1538 first to Robert Grampton, then to Mr Horton and, after 'disobedience and mislanguage towards the wardens' to Edward Gylbert. He came into the Livery in 1555, served as Warden in 1569, 1572 and 1578, signed his will in 1601 which was proved the following year. My thanks to David Beasely for access to these sources.

Among his known works are the Browne Reliquary on loan to the V&A Museum (1551); a mounted rock crystal cup and cover in the Schroder Collection (1554) (Schroder, as at note 22, pp. 139–41); the Trenchard nautilus cup in the V&A Museum (1557) (Glanville, as at note 10, pp. 398–99); the Goodricke Cup in the British Museum (1563) (Anthony Wells-Cole, *Art and Decoration in Elizabethan and Jacobean England*, New Haven and London, 1997, p. 202); the twelve Labours of Hercules engraved plates, also once owned by J. Pierpont Morgan (1567) (Timothy Schroder, *The Francis E. Fowler, Jr., Collection of Silver*, Los Angeles, 1991, pp. 15–16); the Vintners' Company Salt (1569) (Lee, as at note 13, pp. 24–25); Archbishop Parker's tankard at Corpus Christi College, Cambridge (1572) (Oliver Rackham, *Treasures of Silver at Corpus Christi College*, Cambridge, 2002, pp. 87–88 (and possibly its apparent 'twin' in the Schroder Collection (Schroder, as at note 22, pp. 13–14); 'Queen Elizabeth's Salt' among the Regalia in the Tower of London (1572) (Grimwade, as at note 14, pp 283–93); the Bacon Cups in the British Museum (1574) (Glanville, as at note 10, pp. 52–53); a mounted rock crystal salt at the Museum of Fine Arts Boston (1577) (Alcorn, as at note 19, pp. 58–60); the Drapers' Company cup (1578) (Glanville, as at note 10, pp. 254–55); and the Glynne Cup (1579) (Glanville as at note 10, p. 167). Timothy Schroder has reported a fine mounted stoneware tankard with characteristic Partridge features, c. 1558, at the Middle Temple *Silver Society Newsletter*, no. 86, September 2014, p. 4.

The Parlington Triumphal Arch by Thomas Leverton, 1782–83. An early photograph, probably taken in the 1860s, either by Colonel Charles Gascoigne or his butler John Shelton. The photograph is one of a pair, designed to be viewed through a stereoscope which produced a three-dimensional image (Photo: courtesy of Don Cathie and Brian Hull (Parlington Hall website)).

Sir Thomas Gascoigne and Crevier's History of the Roman Emperors

Adam White

An enigmatic manuscript came to light some years ago in the cash safe at Lotherton Hall. Lotherton is the former home of the Gascoigne family; it was given to the City of Leeds in 1968 and opened its doors to the public in 1969, the year in which Terry Friedman was appointed to the staff of the Leeds City Art Galleries. He took a passionate interest in Lotherton's art collections, some of which came from the family's previous and much larger residence, Parlington Hall which stood nearby, on the west side of the Great North Road.

When found, the manuscript bore no museum number and had evidently been put in the safe because it seemed to be worth preserving but no-one quite knew what to do with it.[1] A title page identifies it as *Extracts from Crevier's Lives of the Roman Emperors, presented to . . . by . . .* with the date 1770. In place of the names of the donor and recipient, there are two armorial shields (fig. 1). The first shield, taken in

1 The manuscript was rescued from the Gascoigne almshouses in Aberford, the estate village of Parlington in the late 1960s/early 1970s and appears on an undated typescript list of books taken from the building at about that time (Lotherton archive). It has now been accessioned into the Lotherton archive with the number DM 105.

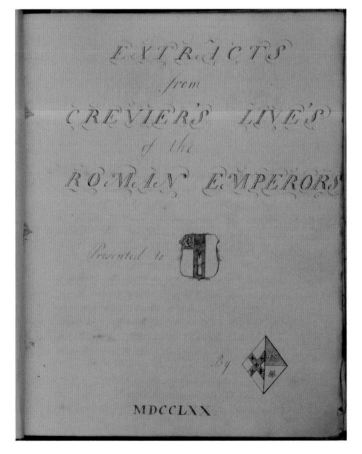

1.   *Extracts from Crevier's Lives of the Roman Emperors.* Manuscript presented to Sir Thomas Gascoigne, Bt. by Isabella Crathorne, 1770. Titlepage. Pen and ink on paper, 24.0 × 18.5 cm. Leeds Museums and Galleries

conjunction with the date, is readily identifiable as bearing the arms of Sir Thomas Gascoigne, 8th Baronet of Parlington (1745–1810). The arms comprise an upward-pointing pike's head on a black vertical stripe (a *demi-luce erect on a pale sable*)[2] for the Gascoigne family with an inescutcheon of the royal arms of Scotland for the baronetcy of Nova Scotia granted to Sir Thomas's ancestor, Sir John Gascoigne in 1635.[3] The second shield is a lozenge (diamond shape), so it was borne by a woman, the author of the dedication. She does not give up her secret so easily.

The manuscript consists of 219 pages extracted from *The History of the Roman Emperors from Augustus to Constantine* by Jean Baptiste Louis Crevier (1693–1765). Crevier was a Frenchman, as his name suggests and his work was first published in Paris 1749–55 under the title *Histoire des empereurs romains, depuis Auguste jusqu'à Constantin*.[4] An English translation by John Mills was issued in London in 1755–61 and it is from this that the extracts were almost certainly taken, there being no other version of the work, so far as is known, between this time and the date on the title page of the manuscript.[5] The *Extracts* of the title more or less live up to their name in the text: the manuscript follows the original quite faithfully from beginning to end, though not all of it, by any means, has been copied out. The title page tells us that the book is 'illustrated with maps, medals, gems and other copper plates' and several of these are reproduced, delicately copied in pen and ink with wash (figs 2 and 3). The whole is bound between soft covers of marbled paper.

So who was the lady prepared to devote so much time to making a hand-made present for Sir Thomas? She turns out to have been Isabella Swinburne, an elder sister of Henry Swinburne, known as 'the traveller' who was later to accompany Sir Thomas on his second Grand Tour of Europe in 1774–79.[6] In 1755 Isabella married Thomas Crathorne, the son of Margaret and George Crathorne of Crathorne Hall in the North Riding of Yorkshire[7] and he thereupon assumed the coat of arms which appears on the title page, *Argent, a saltire sable charged with five crosses paty or* (Crathorne), impaling Swinburne, *Per fesse gules and argent three cinquefoils counter-changed*. The Swinburnes were a Northumberland family, their main seat being Capheaton Hall, Capheaton to the north-west of Newcastle where they still live.[8] She was clearly a lady of literary tastes and appears seated with a book open at a table in a double portrait with her husband by Francis Cotes (fig. 4). Apart from this, very little, if anything appears to be known about her, beyond the bare outline of her life. She was born in 1736 so would have been in her early thirties when she made her present to Sir Thomas.[9] Her family was a large one, she being the eighth of eleven children of Sir John Swinburne, 3rd Bt. of Capheaton and Mary his wife. By her husband she in turn had five offspring. He died young in 1764 aged forty-three, leaving her as the sole administrator of his estate which was held in trust for Henry Ralph Crathorne, their seven-year-old son and heir. She died on 7th April 1789 aged fifty-two and is buried at Holy Trinity, Kendal, Cumbria where there is a monument to her memory.[10]

The Swinburnes were Roman Catholics. This was an important consideration when Sir Thomas Gascoigne chose travelling companions for his Grand Tour, for he was also a Catholic and a journey to Rome, his main destination, clearly had a religious meaning which for Protestants it lacked. The story of Sir Thomas's second Grand Tour of Europe and the art collecting associated with it is the subject

2 For the origin of this curious device, see F. S. Colman, *A History of the Parish of Barwick-in-Elmet in the County of York*, Thoresby Society Publications, 17, 1908, pp. 129–30.

3 *Ibid.*, p. 148.

4 J. Balteau, M. Barroux, M. Prévost et al. (eds.), *Dictionnaire de Biographie Française*, Paris, 1933 et seq., 9, p. 1246. This first edition appears to be rare; the only one known to the author is in the University Library, Leeds. Another French edition was published simultaneously in Amsterdam and Paris 1750–56. There appears to be no evidence for the edition of 1730 which is mentioned in *Wikipedia, s.v.* Crevier.

5 London, printed for J. and P. Knapton.

6 For Swinburne, see *O.D.N.B., s.v.* Swinburne, Henry; John Ingamells, *A Dictionary of British and Irish Travellers to Italy, 1701–1800*, New Haven and London, 1997, *s.v.* Swinburne; and Anne French, *Art Treasures in the North. Northern Families on the Grand Tour*, Norwich, 2009, *passim* and John Baker's diary, as at note 14, below.

7 Details from Huntington website (http:www//huntington.org/view/objects/asitem/People).

8 A pedigree of Swinburne of Capheaton is given in John Hodgson's *History of Northumberland*, part 2, vol. 1, 1827, pp. 231–34. See facsimile reprint, Newcastle, 1973–74.

9 Not 1731 as stated on the Huntington website, cited at note.7, above. Hodgson's pedigree (cited at note 8, above) gives her date of birth as 17 August 1736 (see p. 233).

10 These biographical details are taken from the Huntington website and Hodgson's pedigree with the exception of the details of her death and memorial, which come from the website of the church (http://www.kendalparishchurch.co.uk/memorialsin2.html). The Huntington website states curiously that her date of death is not known.

Ex Museo Florentino.

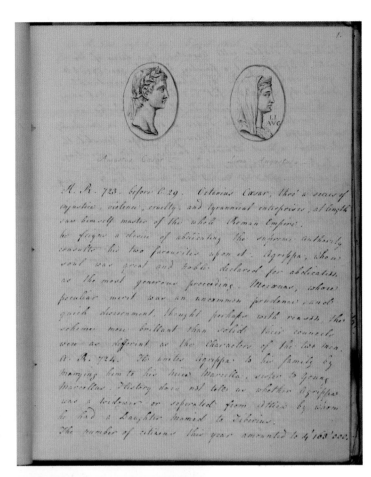

2. Illustrated page from Crevier's *History of the Roman Emperors*, English translation, 1775–81.

3. Page from Isabella Swinburne's *Extracts . . .* with portraits of Augustus Caesar and Livia Augusta. Compare fig. 2, top.

4. *Portrait of Isabel[la] Swinburne and Thomas Crathorne* by Francis Cotes, 1767. Huntington Art Collections, San Marino, USA. Oil on canvas 133.4 × 151.1 cm

5. Portrait of Sir Thomas Gascoigne in Rome by Pompeo Batoni, 1779. Leeds Museums and Galleries. Oil on canvas 248.9 × 172.7 cm.

11 'Sir Thomas Gascoigne and his Friends in Italy', *Leeds Arts Calendar*, 78, 1976, pp. 16–23.
12 Paola Bianchi, '"Quel Fortunato e Libero Paese". L'Accademia Reale e I Primi Contatti del Giovane Alfieri con in Mondo Inglese', proceedings of the conference *Alfieri e il suo Tempo*, Florence, 2003, p. 112. His name is recorded as *mons. Gascoigne*.

of one of Terry Friedman's best academic articles published in the *Leeds Arts Calendar*.[11] He may or may not have been aware of Sir Thomas's first Grand Tour which had taken place in the previous decade and had ended in disaster. In 1764 Sir Thomas enrolled at the Accademia Reale in Turin, a popular place of study for young Englishmen of ample means who wished to acquire gentlemanly accomplishments.[12] The next we hear of him is that on 6 September 1765 a papal pardon was issued to him and another Englishman Sir George Damer, later Earl of Dorchester for their part in an incident which had taken place that March in Rome and had resulted in a wounding and the death of a coachman. It caused Gascoigne to flee the city, assisted by the Governor.[13]

Gascoigne was clearly a young man in need of some guidance. He was born the sixth child and third son of Sir Edward Gascoigne, sixth baronet of Parlington. His father died when he was only five years old and he became the ward of three English Catholic Guardians, all Yorkshire gentlemen. He was educated abroad, first by the Benedictine monks at Douai in Flanders, then at the Collège des Quatre Nations in Paris. As a third son, he did not expect to inherit the family title and estates but his two elder brothers predeceased him and, in 1762 aged seventeen, he came into the family inheritance. The move to Paris had been contrived by his guardians in an attempt to cure his laziness and lack of application to his studies. In the following year they finally allowed him to visit England, seemingly for the first time as an adult.

The earliest record of Sir Thomas in connection with the Swinburnes comes from the diary of Henry Swinburne's father-in-law, the lawyer John Baker who in the early 1750s had served as Solicitor General of the Leeward Islands. On 11th March 1770 he and his wife Mary dined in London at the house of a Mrs Tuite in the company of Sir Thomas.[14] It will be recalled that 1770 is also the date on the Crevier manuscript, so it is possible that this meeting led to a general friendship with the family. Isabella's interest in the ancient world was shared by her brother Henry and by Henry's wife Martha, John Baker's daughter, whom he had married in 1767. Henry and Martha (who was a Catholic convert) had received a similar education to Sir Thomas and, in Henry's case, it was followed by a spell of travel on the Continent, seemingly with more productive results than had accrued to the young baronet of Parlington. They were both independently wealthy, or expected to become so and could afford to indulge their taste for travel which became a passion for the rest of their lives.[15] They were thus ideal travelling companions for Sir Thomas and busts of them both appear in the background to a grand, full-length portrait of him he commissioned in Rome from Pompeo Batoni (fig. 5).

The iconography of the Batoni portrait is worth studying. It is by no means a typical image of a rich young Englishman visiting the Eternal City on his Grand Tour. After the artist's signature comes the word ROME, painted inconspicuously along the top edge of the table at which Sir Thomas stands but, apart from this, there is nothing to show where he is — no ruins in the background or famous statues by his side. In this respect the painting stands in marked contrast to the Grand Tour portrait of his father, Sir Edward Gascoigne which now hangs opposite to it at Lotherton Hall (fig. 6). This shows Sir Edward in conventional style with the Coliseum in the background. For Sir Thomas, the whole emphasis is on book learning, on the process of travel and the collecting of educational objects; he stands in a library. Behind him are busts of Henry and Martha Swinburne,[16] he bare-chested like a Roman worthy and she swathed in classical drapery. In front of them is a globe. The message is clear, that they are the educated ones, instructing him on his travels and enabling him in turn to complete his education.

This is Sir Thomas as his guardians wished him to be — sober, serious, accomplished and taking his place in the world. The world in which he in fact took his place was not always the one which they would have wished him to inhabit. John Baker noted in his diary for June 1772 that, in the ten days up to the middle of that month, Sir Thomas and a companion had lost the enormous sum of £5,000 by

13 West Yorkshire Archive Service, Gascoigne papers WYL 115/XC/ Box 70, no.5; O. D. N. B, on-line (2013), s.v. Gascoigne, Sir Thomas (entry by Alexander Lock). For a fuller account of this incident, see Alexander James Lock, *Sir Thomas Gascoigne (1745–1810): English Catholicism, Politics and Estate Management in the Late Eighteenth Century*, Ph.D. thesis, University of Leeds, 2011, ch. 2. It is very much to be hoped that this excellent thesis will eventually be published.
14 Philip C. Yorke (ed.), *The Diary of John Baker*, London, 1931, p. 190.
15 Ibid., pp. 24–28.
16 The busts formed part of the Gascoigne Gift to the City of Leeds in 1968. They are attributed to the Irish sculptor Christopher Hewetson

6. *Portrait of Sir Edward Gascoigne in Rome*, attributed to Francesco Trevisani 1724-6,. Leeds Museums and Galleries. Oil on canvas 133.4 × 98.5 cm.

7. Sir Thomas Gascoigne's bookplate for his library at Parlington Hall by Hughes of London, late eighteenth century. Leeds Museums and Galleries. Print on paper 11.0 × 7.5 cm.

17 Yorke, as at note 14, p. 237.
18 The Gift included the Batoni portrait.
19 Friedman, as at note 11, p. 20.
20 Friedman, as at note 11, pp. 19–20. All three busts are on display at Lotherton Hall.
21 Lindsay Stainton, 'A Rediscovered Bas-relief by Thomas Banks', *Burlington Magazine*, June 1974, pp. 327–29; Friedman, as at note 11, pp. 21–2.This, too is now at Lotherton, somewhat regrettably embedded in a wall of the outer vestibule of the house. The subject is from Ovid's *Metamorphoses*.

gambling at the Cocoa Tree Club in London, half of it in a single evening.[17] His second Grand Tour, under the tutelage of the Swinburnes, seems to have passed off without serious incident and he arrived home with a fine haul of works of art, several of which were handed down in his family and formed part of the Gascoigne Gift to the City of Leeds in 1968.[18] By Sir Thomas's left hand in the Batoni portrait is a case of gold coins or medals. Terry Friedman suggested that they were part of the Petroni Collection of medals which Sir Thomas bought in Naples in 1779.[19] This was a purchase very much in the spirit of Crevier's *Lives* and it is all the more a pity that it is not known to have survived. The Swinburne busts which appear to be plaster models in the Batoni portrait were cast in bronze, probably by Luigi Valadier whose signature appears on a companion bust of Sir Thomas himself.[20] The Swinburnes also secured for Sir Thomas a highly important piece of neo-classical sculpture, the contemporary bas relief of *Alcyone Discovering the Body of her husband Ceyx* by Thomas Banks which they won in a raffle and gave to him.[21]

On his return to England Sir Thomas began his long reign as the resident squire of Parlington which lasted until his death in 1810. One of his first actions was to renounce Roman Catholicism. On 9th January 1780 he 'read his recantation from the errors of the Church of Rome, before the Archbishop of Canterbury, and received the sacrament'.[22] This he did so that he could stand for Parliament which, as a Catholic, he would have been forbidden; later that year he was duly elected as the member for Thirsk.[23] He was, however, keen to parade his new learning. For his library at Parlington he commissioned a fine pictorial bookplate with his name and seat in the top right-hand corner and his coat of arms below (fig. 7). The general design owes a good deal to the Batoni portrait. Sir Thomas's own place in the composition has been replaced by allegorical figures of Literature and Music but there are still books behind a screen of classical columns and a globe in the foreground. The heraldry provides a minor correction to what Isabella Swinburne drew on the Crevier titlepage by placing the Scottish saltire (St Andrew's cross) behind the royal arms on his baronet's badge.

In 1782 Sir Thomas commissioned the London architect Thomas Leverton to rebuild Parlington in the form of a Roman villa around a courtyard.[24] Unsurprisingly, this was not proceeded with, but he did erect a Roman triumphal arch which stands in the park to this day. It carries a political message carved on the frieze, LIBERTY IN N[ORTH] AMERICA TRIUMPHANT with the date 1783, an assertion of Sir Thomas's support for the Rockinghamite Whigs who had been opposed to the government's pursuit of the American war and wanted to make peace with the colonies.[25] In the early 1970s the architectural historian Sir Nikolaus Pevsner suggested that it be dismantled and taken across the Atlantic as a gift from the British Parliament to the US Congress, to mark the bicentenary of American independence but the proposal was rejected by the Foreign and Commonwealth office on the grounds that it did not have 'sufficient historical significance or contemporary relevance to make it a worthy gift'.[26]

Poor Sir Thomas, that his grand gesture should be so looked down upon by posterity! There is a touch of the absurd about him with his pretensions and portly figure, faintly reminiscent of Mr Toad of Toad Hall. But he made his mark on the physical as well as the cultural landscape, a characteristic figure of the Georgian era: refined and elegant, cultivated, coarse and comic, all at the same time.[27]

22 Joseph Foster, *Pedigrees of the County Families of Yorkshire*, London, 1874, s.v. Gascoigne of Gawthorpe and Parlington.
23 Lock in *O. D. N. B.*, cited as at note 13.
24 Terry Friedman, 'Romanticism and Neoclassicism for Parlington: the tastes of Sir Thomas Gascoigne', *Leeds Arts Calendar*, 66, 1970, pp. 16–17. The design, which is among the Gascoigne papers on deposit at the West Yorkshire Archive Service in Leeds, is reproduced on fig. 1.
25 Friedman, as at note 24, pp. 16,20–21 and fig. 5.
26 Letter, J. A. L. Morgan, Cultural Relations Department, F. C. O. 13 January 1975 and report attached, TNA, FCO/13/1774. I am grateful to Dr Alexander Lock for this reference.
27 There is a caricature of him paying court to an Italian lady in the British Museum. See Lindsay Stainton, 'A Caricature of Sir Thomas Gascoigne by Richard Cosway, RA (1742–1821)', *Leeds Arts Calendar*, 85, 1979, pp. 20–24

Championing James Gibbs at Wentworth Castle

Patrick Eyres

When Terry Friedman retired in 1993, the editor of the *Leeds Arts Calendar* applauded him for '24 years of high achievement' as a curator and as 'an exceptionally able professional art historian; James Gibbs's modern biographer; a world authority on sculpture but also possessing a versatile knowledge of the fine and decorative arts'.[1] This chapter salutes him as the champion of James Gibbs at Wentworth Castle, the Georgian country estate outside Barnsley. This task was launched as soon as he arrived in Leeds. It was first articulated in the *Leeds Arts Calendar* during 1970 and came to a mighty crescendo in 2012 with his chapter, 'James Gibbs at Wentworth Castle', in the proceedings of the first Wentworth Castle conference.[2]

His authoritative monograph on James Gibbs was published in 1984 and constitutes a major contribution to Georgian architectural history. However Gibbs's work at Wentworth Castle is tantalisingly intimated only by the inclusion of his name in the contract dated 28 July 1724, wherein the master joiner Charles Griffith agreed to: 'wainscout the Gallery att Staineborough as Desined by Mr Gibbs' (fig. 1). Consequently Terry's discussion of Stainborough Hall, re-named Wentworth Castle in 1731, is confined to a couple of pages.[3] Nevertheless the design of the mansion and garden buildings had convinced him that Gibbs's involvement extended much further than the Gallery and that the place merited further investigation. His intentions, though, were frustrated by the inaccessibility of the semi-derelict garden and park buildings, which were engulfed by a rampancy of rhododendrons, ivy and scrub woodland.

The decline of the estate appears to have begun before the Second World War. The war and post-war years brought the army, the ploughing up of much of the parkland for arable crops and the destruction of Georgian woodland by opencast coalmining. Then the early 1960s brought a new phase of coalmining beneath the gardens and the consequent subsidence undermined the gatehouse-keep of Stainborough Castle — the monumental, early-eighteenth-century castellated folly that crowns the summit of the Wentworth Castle estate — so that it collapsed into partial ruin. By the late 1960s the northern advance of the M1 motorway had demolished the south-eastern part of the estate where the vestigial structures and sculpture were lost either to the bulldozers or to theft. It was in 1969, the year after the motorway opened, that Terry Friedman arrived in Yorkshire to take up his post with Leeds City Art Galleries. He immediately visited Wentworth Castle and made contact with Keith Wark, historian at the Wentworth Castle College of Education, with whom he corresponded well into the 1970s. Unlike the estate fabric, the

1 A. Wells-Cole, 'Editorial', *Leeds Arts Calendar*, 112, 1993, p. 2.

2 T. Friedman, '"an unbounded prospect of a very rich Country": James Gibbs at Wentworth Castle', in P. Eyres (ed.), *Wentworth Castle and Georgian Political Gardening: Jacobites, Tories and dissident Whigs*, Stainborough, 2012, pp. 71–90.

3 For Griffith's contract, see T. Friedman, *James Gibbs*, New Haven and London, 1984, pp. 321–22; see also pp. 123–25 and fig. 124.

1. James Gibbs, The Long Gallery, Wentworth Castle, photograph, 1903 (photo: © *Country Life*).

4 See D. Lambert, 'Wentworth Castle in the Welfare State: The Road to a Public Landscape', in Eyres, as at note 2, pp. 177–90.

5 See 'Index to the Leeds Art Calendar, nos 1–116 (1947–95)', in *Leeds Arts Calendar*, 117–18, 1996–97, pp. 7–38, which lists the 21 articles.

mansion had been saved after the war when Barnsley Council had purchased it for conversion into a teacher training college. When in 1978 the college was transferred into Sheffield Polytechnic, the mansion became the home of the Northern College of Residential Adult Education.[4]

Despite the parlous state of the Georgian landscape and its buildings, Terry began to champion the place in his occasional articles on architecture and sculpture in the *Leeds Arts Calendar*. Between 1970 and 1992 he contributed twenty-one articles,[5] of which one fifth ingeniously promoted Wentworth Castle and their publication between 1970 and 1981 coincided with the preparation of his book on Gibbs. Indeed, in his first contribution he asserted the importance of Stainborough Castle (1726–30) in the 'reinterpretation of medieval patterns for modern garden buildings':

a lesser-known but equally remarkable creation of the early romantic landscape garden, here attributed to James Gibbs (1682–1754): the 'fortress' erected before 1739 in the grounds of

Stainborough (renamed Wentworth Castle) near Barnsley. Here, a circular mound — the site of an ancient Danish Camp (in the centre of which is Rysbrack's life-size, marble statue of the owner, Thomas Wentworth, Lord Raby and 1st Earl of Strafford, in Roman general's dress) — is encompassed by crenellated walls, four squat embattled towers and a taller, square gatehouse with turreted corners.[6]

Terry must have been among the last to experience the Strafford memorial statue within Stainborough Castle (fig. 2). At about this time the figure was mysteriously beheaded and the repaired statue relocated for safe keeping to its present position outside the north end of the mansion's Baroque wing.

In his next article he linked Gibbs with Gaetano Brunetti, the Paris-based Italian artist and designer, noting that they were 'closely associated during the 1730s'.[7] This has proved to be especially useful due to the subsequent linkage between Brunetti's designs and the plasterwork of Francesco Vassalli who, like Charles Griffith, was another associate of Gibbs to work at Wentworth Castle (fig. 3).[8] The other two articles emphasised the significance of the place in the mid-eighteenth century as represented by the estate landscapes commissioned from the painter, Thomas Bardwell,[9] and through the role of the Rotherham builder, John Platt in the construction and sculptural embellishment of the Palladian front of the mansion.[10]

It was not until the beginning of this century that the organisation was created that has enabled the estate to be plucked from the brink of dereliction in the very nick of time — and when the Wentworth Castle Heritage Trust was established in 2001, I was invited to become the Georgian Group representative on the Board of

6 T. Friedman, 'Romanticism and Neoclassicism for Parlington: The Tastes of Sir Thomas Gascoigne', Leeds Arts Calendar, 66, 1970, p. 19.

7 T. Friedman, 'James Gibbs's Designs for Domestic Furniture', Leeds Arts Calendar, 71, 1970, p. 23.

8 See W. J. and K. Smith, An Architectural History of Towneley Hall, Burnley, Nelson, Heritage Trust of the North West, 2004, pp. 56–62.

9 T. Friedman, 'A Temple Newsam Mystery Solved', Leeds Arts Calendar, 78, 1976, pp. 6 and 8.

10 T. Friedman, 'A Convenient and Pleasant Habitation', Leeds Arts Calendar, 89, 1981, p. 7.

2.   James Gibbs (attrib.), Stainborough Castle, showing the gatehouse (collapsed c. 1961) and the Strafford memorial statue by Rysbrack, postcard, c. 1920 (photo: Wentworth Castle Heritage Trust).

3.   Francesco Vassalli, The Perseus Medallion in the allegory of Peace conquering War, Italian Staircase, Wentworth Castle, postcard, c. 1950. Terry Friedman proposed that the garland of scrolls, foliage and rosettes surrounding the medallion derived from the Ara Pacis Augustae, the Altar of Augustan Peace, excavated fragments of which were on display when Gibbs and Strafford were in Rome in the first decade of the eighteenth century (photo: Wentworth Castle Heritage Trust).

Trustees. In 2003 the place not only featured on the BBC TV programme *Restoration* but also won the financial support of the Heritage Lottery Fund — and from 2005 the Trust has driven forward the ambitious programme of estate restoration that has encompassed the gardens and park, buildings and monuments, home farm and mansion. By 2003 the mansion leaked like a sieve and had it not been completely re-roofed in the autumn of 2006, this fine Georgian building would have been washed out by the torrential rains of 2007 that flooded much of South Yorkshire and many other parts of England. It was also in 2007 that the 600-acre estate was opened to the public for the first time.

My intermittent conversations with Terry about Wentworth Castle were prompted by *New Arcadian Journal* 31/32 (1991), which was devoted to both Wentworth Castle and Wentworth Woodhouse. By 2004, I was ready to bring him up to date about the schedule of the HLF-funded Phase I of the restoration and to ask him specific Gibbsian questions. But Terry was in hospital, and my letter was postponed until the autumn when he was convalescing after his operation. His reply was immediate and characteristically generous: '... I'm delighted that the project to restore the gardens attracted such a substantial grant and that work is proceeding apace. I've been at home from hospital for nearly two weeks and every day get stronger and more like my old self ... My file on Wentworth Castle is fairly thick and you would be most welcome to consult it, as it includes material about both the house and gardens gathered over several years ...'.[11]

It also transpired that Terry had acquired two Georgian prints relating to Wentworth Castle: *Stainborough*, the bird's-eye view engraved by Johannes Kip after Leonard Knyff in 1714, and *The Market Cross at Chichester*, engraved by George Vertue after William Ride, 1749. The latter was the model for the design by Richard Bentley for the exquisite Gothic Umbrello erected at Wentworth Castle, c. 1758 (fig. 4). Bentley was a member of Horace Walpole's Strawberry Hill Committee of Taste. Walpole was a lifelong friend of William, second Earl of Strafford (1722–91), and not only encouraged Strafford's estate improvements but also eulogised them in his publications. Unfortunately, the Umbrello collapsed c. 1950.

The Kip and Knyff is one of the series of engravings that promote the development of the estate and the status of its creator, Lord Strafford (1672–1739).[12] These were distributed both by the patron and the London booksellers, and Strafford also had them incorporated in prestigious architectural publications. As soon as the Baroque mansion had been erected (1710–14), he ensured that two elevations and a plan were engraved after Colen Campbell for Campbell's influential *Vitruvius Britannicus*, vol. 1 (1715). Later, he made sure that the 1713 and 1730 estate prints (see below) appeared in J. Badeslade and John Rocque, *Vitruvius Brittanicus* [sic], vol. 4 (1739), and in David Mortier, *Britannia Illustrata*, vol. 2 (1740), along with the companion French language edition: *Nouveau Theatre de la Grande Bretagne*.

The 1714 version of *Stainborough* by Kip after Knyff had been preceded by their 1711 engraving, which placed the planned new house within the pre-existing gardens and park of the estate Strafford acquired in 1708. The 1714 print displays Strafford's newly erected Baroque mansion and the gardens designed by the royal gardener, George London, amidst parkland clearly under improvement. Both show the ancient earthwork known as Stainborough Law high above the mansion. By 1730 it had become the monumental folly in the form of the replica medieval castle, and was named Stainborough Castle in 1731. Strafford's prints are also instructive on

11 T. Friedman, letter to author, 1 October 2004.
12 This series is the subject of *The Wentworth Rivalry in Georgian Prints: New Arcadian Journal* 77/78, 2017.

4. Richard Bentley, Gothic
Umbrello, *c.* 1758, photograph,
c. 1930, collapsed *c.* 1950 (photo:
Wentworth Castle Heritage Trust).

5. Johannes Kip, engraving after
Leonard Knyff, *Stainborough*, 1711,
bound into *Britannia Illustrata, 1709*
(photo: the Provost and Fellows of
Worcester College, Oxford).

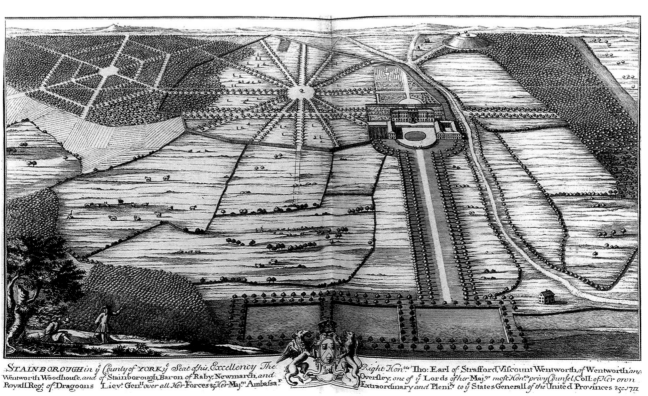

STAINBOROUGH in ý County of YORK ý Seat of his Excellency The   *Right Hon.ble Tho: Earl of Strafford, Viscount Wentworth of Wentworth and*
Wentworth Woodhouse, and of Stainborough, Baron of Raby, Newmarch, and   *Oversley, one of ý Lords of her Major most Honble privy Counsel, Coll: of Her own*
Royall Reg.t of Dragoons Liev.t Gen.ll over all Her Forces, Her Maj.ties Ambassa.r   *Extraordinary and Pleni.ry to ý States Generall of the United Provinces &c 1711*

account of their inscriptions, which are characterised by the first one — on the 1711 bird's-eye view (fig. 5):

STAINBOROUGH in yᵉ County of YORK, yᵉ Seat of His Excellency The Right Honᵇˡᵉ Tho: Earl of Strafford, Viscount Wentworth, of Wentworth and Wentworth Woodhouse and of Stainborough, Baron of Raby, Newmarch and Oversley, one of yᵉ Lords of her Majesᵗʸˢ Honᵇˡᵉ Privy Counsel, Coll: [Colonel] of Her own Royal Regᵗ of Dragoons, Lieuᵗ Genˡˡ over all Her Forces & Her Majesᵗʸˢ Ambassaʳ Extraordinary & Pleniʳʸ [Plenipotentiary] to yᵉ States Generall of the United Provinces &c. 1711.

This is an impressive litany of aristocratic titles as well as political, military and diplomatic achievements. The inscription commemorates Strafford's elevation in the peerage that year, 1711, as the Earl of Strafford (second creation) in acknowledgement of loyal service to the Protestant Stuart crown. It also creates the impression that Strafford owned both the Stainborough estate and neighbouring Wentworth Woodhouse — and therein lies the dramatic tale of the Wentworth family rivalry.

He had become Lord Raby in 1695 on the death of the second Earl of Strafford (first creation). As the senior Wentworth male he had anticipated inheritance of the ancestral estate at Wentworth Woodhouse. Imagine his outrage when he learnt that Woodhouse had been passed not to him but down the female line to a Thomas Watson, who then styled himself Watson-Wentworth. Perhaps there was comfort in the lapse of the earldom in 1695 — because through elevation as Raby and purchase of the Stainborough estate, combined with his success as a soldier and diplomat, he managed to have it revived and bestowed upon himself. This accounts for his propagandist, though legitimate, use of titles associated with the seventeenth-century owners of Wentworth Woodhouse.

The 1714 *Stainborough* reiterated the inscription on the *Wentworth Castle* (fig. 6),[13] engraved by D. Coster after C. Holzendorf in 1713 to show the splendid Baroque front complete with cascade, grottos and pool (though the statues were never installed). The text and image of Strafford's prints consistently promoted his restoration of the Wentworth dynasty, which now eclipsed the neighbouring and rival cousins through his superior status and estate embellishment. Indeed Terry had emphasised in *Country Life* during 1973 that: 'in the architectural race between the two rival branches of the Wentworths, the new house at Stainborough, later to be known as Wentworth Castle, was in the lead'.[14]

The text and image of the 1714 *Stainborough* developed the narrative begun by the 1711 print. The inscription elaborates Strafford's progress by acknowledging that he was Britain's co-negotiator at the peace congress at Utrecht, which brought to an end to the long-running War of Spanish Succession. Historians acknowledge that this treaty (1713) confirmed Britain as a European power with a maritime empire, and that the most popular clause — acquisition of the monopoly of the Spanish imperial slave trade — was the catalyst to British dominance of the Atlantic slave trade.[15] Moreover, Strafford had become (1712) a 'Knight of the most Noble Order of the Garter', an honour bestowed by the monarch alone.

There was a companion to the 1714 *Stainborough*, and together they consolidated his status as Queen Anne's reign came to an end. This portrait, *His Excellency the Right Honourable Thomas Earl of Strafford*, was engraved by John Simon after Jacques D'Agar and shows Strafford sporting the finery of a peer and the insignia of his beloved Order of the Garter while, in the background, a warship fired a broadside to salute him as

13 The title substitutes *Wentworth Castle* for *Stainborough* and thus exemplifies Strafford's practice of having engravings reprinted throughout the 1720s and especially after he renamed the estate in 1731.
14 T. Friedman and D. Linstrum, 'A Tour of Architectural Splendour', *Country Life*, 8 February 1973, p. 335.
15 See *The Blackamoor and the Georgian Garden: New Arcadian Journal* 69/70, 2011.

First Lord of the Admiralty. However the events of 1714 required a further print. The premature death of Queen Anne ushered in the Hanoverians, and the subtle shift in the inscription's emphasis registers the seismic quake experienced by the Queen's Tory ministers with the arrival of Whiggish George I. This portrait, *His Excellency Thomas Earl of Strafford* (fig. 7), was engraved by George Vertue after Sir Godfrey Kneller and a significant phrase was incorporated into the already lengthy inscription: 'One of the Lords Justices of Great Brittain [sic] & Ireland by Act of Parliament during the Absence of his Majesty'. The emphasis is on Strafford as the loyal minister who ensured the smooth transition from one royal dynasty to another thus securing the Protestant Succession. But in vain. George I and the Whigs abhorred the terms of the Peace of Utrecht and were determined to impeach the Tory ministers responsible. For two years Strafford literally fought for his life — and succeeded, though by 1717 he was so alienated by the brutality meted out to him that he threw his lot in with the Jacobite cause and actively conspired to restore the exiled Stuart King James III, half brother to the former Queens Mary II and Anne.

Throughout the 1720s he embellished his Yorkshire estate — completing the interior of the mansion, erecting buildings in the burgeoning gardens and developing the parkland. By 1730 he must have had a sense of completion because he commissioned a new pair of bird's-eye views. Both were engraved by John Harris after Thomas Badeslade and they complete Strafford's engraved narrative of status and achievement.[16] *A Prospect of Stainborough and Wentworth Castle* is a sweeping overview of the estate's splendour that befits the magnificence of Strafford's aristocratic status. The inscription is shorter because it highlights his prized award of the Order of the Garter alongside his now familiar titles in the peerage, which confirm ascendency over the rival Whig cousins and 'coincidentally' imply ownership of Wentworth Woodhouse. In both, the folly castle dominates the terrain and, visible for miles around, it swaggers as a theatrical display of dynastic longevity, apparently present since time immemorial. It was also infused with Jacobite associations for the knowing fellow traveller.

6. (top left) D. Coster, engraving after C. Holzendorf, *Wentworth Castle*, 1713, reproduced in *Britannia Illustrata*, vol. 2, 1740. It is likely that this records the final version of the elevation by Johan Eosander (photo: Wentworth Castle Heritage Trust).

7. (top right) George Vertue, engraving after Sir Godfrey Kneller, *His Excellency Thomas Earl of Strafford*, 1714 (photo: private collection).

16 Their titles are notable because they precede the renaming of the estate in 1731 and thus still describe the mansion as Stainborough and the monumental folly on Stainborough Law as Wentworth Castle.

STAINBOROUGH and WENTWORTH-CASTLE, in the County of YORK, Wentworth, of Wentworth Woodhouse and of Stainborough, Baron of Raby, who at the Death of QUEEN ANN, was one of the Lords of the regency appointed by Act of the Royal Regiment of Dragoons, privy Councellour, Ambassador Extraordinary and

One of the Seats of the Right Honourable Thomas Earl of Strafford, Viscount Newmarch and Oversley, and Knight of the most Noble Order of the Garter, Parliament, as First Lord Commissioner of the Admiralty, was Lieu: General Colonel Plenipotentiary to the States General as likewise for the Congress at Utrecht &c

8. John Harris, engraving after Thomas Badeslade, *Stainborough and Wentworth Castle*, 1730, reproduced in *Britannia Illustrata*, vol. 2, 1740 (photo: © British Library Board).

In *Stainborough and Wentworth Castle* (fig. 8) the focus is on the new Baroque mansion, whose design by Prussian court architects commemorates his years as envoy then ambassador in Berlin (1701–11), as well as on the surrounding gardens which are topped by the enormous folly castle. The inscription reiterates those of 1713–14 as a reprise of all his titles and achievements at the end of the reign of Queen Anne, and includes his successful embassy in The Hague and peacemaking at Utrecht. Nevertheless the wording of this inscription is so particular that it identifies Strafford's Yorkshire estate as the monument to his dynastic and diplomatic achievements as well as to his coded Jacobite affiliation. By retaining the phrase 'Colonel of the Royal Regiment of Dragoons', he signalled the brutality of the Hanoverians who in 1715 had stripped him of this prestigious and lucrative position (and passed it on to Lord Cobham, creator of the landscape garden at Stowe, who was then a loyal rather than a dissident Whig). Was he now, in 1730, also highlighting his legitimate service to the Stuart crown as a surrogate for his treasonous loyalty to the exiled royal dynasty? The clue to such a thought lies in Strafford's addition of the fascinating phrase, that he: 'at the Death of QUEEN ANN, was one of the Lords of the regency appointed by Act of Parliament'. Remember, the final portrait print of 1714 had used a different form of words: 'One of the Lords Justices of Great Brittain [sic] & Ireland by Act of Parliament during the Absence of his Majesty'. So what might account for the change from Lord Justice to Lord of the regency? There is no doubt that Strafford was one of the Lords Justices in 1714. Yet he had also been named as a Lord of the regency in 1722, by the exiled Stuart monarch James III. So are we to think that the change of words between the 1714 and 1730 prints encodes his role as a regent of the absent Stuart king? Fellow Jacobites would certainly draw this conclusion.

Moreover he would shortly translate this use of language from print to stone through inscription on the Queen Anne Obelisk, which he erected during 1734 at the edge of the park beside the public road to mark the twentieth anniversary of the death of the last Stuart monarch. The lengthy inscription only slightly elaborates on those of the prints and proclaims that he: 'was one of the seven appointed by act of PARLIAMENT to be REGENTS of the KINGDOME during the absence of the SUCCESSOR'. Unusually for a monument dedicated to royalty, both the Queen's successor, Hanoverian George I and his successor George II, are omitted — doubtless because 'the SUCCESSOR', Stuart James III, remained absent. In so doing Strafford created a Jacobite monument that is unique in a Georgian country estate. Characteristically, he concludes the inscription by commemorating his embassy to the Dutch Republic and co-negotiation of the epoch-defining Peace of Utrecht. He clearly relished flourishing in print and stone the name of the treaty so despised by Whigs and Hanoverians. Naturally Utrecht was integral to the posthumous inscription on the pedestal of Rysbrack's memorial statue when it was installed in the bailey of Stainborough Castle during 1744. Substantially the same as the inscriptions on the prints of 1713–14 and 1730, as well as that on the Queen Anne Obelisk, it concludes: 'How deservedly he was elevated to these honours, his public acts must testify'. [17]

Although the text of his engraved inscriptions became translated into the stone of monuments in the 1730s and 1740s, their content was already evident in the symbolism of mansion and garden. The question remains: who was the designer who visualised Strafford's iconography? As a deposed Tory minister and Jacobite conspirator, who else would Strafford turn to than the fellow traveller, James Gibbs?

By the summer of 2007 the mansion had been re-roofed and the key garden buildings were visible after consolidation. The time had come to take Terry back to Wentworth Castle. Both in the mansion and gardens his pleasure was palpably rapturous. He applauded both the Trust's restoration programme and the new research published in the New Arcadian Journal devoted to the development of the Georgian estate and its iconographies. [18] The latter established that the design and decoration of the mansion as well as specific garden and parkland features commemorated Strafford's diplomatic achievements in the service of the Protestant Stuart Queen Anne — as envoy then ambassador to the Prussian court in Berlin, 1701–11; as ambassador to the Dutch Republic in The Hague, 1711–14; and as Britain's co-negotiator of the Peace of Utrecht, 1711–13. [19] It also confirmed that, after his political downfall, Jacobite associations became encoded within the legitimately Stuart symbolism. [20] Moreover the New Arcadian Journal also revealed that it was the architects of the Prussian court in Berlin who had designed the Baroque wing — Jean de Bodt and Johann Eosander — thus answering the question that had vexed architectural historians for the past half century. [21] In addition, Francesco Vasalli was established as the mansion's stuccoist, probably with Martino Quadri, rather than Giuseppe Artari and Giovanni Bagutti to whom the plasterwork had previously been attributed. [22]

The visit prompted Terry's enthusiastic re-engagement with the place, and a mutually stimulating collaboration:

17 For the inscriptions on the obelisk and pedestal, see M. Charlesworth in The Georgian Landscape of Wentworth Castle: New Arcadian Journal 63/64, 2008, pp. 50, 70.

18 Wentworth Castle: New Arcadian Journal, 63/64, 2008, as at note 17, with articles by M. Charlesworth, P. Eyres, W. Frith, J. Furse, C. Margrave, J. Woudstra; 1st edn., 57/58, 2005.

19 See P. Eyres and M. Charlesworth, as at note 18, Wentworth Castle, pp. 15–47 and pp. 49–79; elaborated further by Charlesworth, 'Lord Strafford's Need for a Past and British National Identity', and Eyres, 'Jacobite Anticipations: Lord Strafford, Wentworth Castle and Dissident Political Gardening' in Eyres, as at note 2, Wentworth Castle and Georgian Political Gardening, pp. 53–70 and 91–112. See also Charlesworth, 'Lord Raby in Berlin: Art, Architecture and Amour', and Eyres, 'Lord Raby's Embassies and their Representation at Wentworth Castle', in P. Eyres and J. Lomax (eds.), Diplomats, Goldsmiths and Baroque Court Culture: Lord Raby in Berlin, The Hague and Wentworth Castle, Stainborough, 2014, pp. 23–41 and 42–63.

20 See Eyres and Charlesworth, as at note 18, Wentworth Castle, pp. 15–47 and 49–79; elaborated further by Eyres in 'Jacobite Patronage: Lord Strafford, James Gibbs, Wentworth Castle and the Politics of Dissent' in S. Kellerman and K. Lynch (eds.), With Abundance and Variety: Yorkshire Gardens and Gardeners across Five Centuries, York, 2009, pp. 63–92; and in 'Wentworth Castle: Gibbs and Garden Buildings', in C. Boot (ed.), Gibbs and Gardening: The Work of the Eighteenth-Century Architect James Gibbs, Buckingham: Buckinghamshire Gardens Trust, 2010, pp. 23–30. See also Eyres and Charlesworth, as at note 18, Wentworth Castle and Georgian Political Gardening.

21 See Charlesworth, as at note 18, Wentworth Castle, pp. 49–79; elaborated further in Charlesworth, as at note 19, Diplomats, Goldsmiths and Baroque Court Culture.

22 See Eyres, as at note 18, Wentworth Castle, pp. 15–47 (n. 8, p. 39). Terry's imagination was also caught by confirmation that John Platt had rebuilt Stainborough Castle in the 1750s prior to the building of the Palladian front; see J. Furse, as at note 18, Wentworth Castle, pp. 115–43.

I write finally to thank you for a most memorable visit to Wentworth Castle and all the amazing dividends that it paid off for both of us. I am full of admiration for the Trust's achievement in restoring the mansion and gardens to their rightful place in the history of British art. A great triumph. Needless to say, I am thrilled by the revelation of the 'Gun Room' which now has become a most poignant landmark in the garden circuit, as it surely must have been intended at the start, and of course it opens up fascinating possibilities of Gibbs's involvement beyond the mansion . . . .[23]

Terry's encouragement, appreciation and support for the research into Strafford's career and iconography knew no bounds and combined a generosity of spirit with demanding critique – which puts me in mind of the retirement tribute in the *Leeds Arts Calendar*: 'a great enthusiast with boundless energy, always very willing to share his expertise with colleagues and students'.[24] My own interest was in the Jacobite context to Strafford's patronage of Gibbs. I had already gathered evidence of Gibbs as the design consultant who advised throughout the interior decoration (1717 to mid-1730s), even in the upgrading of the Earl's domestic accommodation within the pre-existing Cutler House.[25] I had also, with Terry's guidance, brought together evidence that supports Gibbs as the designer of Strafford's garden buildings.[26] My purpose was to make a case for the influence of the Strafford-Gibbs collaboration on dissident political gardening elsewhere, for example at Cirencester Park, Hartwell and Stowe.[27] Terry's principal interest however was in substantiating an overview of the architect's involvement with the buildings and sculptures of the gardens and park for both the first and second Earls of Strafford — a role far greater than he had thought in the early 1980s — and it was this that he presented to the first Wentworth Castle conference in August 2010.

In 'James Gibbs at Wentworth Castle', Terry eloquently promoted the architect as Strafford's ideal collaborator, especially as during the 1720s Gibbs's practice began to encompass the design of garden buildings. Thus Gibbs offered site specific designs as well as published designs that could be adapted by local workmen to suit the needs both of the owner and topography. Consequently Terry's key point was that Wentworth Castle demonstrated: 'the contributions made . . . by the architect himself or within a Gibbsian sphere of influence'.[28] Moreover 'It should be no surprise that . . . Gibbs's participation spread into the surrounding parkland, or that that should occur around the time he was preparing *A Book of Architecture* [published in 1728], containing among much else thirty-five designs for garden buildings and ninety-three for outdoor ornament, all conceived by one person in the manner of Italian models, the first English pattern book of its kind. The Earl was a subscriber'.[29]

Terry emphasised that in the volume's Introduction Gibbs had stressed the pragmatic usefulness of his designs: '. . . to such Gentlemen as might be concerned in Building, especially in the remote parts of the country where little or no assistance for Designs can be procured . . . with Draughts . . . which may be executed by any Workman who understands Lines, either as here Design'd or with some Alteration . . . easily made by a person of Judgement'.[30] Marshalling the evidence of the pattern book, along with that of the architect's garden buildings elsewhere, Terry attributed those at Wentworth Castle — Strafford's obelisks, the so-called Gun Room, Stainborough Castle and the now vanished Law Temple and Constantine's Well — to James Gibbs. He also — noting the Rotunda, Argyll Column and Strafford memorial statue (fig. 9) — observed that it is hardly coincidental that the son,

23 T. Friedman, letter to author, 17 August 2007.
24 Wells-Cole, as at note 1, p. 2.
25 For evidence of artists and craftsmen associated with Gibbs working at Wentworth Castle, see Eyres, as at note 20, 'Jacobite Patronage', pp. 69–70, and nn. 13–18.
26 See Eyres, as at note 20, 'Jacobite Patronage', pp. 74–75; and Eyres, as at note 20, 'Gibbs and Garden Buildings', pp. 23–30.
27 See Eyres, as at note 20, 'Jacobite Patronage', pp. 85–92; and especially Eyres, as at note 19, 'Jacobite Anticipations', pp. 101–09.
28 Friedman, as at note 2, p. 72.
29 Ibid., p. 76. Edward Reeves, who was also a subscriber, had supervised the building of the Baroque mansion and appears to have implemented Gibb's designs at Wentworth Castle into the 1730s; see Eyres, as at note 20, 'Jacobite Patronage'. The 2nd edition of *A Book of Architecture* was published in 1739.
30 James Gibbs, *A Book of Architecture*, cited by Friedman, as at note 2, p. 78.

9. Chris Broughton, *Overview of Wentworth Castle*, drawing, 2013, reproduced in *Wentworth Woodhouse: New Arcadian Journal*, no. 73/74, 2014. Anti-clockwise from top: Stainborough Castle, Lady Mary's Obelisk, Arcade, Union Jack Gardens, Corinthian Temple and, in the park, Argyll Column, Rotunda, Queen Anne Obelisk, Serpentine River, Palladian Bridge, Strafford Gate — and the Home Farm (right) with Long Barn, Stables and Estate Church, and (far right) Steeple Lodge and Pillared Barn; and the mansion's Baroque Wing (centre) with Gun Room (to right), and Palladian Wing (centre left) with (above) the Victorian Conservatory (photo: the artist, the Wentworth Castle Heritage Trust and the *New Arcadian Press*).

William the second Earl, initially operated within a Gibbsian sphere of influence: both his father and father-in-law, the second Duke of Argyll, had been patrons of the architect and Rysbrack, who sculpted the memorial statue, was professionally associated with Gibbs.

Doubtless other architects will continue to be proposed for particular garden buildings. However none to date have the same claim to Strafford patronage as Gibbs, and Terry Friedman's case remains compelling — though he would be the first to remind us that further discoveries are yet to be made in the voluminous family archives. With eye-twinkling mirth, he would solemnly pronounce that it would be easier for Barack Obama to track down Osama Bin Laden than for a single scholar to excavate the Strafford Papers in the British Library. History has already proved him correct!!

Gibbs at Raby Castle

Richard Hewlings

The transformation by successive Lords Barnard of the Nevilles' great castle at Raby, Co. Durham, into a modern country house was described by Alistair Rowan in three articles in *Country Life* in 1970 and one article in *Architectural History* in 1972.[1] A single article in *County Life* in 2012 by the present author interpreted the same evidence slightly differently, and necessarily in a somewhat compressed form.[2] The purpose of the present article is to set out the evidence for one of the conclusions presented in 2012, a conclusion of interest to Terry Friedman since it revealed that Raby had been the subject of a proposal by James Gibbs, whose biography he published in 1984.[3]

The proposal, in alternative drawn forms (figs 1 and 2), was first recognized, described and illustrated by Alistair Rowan in his 1972 article.[4] Both designs are

1 Alistair Rowan, 'Raby Castle, Co. Durham', *Country Life*, CXLVII, 1, 8 and 22 January 1970, pp. 18–21, 66–69, 186–89; Alistair Rowan, 'Gothick Restoration at Raby Castle', *Architectural History*, XV, 1972, pp. 23–50.

2 Richard Hewlings, 'The result of an unnecessary provocation', *Country Life*, CCVI, 1 August, 2012, pp. 51–55.

3 Terry Friedman, *James Gibbs*, New Haven and London, 1984.

4 Rowan, 'Gothick Restoration', as at note 1, pp. 26–27, and figs 5–6.

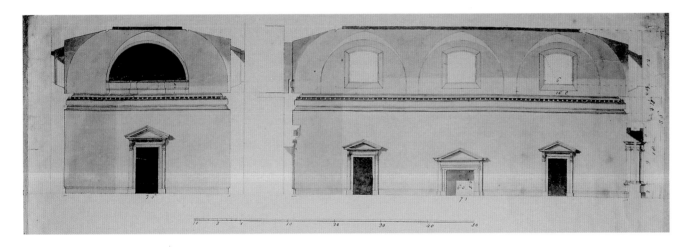

1.   James Gibbs, alternative proposals for the High Hall, Raby Castle, Co. Durham. The two drawings are pasted onto the same sheet, and thus appear in the same photograph (photo: Clare Owen).

2. James Gibbs, alternative proposals for the High Hall, Raby Castle, Co Durham. The two drawings are pasted onto the same sheet, and thus appear in the same photograph (photo: Clare Owen).

evidently for the reconstruction of the upper of two superimposed great halls at Raby Castle, the one known as the High Hall. Professor Rowan noted their 'Palladian' character, but did not attribute them to a particular architect. Nor was it possible to date the drawings, although a window proposed in the south end indicates that they must have been made after the destruction of rooms south of the High Hall by a fire whose date is also not certainly known. It is still not possible to date them accurately, but the discovery of their author makes one hypothesis possible.

This author was Gibbs. The attribution rests on a single pen-stroke, the representation of zero on the scale-bar by a lower-case v with the second part of the stroke slightly curved, almost like a lower-case r (figs 3 and 4). This was Gibbs's signature scale-bar, and it can be found on numerous drawings by him in the RIBA, the Ashmolean and elsewhere.[5] Detailed accounts for work at Raby cover the years 1736–55 (and resume in 1770), and do not include payments to Gibbs, so the drawings may pre-date those years. But Gibbs was paid £2,528 10s. by the first Lord Barnard in instalments between 11 April 1722 and 18 May 1723; these payments are recorded in Lord Barnard's bank account, although this does not specify what they were for.[6] However, Gibbs built the parish church of Shipbourne, Kent, for Lord Barnard, and designed a monument there for him, his wife and his mother; both church and monument were complete at the consecration on 29 June 1723. Not

5 This point is made in Richard Hewlings, 'Sir George Savile's Architectural Drawings', *English Heritage Historical Review*, VI, 2011, pp. 89–90; and not made, but assumed, in Richard Hewlings, 'Adderbury House', in Malcolm Airs (ed.), *Baroque and Palladian: The Early Eighteenth-Century Great House*, Oxford, Universty of Oxford, 1996, pp. 128–29.

6 London, C Hoare and Co., Ledger G,

The Rt. Hon:ble ye. Lord Barnard

[fol.] 46	1722	April 11
To Jas. Gibbs	500.—	
		July 5
To James Gibbs	500.—	
[fol.] 235	1722	Oct:r 1
To James Gibbs	500.—	
	[1723]	Jan 11
To James Gibbs	400.—	
[fol.] 116	1723	May 18
To James Gibbs	628. 10.—	

dated, but presumably near-contemporary, is the room which Gibbs added to Lord Barnard's house, Fairlawne, in the same parish.[7] Gibbs's large receipt presumably covered these works, but it may have covered the preparation of the Raby drawings also.

In any case Lord Barnard died on 28 October 1723, not long after the consecration of his church, and Lady Barnard died two years later, on 9 November 1725. Relations with his eldest son, the Hon. Gilbert Vane, were not cordial. Gilbert had brought an action in court against his father between 1714 and 1716;[8] and, although he inherited Raby as second Lord Barnard, Fairlawne was left to his younger brother, the Hon. William Vane.[9] The second Lord might have employed his father's architect, but it seems unlikely. Gibbs's proposals for Raby are therefore more likely to pre-date October 1723.

There also exist three unsigned, undated, uncaptioned (and unexplained) drawings in the collection of Lord Burlington, which are at least identifiable as surveys of Raby Castle. They do not appear to have been drawn by Burlington, and

7 Friedman, as at note 3, pp. 302–03. The church at Shipbourne, demolished in 1880, is illustrated on p. 72, and the monument on p. 93. Under Fairlawne, Friedman noted the possibility that these payments may also 'relate to work at Raby Castle'.

8 Rowan, 'Gothick Restoration, as at note 1, p. 24.

9 E[veline] C[ruickshanks], in Eveline Cruickshanks, Stuart Handley and D. W. Hayton, *The House of Commons 1690–1715*, V, Cambridge, Cambridge University Press, 2002, p. 718. Even this inheritance was disputed.

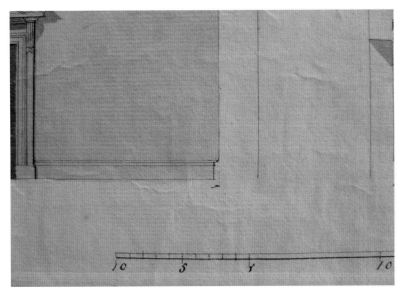

3. (left)   James Gibbs, detail of fig. 1, showing the scale bar (photo: Richard Hewlings).

4. (bottom left)   James Gibbs, detail of fig. 2, showing the scale bar (photo: Richard Hewlings).

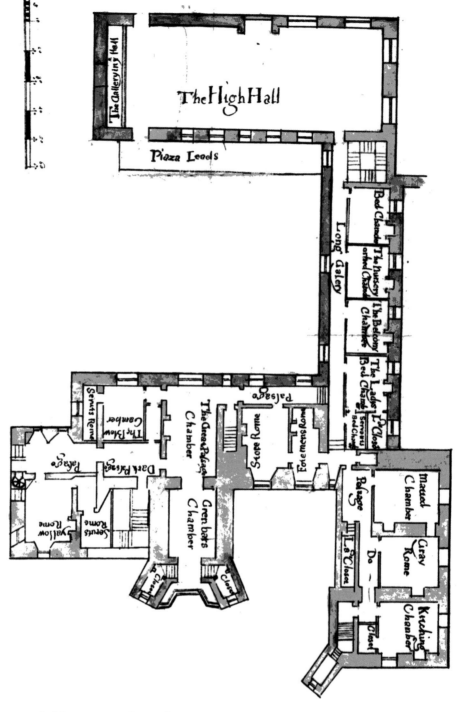

10 Rowan, 'Gothick
Restoration, as at note 1, p. 24;
Hewlings, as at note 2, p. 52.
Dickinson, carpenter and joiner,
paid 6 gns in 1737 [Raby Castle,
Account Book A, 13 and 47],
and Perritt, plasterer, paid £19
19s. 6d. for work done in 1739
[Raby Castle, Account Book A,
122], and £229 11s. for work
done between 1743 and 1746
[Raby Castle, Green Account
Book, 68], had worked at York
Assembly Rooms in 1730–32
[Royal Commission on the
Historical Monuments of
England, York, v, London, 1981,
p. 45]. Bagnall, plasterer, paid
£38 19s. in 1754 [Raby Castle,
Green Account Book, 148
(where his name is spelt
Bagnell)], had worked in
Burlington's own house at
Londesborough in 1730 [ex inf
the late Dr R. T. Spence].
11 Chatsworth House, Archives,
Lord Burlington's drawings, Boy
[11], 1.

were probably sent to him for an opinion. We may at least infer that Lord
Burlington offered an opinion, since two of Lord Burlington's protégés, Daniel
Garrett and James Paine, were to work at Raby Castle, and so were at least three
building tradesmen, Bernard Dickinson, Thomas Perritt and John Bagnall, whom
Burlington had engaged elsewhere.[10]

One of the three drawings (fig. 5) is a first-floor plan, or strictly a part-plan, as
it only shows the western half of the south range and the southern half of the west
range, but it includes the High Hall.[11] It is not entirely accurate, the rooms are
identified in a naïve printed hand, and the scale bar is not very well drawn; so it

may have been drawn by a local surveyor, such as the joiner-architect Thomas Shirley.[12] But it is of great value in showing the arrangement of the first-floor rooms before the transformations which began around 1736, and in particular it shows the High Hall unaltered by Gibbs. It could of course have been made before Gibbs drew up his proposal, but the other two drawings (figs 6 and 7) in the Burlington collection are annotated in the hand of Daniel Garrett,[13] who was working at Raby in 1748, and thus (from the reasoning put forward above) almost certainly after Gibbs.[14] All three also show what is recognisable as the High Hall without Gibbs's proposed alterations, and we may conclude that the latter were never implemented.[15]

Gibbs inherited a two-storey-high volume from the medieval castle, and his proposals would have transformed this into a room like the two-storey-high public rooms which he designed for Cambridge University in 1722 and St Bartholomew's Hospital in 1730.[16] One of his proposals shows Ionic pilasters and panelled walls in the lower storey, with seven windows in long walls and three in the short walls of the upper storey, set into vaulted penetrations in the cove, the system which he had

12 Howard Colvin, *Biographical Dictionary of British Architects 1600–1840*, New Haven and London, 2008, p. 921.

13 Chatsworth House, Archives, Lord Burlington's drawings, Boy [11], 2 and 3. Garrett's hand is discussed and illustrated by Howard Colvin and John Harris, 'The Architect of Foots Cray Place', *Georgian Group Journal*, VII, 1997, 5–7. There are drawings by Garrett for Wallington Hall at Wallington (e.g. Wall. 85, 91, 109); for Gibside at Glamis Castle, noted in Margaret Wills, *Gibside and the Bowes Family*, Newcastle, 1995; and for Aldby Park, Buttercrambe, in North Yorkshire Record Office, DAR MP 27 and 28.

14 One of Garrett's signed drawings at Raby is dated 16 July 1748 [Raby Castle, drawings, unnumbered].

15 The most distinctive feature, shown in all three drawings, is the four-foot-wide gallery at the north end, which is still there today. All three show two doors at the north end of the east and west elevations, and one at the south end of the east elevation. All show a fireplace in the east wall. All three agree in showing seven tall windows on the west side and three on the east side, the former evenly distributed, the latter in the southern half only, but the plan differs from the east elevation in positioning the northernmost of these three windows over the fireplace.

16 Friedman, as at note 3, figs 243 and 254.

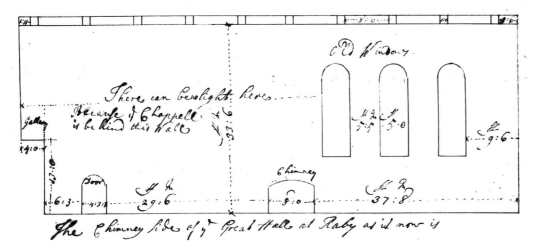

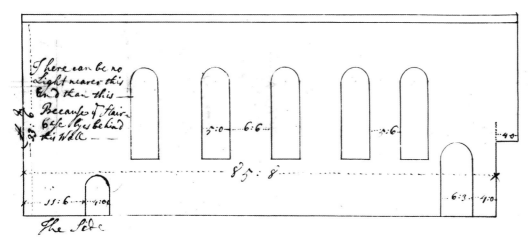

6.   Daniel Garrett (here attributed), survey elevation of the east side of the High Hall, Raby Castle (photo: Geremy Butler, Trustees of the Chatsworth Settlement).

7.   Daniel Garrett (here attributed), survey elevation of the west side of the High Hall, Raby Castle (photo: Geremy Butler, Trustees of the Chatsworth Settlement).

used for Sudbrook (1715), Orleans House, Twickenham (1716) and Ragley (1750), although without the Rococo ornament in these houses.[17] The other proposal is even more austere. It omits the pilasters in favour of bare walls, against which doors and chimneypiece stand out in greater contrast, gaining further emphasis by the addition of pediments. It retains the entablature, slightly enlarged, and further emphasised by the addition of modillions. The seven and three windows of the upper storey have been reduced to three and one respectively, and the cove much enlarged, so that it springs from immediately above the entablature. By reducing and enlarging the details Gibbs created an effect like that of an ancient Roman bath. Gibbs was not incapable or averse to the recreation of antique forms, as his temple-like designs for St Mary-le-Strand and St Martin-in-the-Fields indicate. The attribution to Gibbs of these drawings for Raby delighted Terry Friedman in revealing that Gibbs was as receptive to awesome antique sensation as Burlington, and perhaps better at recreating it.

Acknowledgements

I am grateful to Lord Barnard for permission to consult his archives at Raby Castle; to Clare Owen and Rachel Milner for their assistance there on two different occasions in 2012, and to Clare Owen for the photographs reproduced here as figs 1 and 2. I am grateful to the Trustees of the Chatsworth Settlement for permission to reproduce three drawings, figs 5, 6 and 7 in this article.

17 Ibid., figs 141–42, 164 and 169

'So gross an imposition': tradesman v. client in the 1790s

Karin Walton

I t might be supposed that in the eighteenth century, in any dispute between a well-off client and a tradesman, the client would always triumph. However, as the following shows, this was not invariably the case.

In the summer of 1793 John Pinney (1740–1818) was putting the finishing touches to his new house, No 3 Great George Street, Bristol, now No 7 and, since 1939 The Georgian House museum. He had purchased the leasehold of land in May 1788 and employed the leading Bristol architect William Paty. After numerous delays John, his wife Jane and their younger children were finally able to move in in 1791 although work continued on the interior for a further two years.

John Pinney was born in Somerset (fig. 1). His father Michael, described as a 'Gentleman', died when he was three and John was dependent on his wealthy

1. William Whitby, *Portrait of John Pinney*, 1792/3, oil on canvas, 730 × 600 mm (sight) on loan to The Georgian House Museum, Bristol, and reproduced by kind permission of the Pinney family (Image © Bristol Museums, Galleries & Archives).

cousins, Azariah and John Frederick who apprenticed him to a 'Warehouseman' in London. On John Frederick's death in 1762, John inherited estates in Somerset and Dorset and sugar plantations on the island of Nevis in the West Indies. He spent the next twenty years on Nevis but, spurred on by the threats of French invasion, he moved his family, consisting of his wife Jane whom he had married on Nevis, and four surviving children, to England in 1783 and set about finding a home. Bristol was still the principal port trading with the Americas and so was the obvious choice.

John took a close interest in the building and fitting out of the house and must have been an exacting client, continually complaining about delays, below-standard work and being overcharged. The evidence for this is in his Letter Books, deposited in the University of Bristol Library[1] but it is a somewhat one-sided account; only rarely do we get the tradesman's side of the story although it is usually possible to piece together the facts from Pinney's detailed expositions.

Although Pinney had favoured a local architect, when it came to furnishings, he preferred to employ London tradesmen. Gilt mirrors, chimney-pieces and the glass for his best bookcases all came from London and it was to London he turned for window curtains for his first-floor drawing room. His agent in securing the most fashionable items was a family friend, Mrs Judith Butler Dunbar, who was delegated to pass on measurements and orders and to take delivery of items until they could be despatched to Bristol, usually by 'Wiltshire's Waggon'.

In July 1793 Pinney himself went to London and ordered curtains for the three windows in his drawing room from Richard Taitt of 92 Jermyn Street, St James's. Taitt who was around forty years of age had built up a successful business. In 1787 his household goods, utensils and stock in workshop were insured for £2,300 and in 1794 he supplied furniture and furnishings to the royal household.[2] The curtains were delivered on 18 September but the first sign of trouble came two days later when the bills arrived. Pinney sent off a flurry of furious letters. The first was to Taitt:

Mr Richard Taitt, No 92 Jermyn Street, London
Bristol, Septem[r] 20th 1793.

Sir,
This moment I have received your Acco[t] from M[r] Tobin; and notwithstanding I am pressed for time, I cannot omit expressing my astonishment at it — The Curtains are by no means according to order, they were not to be trimmed with Silk &c. but to be made in a proper manner for <u>linen</u> not silk Curtains — The Charges appear to me so extravagant that I know not what to say — they still remain in the Case you packed them in, where they shall stay until it is determined what is to be done with them — To avoid contention I will gladly lose ten or twelve Guineas on the Contents of the box and charges you sent me. I flatter myself you will be able to dispose of them amongst some of your noble Customers, for such amazing expence for <u>linen</u> Curtains will not suit the pocket of a private Gentleman.
I am Your hble Ser[t3]

He then looked at the bill for the materials supplied by Messrs Pritchard & Dudding, owners of a Chintz Warehouse off Bond Street, and this led him to open the crate. Another letter followed:

Mess[rs] Pritchard & Dudding
Lower Brook Street London

Gentlemen!

1. University of Bristol Library, Special Collections. I am grateful to Hannah Lowery and Michael Richardson for access to the papers and to the Pinney family for permission to quote from them.
2. Geoffrey Beard and Christopher Gilbert (eds), *Dictionary of English Furniture Makers*, Leeds, 1986, p. 870.
3. Pinney Papers, Letter Book 10, p. 334.

This day Mr Tobin arrived here in the Mail Coach, and he has just delivered me your Acco^t of Chintz and green Callicoe for lining the Window Curtains, you delivered Mr Taitt — the quantity of Lining struck me with the greatest astonishment, as I could not conceive how it was possible for him to dispose of it in lining Curtains for three Windows I dare say, you perfectly well recollect that you calculated it might take three or four yards more than two pieces for the lining, and about the same quantity of the Chintz and in consequence thereof I ordered two pieces of the lining with two pieces of the Chintz for the Curtains, with an order for you to supply the few yards that might be deficient ... and I observe, agreeable to the above order, you sent Mr Taitt, the 20th of July, the two pieces of green Callicoe for lining the Curtains with the Chintz. Your calculation of the quantity corresponded with what I understood from Mr Taitt, when I was at his House with Mrs Ford and gave my order to you accordingly — Judge then how great must be my surprize to find a charge ten days after, without my knowledge or consent, of no less a quantity than the addition of 103 yards of green Callicoe lining, instead of about three or four yards as I was taught to believe.[4]

Now he had discovered what had gone wrong, he wrote again to Taitt:

Upon looking into Messrs Pritchard & Dudding's Acco^t (since writing to you this day) I was not a little surprised at the large quantity of green lining they had delivered you to line the chintz Curtains I gave you directions to make. This induced me to look into the box you sent to endeavour to find out where the quantity was disposed of: when, upon removing the top-piece, to my very great astonishment, I found that you had made the Curtains of the lining, instead of the Chintz sent for that purpose. What induced you to do it, is best known to yourself, but it being so palpable an error and so contrary to my <u>express</u> order, in the presence of a young Gentleman with me, that you cannot be surprized at my desiring you to inform me what you wish to have done with them, for I consider them your property. I would not use them in there present state, if you were to make me a compliment of the trimmings and making.[5]

Pinney was well used to taking on impudent tradesmen. When he deemed he had been overcharged for a chimney-piece, he simply sent what he claimed had been the amount of the estimate.[6] On the positive side, he was quick to pay his bills although he expected a discount for prompt payment and deducted it from the total whether it was offered or not.

In Taitt, however, Pinney had met his match. If he was expecting Taitt to give in, he was to be disappointed. Taitt replied on 23 September and Pinney's next letter, of 30 September, is marginally more placatory, but with a sting in the tail:

On my return from Race down I found your letter of the 23rd and am sorry to find your assertion so contrary to the <u>real</u> fact, which can be authenticated upon oath. But notwith-standing, being desirous to avoid contention, and ever willing to put an end to any dispute or misunderstanding by the cool unbiased decision of respectable & disinterested men, I shall cheerfully submit our affair to Arbitration — An Arbitrator to be chosen by each party and if they disagree to elect an Umpire — To examine all evidence, upon Oath. This appears to me the most easy and satisfactory way of settling it: But if you should wish to compromise matters, in order to put an end to such unpleasant business without further investigation I will readily meet you on that ground, and shall beg leave to propose your receiving back the three pair of Curtains, made with Calico, <u>instead of Chintz</u>, and to remove the outside Callico & to replace it with Chintz. To take back the Gimp on the Curtains & half the Silk Tassels as the Curtains are to be quite plain. The Callico, Gimp & Tassels, in your extensive business, can be of no consequence, you can easily dispose of them amongst your numerous Customers.

... I could say much more on the subject but shall not enlarge unless I am compelled to appeal to the laws of my Country for redress, which I hope & flatter myself you will not oblige me to do.[7]

4. Pinney Papers, as at note 3, pp. 337–38.
5. Pinney Papers, as at note 3, p. 337.
6. Pinney Papers, as at note 3, p. 44.
7. Pinney Papers, as at note 3, pp. 339–40.

At this point, it may be helpful to examine the different curtain arrangements fashionable during the eighteenth century. While humbler homes, if they had curtains at all, would have had a single curtain or a pair of curtains hung on rings from a plain rod throughout the period, more affluent homes followed changing fashions. During the first half of the century, the 'festoon' curtain was in vogue. This consisted of a single curtain fixed across the top of the window and drawn up horizontally by a series of cords and pulleys (fig. 2). The festoon was superseded from the 1760s by the draw-up or drapery arrangement (now called 'reefed' or 'Italian strung') where a pair of curtains is drawn up towards the corners of the window (fig. 3). Then, towards the end of the century, there was a return to plain pairs of curtains, now operated along their rods by strings and pulleys concealed under an elaborate draped valance and often referred to as French draw curtains (fig. 4). Terminology was not standardized and this was at the root of the Pinney/Taitt affair. This is explained in a letter from Pinney to his attorney, Charles Martin, setting out the facts as he saw them:

The order to Taitt was to make three fashionable window curtains of Chintz and to line them with green calico swissed — To be made with aprons or festoons on the tops to cover the rods and the curtains to draw up in a kind of festoon on each side the windows, and that the two pieces of green calico which I had ordered P.& D. to send him in, would be sufficient to finish the curtains, <u>save three or four yards</u>, which quantity <u>only</u> I authorized him to send to P.& D.'s for in case he wanted it — This, and other particulars in the narrative, my son Frederick can prove. Now Taitt instead of attending to my order of making <u>the Curtains to draw up in a kind of festoon on each side the windows</u> has made what he calls drapery, to imitate Curtains on each side the windows and has made the Curtains, <u>of lining, instead of Chintz</u>, to run on a rod within side these sham Curtains, called drapery, which he could only have done for the sole purpose of enabling him to raise against me so enormous a bill: thinking, I presume, that I would sooner submit to so gross an imposition than to contend it at law.[8]

8. Pinney Papers, Letter Book 12, p. 7; 'swissed' refers to the glazed finish on the chintz.

2. Antoine Jean Duclos after Augustin de Saint-Aubin, *Le Concert*, 1774, etching, 320 × 430 mm (© Trustees of the British Museum).

Festoon curtains are depicted here in three different positions: fully down, half drawn and fully drawn up.

A NUN confeſsing her paſt FOLLIES to FATHER SLY-BOOTS. 126

At _Twelve_, I began to think of a Man. At _Fourteen_, I was Violently in Love with a Man.
At _Thirteen_, I Sighed for a Man. At _Fifteen_, I run away with a Man.
But he was a Very Pretty Man — therefore I hope youll Pardon me Sir.

Publiſhed 1ˢᵗ Octᵣ 1794 by LAURIE & WHITTLE, Nᵒ 53 Fleet Street London.

3. Published by Laurie
& Whittle, after W.
O'Keeffe, _A nun confessing
her past follies to Father Sly-
Boots_, 1794, etching, 198 ×
247 mm (© Trustees of
the British Museum).

The tasselled cords at
the side of the window
show that these curtains
are of the drapery type,
albeit somewhat
exaggerated in form,
which John Pinney
insisted he had ordered.

4. Thomas Sheraton, _The
Cabinet-Maker and
Upholsterer's Drawing-Book_,
1793, plate 51 (© Leeds
Museums and Galleries,
Temple Newsam House).

Two designs for
French draw curtains
with drapery valances.
Sheraton explains: 'When
the cords are drawn the
curtains meet in the
centre at the same time,
but are no way raised
from the floor. When the
same cord is drawn the
reverse way, each curtain
flies open, and comes to
their place on each side
. . .'

Nº 16: pl.1.   Cornices, Curtains & Drapery for Drawing Room Windows.   Plate 51.

T. Sheraton. del   Published as the Act directs, by G. Terry.— June 11. 1792   Terry Sc.

So Pinney had ordered, or thought he had ordered, drapery curtains made of chintz and lined with calico but Taitt had supplied French draw curtains of the calico with a draped valance of chintz. In fairness to Taitt, draw-up curtains would no longer have been fashionable among his London clientele by 1793. It is unclear whether Pinney's order is an indication that even a major city like Bristol lagged behind the capital's lead or simply that John Pinney himself had conservative tastes.

The case moved swiftly. Pinney's offer of compromise — that he would accept the French draw curtains if Taitt replaced the outer calico with chintz and removed the gimp trimming and half the silk tassels — was delivered to Taitt by his son, Azariah, who duly reported back, adding some extra information:

I told him it was your wish to have the business amicably settled, without bringing it into Court, he said he would much rather wait the issue of a Process at Law, and that he would appeal to Mrs.Ford to corroborate his assertion, at which I of course laughed and told him that was impossible as Mrs.Ford was not present when the order was given. I then wished him a good morning, and repaired directly to Mrs.Fords, ... I introduced the circumstance of your Curtains, she then began to relate all circumstances, and mentioned one circumstance which I believe you are not acquainted with, that is, that she was walking one day with a relation of hers who was going to furnish a House, and they went into Mr.Taitts, where your Curtains were hung up, as they appeared very handsome they were induced to ask who they were for and directly he said they were for you, she wondered how you could order your Curtains of Calico, especially as they were for your best Drawing room, she was so astonished that she asked Mr.Taitt repeatedly whether they were made according to order, and he always answered in the affirmative.[9]

On 5 October, Pinney apprised Pritchard & Dudding of Taitt's intransigence:

Mr Tait having refused to submit his dispute with me to the arbitration of disinterested and respectable men, or to compromise the matter in any other way, I am compelled to appeal to the Laws of my Country for redress, as I cannot tamely submit to such gross imposition.[10]

On the advice of his Bristol lawyer he sent the curtains back to London and asked Pritchard & Dudding to take custody of them.

On 21 October, he was still prepared to compromise:

I have offered to leave our dispute to the determination of Arbitrators, or, if it was your wish to have it compromised without further trouble, I laid before you a plan for that purpose, which I conceived you would not have objected to, as it was an unfortunate piece of business — Was it possible to have shewn a greater regard to Lenity? or a greater inclination to avoid contention? & give me leave to add that every honest & worthy character must approve of so fair a proposal, & allow, that it is doing all in my power to prevent litigation — That nothing may be laid to my door, I shall beg leave, once more, to offer the same, & to request you will indulge me with a positive refusal or acceptance.[11]

His appeal fell on deaf ears and Taitt, claiming he had been 'driven ... to the last resource',[12] filed his declaration on 9 November; on the 13th Pinney sent a detailed account of the affair to his attorney, Charles Martin of Haydon Square, London. There was an added complication because of confusion over when the order was placed and in whose presence:

My order to Pritchard & Dudding, as well as to Taitt, was decisive, to supply Taitt with only three or four Yards of green Calico, above the two pieces ordered to be sent in, if wanted, to finish my Curtains. Notwithstanding this express direction from me, Taitt on or ab^t the 5th of August without my knowlege or consent, and contrary to my positive orders, did take up in my name no less a quantity than 103:Yards of green Calico swissed above the two pieces

9. Pinney Papers, Box S3: 6, typed transcript.
10. Pinney Papers, Letter Book 10, p.341.
11. Pinney Papers, as at note 10, p. 343.
12. Pinney Papers, as at note 10, p. 343.

sent him by Pritchard & Dudding the 27th July. Taitt went to P.&D. himself and Mr Pritchard informed him of the quantity I had ordered to be delivered and that they were not authorized by me to deliver him above three or four Yards in addition to what they had sent in. This did not stop him but he still persevered, being determined to make as much out of me as possible as it was not likely I should ever deal with him again . . . .[13]

The order was given to Taitt — himself not another Person besides us three were present, and we did not see or hear any other Person in or about the Rooms — but you will notice that he boldly asserted to my Son Azariah, who was authorised by me to wait upon him, that Mrs Ford was in an adjoining Room and therefore could easily confute the testimony of my eldest Son.[14]

The trial was set for some time after 29 November and two of John's sons, John Frederick, who had been present when the order was placed, and Azariah, who had acted as his emissary, were instructed to hold themselves in readiness as witnesses. Pinney was clearly smarting under the indignity of his position; he wrote to Martin:

I hope you will take particular pains to have the materials used and supplied by Taitt measured and valued by proper people, . . . let not the smallest minutiae escape you, for I contend the whole is a gross imposition and any man capable of such conduct ought to be exposed to the Public.[15]

Messrs Pritchard & Dudding, it appears, were starting to be less certain about the facts:

[I] am rather surprized to hear that Pritchard & Dudding do not come forward in the manner you expected; as they both carefully read over their whole evidence and corrected where-ever any word varied from what they understood — Subpenae both of them . . .[16]

Pinney's barrister was one 'Mr Garrow', presumably William Garrow who was making a name for himself as a defence counsel through his effective use of cross-examination.

The case was heard at the Court of King's Bench on 3 December 1793. Azariah reported back to his father the same day:

Dear Father,

This day an iniquitous Verdict was pronounced against you, in favr of that Man Taitt, who brought three perjured witnesses to prove that the Order was given when you first went to his house, with Mrs.Ford, . . . one of his witnesses gave evidence that they were not ordered that day, and Mrs.Ford gave a very clear testimony to the same effect, and Jack gave a very good evidence, your Council thought it was so good a cause that mine was not needed, the Judge appeared very much in our favour, and Mr.Garrow says if you will have it tried again by a special Jury, you will most undoubtedly gain your Cause, because the Verdict was contrary to evidence.[17]

After a night to consider the outcome, he wrote again the following day:

Your trial I hear has been published in today's Paper, and has been accurately stated, by which I make no doubt you will see that there was no exertion wanted in your favor on the part of the Council who made a very masterly speech, which carried full conviction with it, but it is impossible to account for the wicked and malicious and partial decision of our depraved and corrupted Juries, who decide in favour of a tradesman, in order that they may continue in their infamous and unjustifiable practices, but I am confident when the affair is investigated by men of character and responsibility, you must gain it, or our laws must be those of iniquity and not those of equity.[18]

13. Pinney Papers, Letter Book 12, pp. 7–8.
14. Pinney Papers, as at note 13, pp. 16–17.
15. Pinney Papers, as at note 13, p. 17.
16. Pinney Papers, as at note 13
17. Pinney Papers, Box S3: 6, typed transcript.
18. Pinney Papers, as at note 17

A report of the trial did indeed appear in *The Times* on 4 December. Pinney's first instinct was to have the case re-tried. He wrote to Martin:

I have only time to say that you will settle with Mr Garrow what is proper to be done — As I wish for my son Fred^k to be absent from the Kingdom until August next, let me know whether the tryal can be put off, in case a new one should be granted.[19]

After careful reflection, however, he changed his mind.

Receiving your letter a few minutes before the post set off yesterday, caused me to adopt the opinion of a new trial, without reflecting on the probability of my going to the West Indies in the present fleet, which I have a full intention of carrying into execution & my son Fred. will go with me — therefore it will be very unpleasant to have a suit of this kind hanging over me — Being thus circumstanced I believe you will join with me it is best to put up with the first loss – therefore be so good as to let me know what I have to pay & I will send up a draft for the money — Don't suffer Taitt to put me to any additional expense by proceeding further.[20]

What he had to pay is itemized in his 'House and Furniture Account':

19. Pinney Papers, Letter Book 12, p. 22.
20. Pinney Papers, as at note 19, pp. 23–24.
21. Pinney Papers, Account Book 41, p. 68.

1794
Janu^y 10th ... p^d Richd Taitt Jermyn Street for Curtains
                                  Made contrary to Order   43 4 — [21]

Charles Martin's bill was £36 10s 5d and there was a further payment of £38 for 'the taxed bill of Cost', i.e. costs awarded to Taitt. Pritchard & Dudding's bill for the

5. Drawing Room of The Georgian House, Bristol, with modern, simplified drapery curtains of chintz lined with green calico (©Bristol Museums, Galleries & Archives).

chintz and calico came to £34 8s. 6d. So, in total, John Pinney's curtains cost him £152 2s 11d. To put this into some sort of context, in the same account, he paid £100 to his architect, £1 10s for six Windsor chairs and £27 6s for two portraits with frames. The final acknowledgment of defeat came in a letter of 7 December to Pritchard & Dudding:

Gentlemen!
Though I have the strongest assurance of success against that R — Taitt on a re-hearing of the matter before a special Jury, yet as my Son is going out of the Kingdom for some months, I am obliged to give up the question. — you will therefore be so good as to send down the Box with the Curtains by Wiltshire's Waggon and put your Acco^t therein.[22]

It is difficult to get to the truth of the matter over two hundred years later. Clearly there was some misunderstanding over the original order which does not appear to have been put in writing but Taitt seems to have overstepped the mark in ordering the extra fabric despite Pritchard and Dudding's reservations. On the other hand, it was unusual for Pinney to give in so easily; was it simply because he was called abroad?

Whatever the rights and wrongs of the affair, it created an interesting curatorial dilemma when new curtains were required three years ago. Should we have the drapery curtains originally intended or the French draw curtains supplied — and presumably installed? Fearful of distressing John Pinney's spirit, we chose the drapery curtains (fig. 5).

22. Pinney Papers, Letter Book 12, p. 25.

Thomas Hardwick's Album: an architect's record

Charles Hind

I first met Terry Friedman about 2000 through his old friend Derek Linstrum.[1] Derek had decided to offer the RIBA the greater part of his library as a bequest and I went up to Leeds several times to discuss the terms and to select the books we might take. Terry joined us for dinner a couple of times and gradually the idea emerged that their *joint* collections of books, to be called the Linstrum-Friedman Library, would be the RIBA's Drawings and Archives Collection's departmental library at the Victoria and Albert Museum. This idea has now been realised and the RIBA is deeply grateful to both of them.[2]

Amongst Terry's numerous articles was one published in the *Georgian Group Journal* on the early churches of Thomas Hardwick (1752–1829).[3] It therefore seemed appropriate to contribute to Terry's *Festschrift* an article on an album by Hardwick recently acquired by the RIBA that contains record drawings of a number of his projects, both speculative and realised.[4] A full list appears in the Appendix.

Thomas Hardwick was the son of a master mason of Brentford, Middlesex, after whom he was named. The Hardwick family came originally from Herefordshire. Thomas Hardwick Senior (1725–1798) had worked at Syon House under Robert Adam and he is said to have rebuilt the nave of Brentford church and the whole of nearby Hanwell church to his own designs.[5] His son Thomas became a pupil of Sir William Chambers in 1767 and was admitted to the Royal Academy Schools in 1769. He won the first Silver Medal for Architecture the same year. In 1776, he travelled to Italy with a short stay in Paris, presumably on the advice of his master Chambers, and thereafter he was in the company of the gentleman artist Thomas Jones. They arrived in Rome in November that year and Hardwick returned home in 1779, reaching London in May.[6] He brought with him numerous sketchbooks filled with drawings of ancient and modern buildings and Roman artefacts, now in the RIBA Drawings and Archives Collections. Subsequently he built up a modestly successful practice primarily as an estate surveyor and as a designer of churches and minor public buildings. The best account of his works and career are in Colvin and his entry in the *Oxford Dictionary of National Biography* by Michael Port.[7]

The album that is the subject of the present paper is a quarto vellum-bound volume of some 115 leaves, of which 63 bear drawings whilst a further three loose drawings are inserted.[8] On the flyleaf, under the signature 'Thos. Hardwick, Architect', it is inscribed 'This Book contains Sketches of sundry Buildings already Executed and Original Designs on various subjects — commencing about the Year 1773'. In 1773, Hardwick was still working for Sir William Chambers whilst attending the Royal Academy Schools. The drawings fall into two groups. The first

1 Professor Derek Linstrum (1923–2009), architect, teacher and writer on architecture, architectural history and conservation.

2 In their lifetimes a handsome slate plaque was commissioned from the sculptor Charles Smith and appropriate bookplates based on the plaque now identify the books.

3 Terry Friedman, 'Thomas Hardwick Jr's early churches', *The Georgian Group Journal*, VIII, 1998, pp. 43–55.

4 The album was bought in 2012 from descendants of the architect with the assistance of the Arts Council/V&A Purchase Grant Fund and the Art Fund.

5 For both Hardwicks, see H. M. Colvin, *A Biographical Dictionary of British Architects 1600–1840*, New Haven and London, 2008, pp. 480–82.

6 For an account of Hardwick's Italian Grand Tour, see John Ingamells, *A Dictionary of British and Irish Travellers in Italy, 1701–1800*, New Haven and London, 1997, pp. 464–65

7 See http://www.oxforddnb.com/view/article/12280

8 Howard Colvin observes in a footnote that he saw this album in 1974. Although he makes a few cautious attributions based on its contents in the 1978 edition of his *Dictionary*, these are omitted in later editions.

1. Thomas Hardwick, after Sir William Chambers, Design for a Domed Church, pen and ink and grey and brown washes, 37 × 24 cm. Royal Institute of British Architects, London (VOS/ 322) (photo: RIBA Drawings and Archives Collections).

9 Grove House, Chiswick, was demolished in 1928 and its grounds completely built over. The authorship of the Temple of Bacchus at Painshill is unclear and is presently being reconstructed. The Library at Christ Church was designed by Dr George Clarke.

sequence is numbered, although a few leaves have been removed, and these appear to date from 1773 to 1776, before Hardwick's departure for Italy (ff. 1–17). The second sequence is not numbered and is a mixture of speculative designs, competition entries, commissioned but unexecuted designs and record drawings of executed work (f. 18–63). I shall return to the second group later.

Amongst the earlier, numbered sequence are a perspective view of the Grotto at the Grove, Chiswick (f.15) and elevations of the Temple of Bacchus at Painshill, Surrey (f.12) and the Library at Christchurch College, Oxford (f. 17).[9] These are the only record drawings of work by other architects. The remaining drawings are mostly very much in the manner of Sir William Chambers and indeed one, a view of a domed church (fig. 1), bears the inscription 'Sr W.C.', suggesting it is a copy after a lost Chambers drawing (f. 14). Most of these designs are for garden buildings typically entitled 'A Cold Bath' (f. 1), 'A Temple to the Graces' and 'A Casino' (ff. 2–3). Amongst the most interesting is a 'Grotto, in Imitation of that in the Gardens of Painshill' (f. 16 and fig. 2). Some of the grander designs for palaces or 'Elevation of the Central Part of a Design for a Custom House &tc. Agreeable to a Plan laid down by Mr. Gwyn in his Publication entitled London & Westminster Improved' may have been topics set by the Royal Academy Schools, although Hardwick was exhibiting similar subjects at the Royal Academy in the 1770s and 1780s.

The unnumbered drawings after f. 18 are more assured than the earlier numbered ones, although the style remains firmly in the Francophile tradition of Sir William Chambers. It might be reasonable to assume that these date from after Hardwick's return from Italy in 1779. A very few are dated, such as the accomplished 'Design for a Villa' of 1795 (f. 25), which combines Chambers's Francophile elegance with elements of the increasingly fashionable Greek Revival (fig. 3). These are seen in the Ionic order of the portico and the baseless Doric columns of the window surrounds on the ground floor. Hardwick was interested in the work of James Athenian Stuart and the Ionic columns derive from the Ionic temple on the Ilissus illustrated by Stuart and Revett in the first volume of *The Antiquities of Athens* (1762) whilst the window surrounds are probably inspired by the Stoa of Attalos.

2. Thomas Hardwick, design for a *Grotto, in Imitation of that in the Gardens of Painshill*, pen and ink and watercolour, 37 × 24 cm. Royal Institute of British Architects, London (VOS/ 322) (photo: RIBA Drawings and Archives Collections).

3. Thomas Hardwick, *Design for a Villa*. 1795, pen and ink and coloured washes, 37 × 24 cm. Royal Institute of British Architects, London (VOS/ 322) (photo: RIBA Drawings and Archives Collections).

Hardwick's designs for a house for 'W^m. Newport Esqr. at Belmont in Ireland', were not built. They were commissioned in the late 1780s by William Newport, younger brother of Sir John Newport, an Irish politician and 1st Baronet (1756–1843), of New Park, Kilculliheen, near Waterford.[10] Belmont was an estate close by. The Newport fortune came from a bank in Waterford, in which both William and his elder brother were partners. In the event, it appears that William rejected Hardwick's designs and his new house was built by another architect.[11] The house would have been of considerable grandeur, with a central, three-storey block of five by four bays with large lateral wings containing a kitchen and stables. Hardwick's only other Irish work was the County Gaol in Galway city in 1802 and he was unsuccessful in the competition for the Sligo County Gaol in 1814.[12]

The next named project relates to the Rookery in Kent, 'the House of G. Norman, Esqr., Bromley Common' (ff. 37–39). George Norman (1756–1830) was a merchant in the Norway timber trade. His father, James Norman, bought the estate in 1755 and made alterations and additions to an existing house, recorded as still being incomplete in 1720. He died in 1787. George married in 1792, which may have provided the excuse for thinking about making alterations and one might note that it was in the same year that Hardwick began adding a second quadrangle to Bromley College, on the far side of the town. A topographical view of the house of about 1825 shows a five-bay, three-storey frontage with single storey wings of three bays. The centrepiece has a Venetian window above the front door and a Diocletian window on the second floor. That Hardwick was responsible for this feature may be assumed from its similarity to the design for an unnamed country house on f. 63. But the project is a puzzle for curiously, one of the drawings (f. 28) is a plan for alterations (adding a single storey library) and its title makes it clear that it was

10 See http://www.historyofparliamentonline.org/volume/1790–1820/member/newport-sir-simon-john-1756-1843
11 William became bankrupt in 1820 and shot himself. His house became a private mental asylum in 1885 and was burned down in 1949.
12 See the Dictionary of Irish Architects 1720–1940, http://www.dia.ie/architets/view/2388/HARDWICK-THOMAS%23

an alteration to an existing house. However, the titles of the other two drawings (a five-bay front elevation with a porte-cochère and a section) seem to suggest Hardwick was proposing a brand new house (ff. 29–30). He omits the elaborate centrepiece with Venetian and Diocletian windows. Yet the plan of the main house seems to match the section (fig. 4), whilst the wings in the elevation do not equate to the proposal for alterations. It is also difficult to match any of the drawings and the 1825 view, apart from the central bay described above, with surviving photographs of the Rookery, which was burned down in 1946.[13] Hardwick's drawings in his album may therefore record proposals for altering the existing house as well as replacing it with a similar sized, but more modern house.

Another puzzle house is Stover Lodge, Devonshire, for which there are proposed designs for James Templer (ff. 42–43). Templer bought the estate in 1765, having made a fortune as a government building contractor in India. The present house, which has rainwater heads dated 1776, is a larger and more horizontal version of Hardwick's design and the plan is essentially the same. No architect is known for the house, which has refined Adamesque interiors and good chimneypieces.[14] Could it be the client's version of Hardwick's design working with a local builder? It would have been a very early work for Hardwick, who was only twenty-four in 1776, the year he left for Italy, and still working in Sir William Chambers's office. However, it may be significant that this was exactly the time that Chambers was gradually winding down his country house practice as his workload in the Office of Works was growing heavier. Colvin was evidently dubious about Hardwick's involvement in the present house as the tentative attribution of it to Hardwick in the 1978 edition of his *Dictionary* was removed for the 1994 and 2008 editions.

The location of a villa for John Robinson (ff. 35–36) has proved impossible to identify. Hardwick records a plan and elevation. Robinson was clearly a rich client as the house would have been substantial. It is of nine bays with an attached portico and no less than five reception rooms and an imperial, top-lit staircase.

With the exception of an un-built design for Thomas Johnes, the designs for the London churches in the album are for projects discussed by Terry Friedman in his 1998 article on Hardwick's early churches. St Mary's Church, Wanstead, Essex (1787–90, ff. 44–48) and St James's Chapel, Hampstead Road (1789–93, demolished 1965, ff. 37–40) therefore do not need much further discussion except one should point out that there are more drawings for these two projects (five and four respectively) than there are for any other project in the album. Also the section of St Mary's, Wanstead (fig. 5) is a particularly beautiful feat of draughtsmanship.

Hafod in Cardiganshire was an estate developed by Thomas Johnes from 1786 and over several decades, it became one of the most perfect picturesque ensembles in the country, a key site of the English Romantic movement. Hardwick's name has never before been connected with Hafod, nor indeed with Johnes, but Hardwick's album contains charming designs (fig. 6) for an octagonal Gothick church,[15] dating probably from the mid 1790s (ff. 41–43) that Hardwick noted as '... designed for Thos. Johnes Esqr'. Hardwick was not a natural Goth and the details derive from Batty Langley's *Ancient Architecture Restored and Improved by a Great Variety of Grand and Usefull Designs* (1742), reissued in 1747 as *Gothic Architecture, improved by Rules and Proportions*. In the event, Johnes delayed building for nearly a decade and then employed the more fashionable architect, James Wyatt, whose rather less charming but also Gothic design was begun in 1800.[16] One might speculate that, the commission, albeit

13 See John L. Filmer, 'The Norman Family of Bromley Common', in *North West Kent Family History*, pp. 52–54. However, late eighteenth-century library fittings and an Adamesque fireplace were removed from the house about 1943 when the Norman family sold it to the RAF and the interiors were largely gutted. After 1949 they were installed at West Farleigh Hall (now Smiths Hall), Kent, 'suggesting that at the least Hardwick may have made alterations to the early eighteenth-century house (see the English Heritage Listing under West Farleigh Hall and http://www.smithshall.com/history/index.html). Christopher Hussey believed that the single storey wings were added and the central bay and some interiors were remodelled c. 1770–75 but it seems likely that they are a little later and by Hardwick. See Christopher Hussey, 'West Farleigh Hall, Kent – II', *Country Life*, 21 September 1967, pp. 660–64. The Rookery was clearly much altered in the later nineteenth century.

14 There are photographs of the house in Stover School, *Stover: the story of a school*, Newton Abbot, Stover School, 1982.

15 Hardwick exhibited a *Design for a Church in South Wales* at the Royal Academy in 1795.

16 It was remodelled in 1887 and badly damaged by fire in 1932. Pevsner dismissed Wyatt's design as giving no credit to the architect.

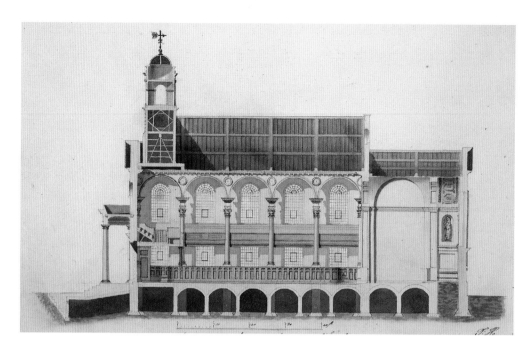

5. (top) Thomas Hardwick, *Longitudinal Section of Wanstead Church*, Essex, pen and ink and coloured washes, 37 × 24 cm. Royal Institute of British Architects, London (VOS/ 322) (photo: RIBA Drawings and Archives Collections).

6. (bottom) Thomas Hardwick, section of a design for a church for Thos Johnes, probably for Hafod, Cardiganshire, pen and ink and coloured washes, 37 × 24 cm. Royal Institute of British Architects, London (VOS/ 322) (photo: RIBA Drawings and Archives Collections).

unfulfilled, came to Hardwick through his relatives in Monmouthshire, as Monmouth was on the route from Hafod to London.

The County or Shire Hall, Dorchester, Dorset (fig. 7), is an austerely Palladian design built 1796–97,[17] though it was much altered internally in the late nineteenth century. It provided two court rooms, one the Nisi Prius Court, the other the Crown Court. Both had substantial galleries for spectators. The building was described at the time as 'very handsome, plain and simple ... the building will contain every convenience and accommodation that can be required, without any superfluity. Real utility has been the first consideration; and the second has been the

17 Clare Graham, *Ordering Law: the Architectural and Social history of the English Law Courts to 1914*, Aldershot, Ashgate, 2003, p. 352.

most strict economy, consistent with durability and good workmanship'. Hardwick's drawing softens the design of the main elevation.[18]

Hardwick's record design for a Chapel for Harbord Harbord, first Baron Suffield, in Albemarle St., London (ff. 63–65) shows a square building with galleries and three doors to the street with two circular windows and a Diocletian window in the middle. The interior is relatively plain, apart from the domed, east apse with decorative plasterwork and paired Corinthian pilasters to either side. This design does not appear to have been built. Eventually the second Lord Suffield built a chapel in 1815 but the architect is unknown. It was opposite the Royal Institution and was demolished in 1906. Proprietary chapels were commercial undertakings, for which the income was derived from pew rents so it appears that the Harbord family delayed their investment until the end of the war with France. Hardwick's design cannot date from before 1786, the year the Suffield barony was created.

Hardwick's design for the Monmouth Gaol (ff. 66–67) was entered into a competition in 1788. The successful architect was William Blackburn (1750–90), a prolific prison designer who based his planning on the ideas of the prison reformer John Howard. Hardwick's proposal was for a monumental but extremely plain classical design, a marked contrast to the elaborate castellated medieval fortress built by Blackburn.[19] Hardwick had cousins near Monmouth, which would doubtless explain why he entered.[20]

Regrettably, Hardwick's album is an incomplete record of his work. The latest dateable building in it is the County Hall, Dorchester, of 1796–97 but significant projects within the time-span of 1773–97 such as the restoration (1788–89) and later reconstruction after a fire of St Paul's, Covent Garden (1796–98), were omitted. Also the reconstruction of Ruperra Castle, Glamorganshire, after a fire in 1784, would certainly have merited inclusion. That he did not exclude alterations is shown by the design for the Rookery, Bromley Common. The order of the drawings does not appear to be strictly chronological. And why did he stop recording his

7. Thomas Hardwick, *Elevation of the County Hall*, Dorchester, Dorset, pen and ink and coloured washes, 37 × 24 cm. Royal Institute of British Architects, London (VOS/ 322) (photo: RIBA Drawings and Archives Collections).

18 Ibid., p. 145.
19 Blackburn's prison closed in 1869 and was demolished in 1884 except for its gatehouse, now divided into private houses.
20 Information communicated to the author by Paul Suan Davies.

work, when he still had over thirty years of productive work ahead of him? We can only speculate.

Appendix

The words in italics are inscribed on the drawings. Many drawings are signed with initials: T. H. or in one case Sir W. C. (evidently After Sir William Chambers). Some drawings have clearly been cut out, explaining the irregularity of the numbering of the first 25 leaves.

1.	*A Cold Bath*	(f. 1)
2.	*A Temple*	(f. 1)
[3–4]	Removed	
5.	*A Park Gate*	(f. 2)
6.	*Temple to the Graces*	(f. 2)
7.	*A Casino*	(f. 3)
[8]	Removed	
9.	A Temple to Shakespeare	(f. 4)
10.	A Triumphal Arch	(f. 4)
11.	A Country House	(f. 5)
12.	A Park Gate	(f. 6)
13.	A Park Bridge with rotunda and flap	(f. 7)
14.	A Town House and Another Town House (2)	(f. 8)
15.	A Prison or Court House and a Ditto (2)	(f. 9)
16.	[River elevation?] *Elevation of the Central Part of a Design for a Custom House &tc. Agreeable to a Plan laid down by Mr. Gwyn in his Publication entitled London & Westminster Improved*	(f. 10)
17.	[Street elevation?] *Elevation of the Central Part of a Design for a Custom House &tc. Agreeable to a Plan laid down by Mr. Gwyn in his Publication entitled London & Westminster Improved*	(f. 11)
[18]	Removed	
19.	*The Temple of Bacchus at Painshill*	(f. 12)
20.	Design for a Temple	(f. 12)
21.	Design for a circular Temple and Plan of same	(f. 13)
22.	Design for a domed church after Sir William Chambers	(f. 14)
23.	*View of the Grotto at the end of the Lake at the Grove, Chiswick*	(f. 15)
24.	*Grotto, in Imitation of that in the Gardens of Painshill*	(f. 16)
[25]	Removed	
26.	*Elevation of the Library of C.C. College, Oxford*	(f. 17)

The leaves hereafter are not numbered

[27]	Design for a Public building	(f. 18)
[28]	[Elevation and section of] *A Museum*	(f. 19)
[29]	[Plan of] *A Museum* (accompanied by two loose drawings for part-plan)	(f. 20, 20a + b)
[30]	Six designs for wall monuments	(f. 21)
[31]	Plan and elevation of a country house	(f. 22)
[32]	Design for a domed public building	(f. 23)
[33]	*Garden Building* and elevation and plan of a large garden pavilion	(f. 24)
[34]	*Design for a Villa, 1795*	(f. 24)

On the final leaf are faint drawings of a façade for a large building and a monument.

R. D. Chantrell: early-Victorian Classicism and Soane's continued influence

Christopher Webster

R. D. Chantrell is justly feted as one of the most successful of the architects who rose to the challenge of designing Gothic churches in the first half of the nineteenth century and much is known about this aspect of his career.[1] However, much less is recorded about his Classical secular designs, an area of professional activity he could have been expected to pursue given his pupilage with John Soane. An article examining four compelling designs for substantial buildings at the beginning of his career was published by this author in 2014[2] and the present essay considers two mansions from the later part of his practice. Taken together, the research leads to the conclusion that his fondness for Classicism, and especially those aspects of it promoted by his former master, was one that never waned.

Sibton Park and the patronage of the Brooke family

The first of these two later houses is Sibton Park in Suffolk (fig. 1), a project linked to the architectural patronage of the Brooke family of Huddersfield, a patronage that first brought them into contact with Chantrell in 1826. In that year Chantrell — by then the region's leading ecclesiastical architect — was chosen to design the new church at Lockwood, a village on the fringes of Huddersfield. It was a project keenly supported by John Brooke (1794–1878) who was a member of the 'local committee' which oversaw its construction.[3] John, with his brother Thomas

1. Sibton Park, built in 1827 by an unknown architect, but one clearly much influenced by Soane (photo: author).

1 For Chantrell's career, see C. Webster, *R. D. Chantrell (1793–1872) and the architecture of a lost generation*, Reading, 2011.

2 For discussion of these, see C. Webster, 'Chantrell in Halifax: Classicism and the Soane Legacy' in *Georgian Group Journal*, XXII, 2014, pp. 167–82.

3 The workings of the Church Building Commission were often complex, but while major decisions were taken by the Commissioners and their staff in London, the selection of site, style and architect were largely delegated to local committees.

2. Louisa Caroline Sayer, Sibton Park, Suffolk, 1844, watercolour, detail (private collection).

(1798–1859), ran the firm of John Brooke and Sons in nearby Armitage Bridge, a business which could trace its roots to the seventeenth century, and in the early nineteenth century, was one of the most successful and innovative textile enterprises in West Yorkshire.[4]

Chantrell must have impressed the Lockwood committee and soon after their first meeting, John Brooke asked Chantrell to design a new residence for his own use, to be named Armitage Bridge House. Progress was rapid and this handsome, Classical mansion, with service wing and stable block, was completed in 1828. Indeed, it was from here that the procession of ecclesiastical and civic dignitaries, accompanied by Chantrell ceremonially carrying his plans, set out for the foundation stone laying ceremony at Lockwood in October of that year. Subsequently, Chantrell was employed by the Brooke family to design a school at Armitage Bridge (c. 1835), to measure and perhaps supervise building work at the mill (1829–38), to design a new church at nearby Honley (1840–44) where the family had much influence, and a new church and vicarage in Armitage Bridge (1844–48), one of the best and most expensive of his later churches. It is reasonable to conclude the relationship went beyond that of patron and architect since both Chantrell and the Brookes shared a commitment to promoting the Established church and an antiquarian interest in medieval architecture. Several Brookes were members of the Yorkshire Architectural Society in the 1840s where Chantrell sat on the committee.[5]

For a family firm that could trace its roots back so far, John might have anticipated that the company would eventually pass to his eldest son John William (1824–81). However, John William was not blessed with a robust constitution and his father concluded that it was not sensible for his son to continue living in the polluted atmosphere of industrial Huddersfield, coupled with the stresses of

4 William Brooke (1763–1846), the father of John and Thomas, remained head of the family business, but from the 1820s was, increasingly, stepping back from the firm's management. For the family and its business activities see Maggie Booth et al, *The Brookes of Honley*, Honley Civic Society, 2011.

5 Unclassified papers of the Yorkshire Architectural Society, York Minster Library.

3. R. D. Chantrell, proposed alterations to Sibton Park, 26 August 1845, pencil and wash, 385 × 278 mm. Design A. (Private collection, photo: author).

4. R. D. Chantrell, proposed alterations to Sibton Park, August 1845, pencil and wash, 347 × 248 mm. Design B. (Private collection, photo: author).

running a complex and demanding company. Accordingly, in around 1843[6] John bought the Sibton Park estate for his son 'situated in the most beautiful part of the eastern division of Suffolk'[7] and, in the autumn of 1844, still in his early 20s, John William left Yorkshire to become a country squire.[8]

6 There is some uncertainly over the precise date at which the Brookes acquitted Sibton. The auction, conducted by Messrs Farebrother & Co of 9, Lancaster Place, Strand, London, took place on 23 August 1843. The *Ipswich Journal* of 2 September 1843 recorded that an un-named buyer had paid £43,000 for the mansion and 995 acres, plus £1600 for the advowsons of Sibton and Peasenhall, plus £2,410 for a further 562 acres of farmland. As the sale particulars remain in the Brooke family archive, one might reasonably conclude that John Brooke was the successful bidder. However, almost a year later, the *Morning Chronicle* (London), 10 October 1844, reported that Messrs Farebrother 'respectfully inform the public that the freehold and copyhold Estate of Sibton Park ... is sold by Private Contract'. And only on 21 June 1845 did the *Ipswich Journal* announced the sale by auction at Sibton Park of 'Modern and Excellent furniture ... the property of Mr Robert Sayer Esq' who had owned the estate from 1825. Furthermore, the *Morning Chronicle*, 8 July 1845, in an advertisement about shares in the proposed Windsor, Ascot and Farnborough Railway, lists the 'Provisional Committee' as including one 'F. Murphy Esq, Sibton Park and Montague Place, London.' Perhaps the Brookes did not purchase the estate immediately after the 1843 auction. The recollection of Mr John Kendall Acton Brooke (b. 1946), John William Brooke's great-great-grandson, and the last of the family to own the estate, is that the date of transfer, as set out in the deeds, was August 1844.

7 The quotation comes from the announcement of the auction, *The Standard* (London), 15 July 1843.

8 Information from Mr J. K. A. Brooke who generously shared his own research into the house and family with me in 2011.

His new house was a handsome, compact mansion, built in 1826–27[9] of rendered brickwork by an unknown architect for Robert Sayer who had bought the estate in 1825.[10] It is a sophisticated design, more-or-less square in plan with five bays on its west side and three wider bays on the south, entrance front. There is a lower, three-bay service wing on its east side. Most of the surface decoration is carefully articulated but restrained; the principal features are the portico on the south front and the block of chimneys which boldly crowns the centre of the roof. A substantial parapet runs around the building. By c. 1843 when the Brookes acquired the property, it must have looked a little dated, especially the entrance front; semi-circular porticos were briefly the height of fashion in the Regency period, but by the mid-1840s were decidedly passé.[11]

No doubt John William was delighted with his new home and almost immediately acquired a detailed watercolour painting of Sibton,[12] one which emphasises its rural setting and opportunities for country life, a life very different from that to be found in Armitage Bridge (fig. 2). Usefully, it records the appearance of the house when he moved in. Then in August 1845, Chantrell visited Sibton and produced two broadly similar proposals for altering the house (figs 3 and 4). He might well have travelled all the way from Leeds in response to a serious desire of Brooke to remodel Sibton, although it is conceivable that it was more of a social visit in which, with a bit of virtuoso flair, Chantrell rattled off a couple of sketches for a relatively easily achieved modernisation.[13] It is possible that Brooke's intended project was the addition of a conservatory as the two drawings include conservatories that are not only significantly different in design, but also in location; a third drawing, dated 1855, shows yet another alternative (fig. 5). However, no building work seems to have been carried out to the mansion — it remains today as it appeared in the 1844 watercolour — and, on one level, the matter can be relegated to a footnote in Chantrell's career. Nevertheless, the drawings are of considerable interest as his last known Classical designs and the two that include the mansion are remarkable in the wider context of the legacy of Sir John Soane, mid-nineteenth-century Classicism, and Chantrell's domestic work in Leeds.

Soane's legacy

By the time of Soane's death in 1837, the Classical tradition was certainly still vibrant, but discerning taste had moved on to the Roman Renaissance Revival led by Charles Barry, Decimus Burton and others; Soane might still be revered for his tireless championing of better professional standards in architecture, but his own style had become decidedly unfashionable. Although the *Architectural Magazine* published a respectful obituary,[14] and a generous biography had appeared in *National Portrait Gallery of Illustrious and Eminent Personages* in 1834 which praised his buildings, his lectures at the RA, his publications and his benefactions,[15] it is likely that T. L. Donaldson's *Review* of his life, published soon after the master's death, would have secured widespread agreement. His assessment was largely critical noting in Soane's later works, 'trivial and unmeaning ... embellishments ... [and] the introduction of meretricious effects [which] lowered the character of the art. ... the results were rarely happy, and show how dangerous it is for an Artist to depart from those examples of the best masters of antiquity.'[16] Soane does not get a mention in either the first or second editions of Gwilt's magisterial *Encyclopaedia of Architecture*

9 *Ipswich Journal*, 24 June 1826, advertised the sale of 'windows and doors' and other materials from the old Sibton Park 'about to be taken down'.

10 Ex inf. J. K. A. Brooke.

11 Among many built examples, one could point to James Wyatt's Bowden Park, Wiltshire (1796) or Decimus Burton's Holwood House, Kent (1823–26). For published examples see, for instance, John Plaw, *Sketches for Country Houses, Villas and Rural Dwellings*, J. Taylor, London, 1800; John B. Papworth, *Rural Residences*, Ackerman, London, 1818.

12 Mr J. K. A. Brooke, who once owned it, stated it was painted by Louisa Caroline Sayer, a talented amateur artist and daughter of Sibton's former owner, Robert Sayer. It was painted in 1844. It is not known whether Brooke commissioned the painting, or received it as a gift. It is not signed and remains at Sibton Park.

13 The two drawings are of a similar, but not identical, size. One of them has a series of pin holes at significant parts of the design indicating at least one more related drawing was produced from it. Indeed, perhaps a whole series of drawings were produced for a seriously considered scheme. And Chantrell did rebuild the nearby church at Peasenhall in 1860–61, paid for entirely by Brooke. For the latter, see *Builder*, 19, 1861, p. 621.

14 *Architectural Magazine*, IV, 1837, pp. 157–60.

15 Vol. V, 1834, p. 2 (but not paginated through the volume).

16 T. L. Donaldson, *A Review of the Professional Life of Sir John Soane*, London, 1837, pp. 26–27. However, three years earlier, John Britton had published a much more flattering assessment: John Britton, 'Brief Memoir of Sir John Soane' in *National Portrait Gallery of Illustrious and Eminent Persons*, vol. V, London, 1834. There was also a generous tribute to him in *Penny Magazine*, 1837, p. 457.

5. R. D. Chantrell, Sketch for the Conservatory at Sibton Park, December 1855, pencil and wash, 320 × 202 mm (private collection, photo: author).

(1842 and 1851), and while he does appear in the 'new and revised' edition of 1867, it is only as a pupil of George Dance;[17] Soane's contemporaries Joseph Bonomi, James Wyatt and Henry Holland receive rather better coverage. Only with the publication of James Fergusson's *History of the Modern Styles of Architecture* in 1862 — precisely a quarter of a century after Soane's death — is it possible to find something approaching a balanced assessment.[18]

No doubt for most of Soane's pupils, their master's influence was fleeting, especially for George Basevi (1794–1845), arguably the most successful of them. Writing from Rome to his sister Emma on 22 March 1817, he observed that: 'Each succeeding day tells me I have done the right thing in quitting Soane. I still continue to think him very clever, but in a particular style. I am of opinion I can form for myself a better [one]. Had I stayed much longer with him I might have become so prejudiced as to see objects with his eyes instead of my own.'[19] Perhaps not surprisingly, Basevi's subsequent work has few obvious Soanian references. Yet for Chantrell — Basevi's contemporary in Soane's office for five years — respect for the master's style remained life-long. Although Chantrell's fame came from a series of accomplished Gothic churches, it might reasonably be concluded that his interest in Classicism remained vibrant. In this respect, the overtly Soanian tower which he added to the existing plain body of the Anglican chapel in Hunslet, Leeds in 1830–32 can be quoted. There, it seems, in a most unlikely setting, Chantrell snatched a rare chance to exploit his favourite idioms.

The Sibton Park designs

On first seeing Sibton in 1845, Chantrell's immediate response was, surely, how similar the house's external design was to Soane's Tyringham Hall, Bucks (1793–c. 1800), arguably his most interesting early house. We might not know the name of Sibton's architect, but he was, unquestionably, familiar with Soane's work. Not only are the two close in size and with similar porticos flanked by pairs of Tuscan pilasters, but the side elevations have near identical articulations. The outer bays of Sibton's west elevation incorporate accentuated panels in its otherwise plain frieze, a feature not found at Tyringham, but certainly in Soane's repertoire, for instance in his unexecuted designs for an Opera House in Leicester Square (1791) and in his New Bank Building (1807–10). Tyringham was completed before Chantrell

17 J. Gwilt, revised by Wyatt Papworth, *Encyclopaedia of Architecture*, London, 867, p. 227.
18 J. Fergusson, *History of the Modern Styles of Architecture*, London, 1862, pp. 301.
19 Quoted in M. L. A. Jordan, 'The Life and Work of George Basevi (1794–1845)', unpublished MA thesis, Courtauld Institute, London, 1979, p. 6. I am grateful to Oliver Bradbury for alerting me to this item.

entered his office, but it is inconceivable that he was not familiar with the project. If Brooke was serious about a remodelling, here was Chantrell's opportunity to update a distinctly Soanian building and present it to a new generation, retaining the obviously Soanian features but repackaging them in the light of the current phase of the Classical Tradition. His response is fascinating: by proposing to remove the semi-circular portico, he dispensed with its most obviously out-dated aspect; it was, indeed, a feature that Soane had used, but it was not characteristically Soanian as so many other late-Georgian architects had exploited it. Furthermore, Chantrell's solution, in reusing the old columns and specifying only limited changes to this façade, was commendably economical. Yet alongside this modernisation, Chantrell proposed to add other, more obviously Soanian embellishments to enliven the design. These, like the portico, were clearly no longer emphatically fashionable, yet in Chantrell's proposal, they take on a new-found currency. Specifically, in Design B, he proposed to crown the centre of the west parapet with a scroll motif copied from those specified by Soane for his Lothbury Front of the Bank of England (1805), the houses for John Robins in Regent Street (1820–21) and for several other commissions. By flattening the portico, the attic storey above the entrance is revealed and in both Designs A and B the addition of urns enhances its significance, bringing it firmly into the tradition of Soane's Bank facades which are punctuated with elaborate attics for emphasis.

In both the Sibton schemes the central block of chimneys was proposed to be transformed into a much more emphatic feature, best described as a squat, windowless tower, not unlike the crown on Soane's Pell Wall, Shropshire (1822–28) or a simplified version of the upper part of his Mausoleum at Dulwich (1811–14). In Design B (fig. 4) the front door and the window above it are given a flamboyant surround which, although not entirely clear, appears to be very much in the spirit of some aspects of Soane's late interiors, for instance the Law Courts and the unexecuted House of Lords schemes.

In both Designs A and B, the plain parapet over the outer bays of the side elevation acquires balusters, further emphasising the visual connection with Tyringham, and the whole parapet is much enlivened by urns, a really interesting addition. On the one hand, parapet urns are not uncommon in Soane's work — although they were generally more slender than Sibton's — for instance at the Bank of England and Dulwich. On the other hand, Sibton's urns transform the house into something much closer to the current Italian Renaissance fashion, led by Charles Barry, seen for instance at Bridgewater House, London (1846–51). At exactly the same time as these Chantrell drawings, Barry was busy remodelling Soane's Board of Trade Offices, London; the result virtually destroyed Soane's design. But in Chantrell's Sibton proposals, the house is brought absolutely up-to-date, yet its emphatically Soanian references are both respected and enhanced.

Keeping in mind what Chantrell proposed to retain, remove and add at Sibton, we have a useful vignette of his domestic Classical interests in the 1840s; it leads to the almost inevitable conclusion that for Chantrell, the style of his master retained a currency well into the decade; interestingly, we might reasonably conclude that he believed it even had the capacity for further development for a new generation. From here, it is revealing to return to Leeds and to the city's most important urban mansion of the early Victorian period, indeed, one that hosted the queen in 1858. This is Woodsley House (now Fairbairn House), Clarendon Road (fig. 6), built for

Peter Fairbairn, a very successful engineer, machine maker and partner in the Wellington Foundry.[20] Fairbairn completed the purchase of the land on 1st and 2nd October 1839[21] and built his new house soon after; he was in residence in time for the census of 1841.[22] The question of its designer is one that has challenged Leeds' historians for many years.

Woodsley House, Leeds

Architectural historians have succeeded in identifying the architects of most of the public and ecclesiastical buildings erected in Leeds in the first half of the nine-teenth century, but have pitifully few facts about the designers of the period's many substantial domestic buildings. A stained glass window at Headingley Castle (c. 1843–46) conveniently records its architect as 'Johanas Child . . . 1846'; there are a handful of helpful documents in the West Yorkshire Archives collection; and the 1858 obituary of John Clark — the only Leeds architect of this period to have had one published — records he was responsible for the city's Gledhow Grove (for John Hives, no dates given, but probably 1835–40) and major alterations to Meanwood Hall (for Christopher Beckett, c. 1834).[23] And that is about the extent of our certainty.

Scholarly research on Leeds' nineteenth-century buildings can reasonably be said to have begun with Professor Derek Linstrum (1925–2009). His first book *Historic Architecture of Leeds*, 1969, does not mention Woodsley House, but his *West Yorkshire Architects and Architecture*, 1978, includes it with 'J. Clark, attrib.' and 'probably by John Clark'.[24] However, in the 'biographical lists' at the end of this book — in small print, often confusingly laid out and without any sources — Linstrum failed to

20 For Fairbairn, see R. V. Taylor, *Biographica Leodiensis*, Leeds, 1865, pp. 491–96.

21 Leeds University Property Deeds, 135. Sadly, the deeds make no reference to Fairbairn's architect.

22 M. Beresford, *Walks Round Red Brick*, Leeds, 1980, p. 92. Fairbairn's former residence in Park Square, was advertised 'To Let . . . from 25 March 1841' in *Leeds Mercury*, 6 March 1841.

23 *Building Chronicle*, May 1857, pp. 197–98. Dates for the buildings are not included in the obituary. These come from H. Colvin, *A Biographical Dictionary of British Architects*, New Haven and London, 2008, p. 253, no doubt supplied by Derek Linstrum.

24 D. Linstrum, *West Yorkshire Architects and Architecture*, London, 1978, p. 106. 'Attrib.' appears with the picture caption, 'probably by' in the text.

include '(attrib.)' after Woodsley House in the Clark list.[25] This is, no doubt, where the subsequent confusion arose. Pevsner, meanwhile, listed the building, but without any reference to its designer. Interestingly, none of the four editions of Colvin's *Dictionary* (1954, 1978, 1995 and 2008) include the house in the Clark entry; although Linstrum provided the details of most of the Clark buildings in the *Dictionary*, Colvin — always a stickler for the documentary sources for authorship and a writer reluctant to include speculative attributions — clearly chose to reject any link between this house and Clark. In 1980 the first edition of Maurice Beresford's *Walks Round Red Brick* appeared, with much detail about the house and its owner, but no hint of its designer. Admittedly, Beresford — Professor of Economic History — was not primarily interested in architects, but his research was always exemplary; certainly, he mentioned architects when he came across them. Sheeran's *Brass Castles*, 1993 has the house as 'thought to be by John Clark'.[26]

In various publications, Linstrum attributed two more significant Leeds houses to Clark: Rose Court, Headingley Lane[27] and Roundhay Hall,[28] the latter now known to be by Samuel Sharp. Yet if these two houses are considered alongside Woodsley House, there is no overwhelming stylistic link within this trio to suggest common authorship, and certainly none to either of the documented Clark houses — Meanwood Hall and Gledhow Hall — beyond the broad umbrella of Classicism. It is hard not to conclude Linstrum's attributions were based solely on the fact that Clark was almost unique in this period as a Leeds architect with demonstrable Classical credentials.

The new millennium seems to have heralded a new age of certainty and both Rose Court and Woodsley House have migrated into the 'by Clark' category,[29] the latter presumably on the basis of Linstrum's misleading 'biographical list'. This would seem a convenient time to revisit the issue of Woodsley House's architect, and this writer will propose that Chantrell be given serious consideration. So far as Clark's authorship is concerned, it is important to remember that his documented buildings of the late-1830s are mainly impeccably composed Greek Revival essays, with details easily traced to Stuart and Revett's *Antiquities of Athens*, occasionally enlivened with highly original Egyptian references; Meanwood Hall is a pioneering example of the fashionable shift towards the Italian Renaissance repertoire.[30] Woodsley House has nothing in common with either of these aspects of Clark's output. Indeed, considering its 1840 construction, it is, in many ways, a conservative composition; put bluntly, had Clark been its architect, one would have expected something rather more innovative. And if Clark had designed it, wouldn't he have included it in the long list of his completed buildings which appeared with his obituary, a list no doubt compiled by Clark himself? Its location would have made it his most prominent mansion and given Fairbairn's pre-eminent political position in the town, it was a building that would have significantly added to Clark's prestige.

One thing that is absolutely certain about the Sibton drawings is that they show Chantrell never lost his interest in Classicism, despite his fame as a designer of Gothic churches. Indeed, given Chantrell's extraordinary Wrenian additions to the tower of Holy Trinity in Leeds in 1839 — elegant, undoubtedly, but an absolutely unnecessary expense for the church — and the designs for an impeccably detailed, temporary Classical pavilion he produced, without charge, for the Leeds Tradesmen's Conservative Association in 1838, one might reasonably conclude he relished any chance to design in this style. Since the architects of Leeds' biggest

25 In a conversation with this author in the early part of the twenty-first century, Linstrum — by this time frail and with a failing memory — could not recall the details.
26 G. Sheeran, *Brass Castles*, Halifax, 1993, p. 151.
27 D. Linstrum, *Historic Architecture of Leeds*, Newcastle upon Tyne, 1969, p. 32.
28 Ibid. and D. Linstrum, *West Yorkshire* [note 25], p. 374. It is now known to be by Samuel Sharp.
29 For Woodsley House, see: S. Wrathmell, *Pevsner Architectural Guides: Leeds*, New Haven and London, 2005, p. 195; P. Leach, *Yorkshire West Riding*, New Haven and London, 2009, p. 479; M. Beresford (C. Hammond, ed.), *Walks Round Red Brick*, Leeds, Thoresby Society, 2012, p. 93.
30 For a fuller discussion of Clark's output, see C. Webster 'John Clark (1798–1857)' in C. Webster (ed), *Building a Great Victorian City: Leeds Architects and Architecture 1790–1814*, Huddersfield, Northern Heritage Publications in association with the Victorian Society, 2011, pp. 117–34.

houses were rarely publicised, it is reasonable to conclude that Chantrell might well have been responsible for several of the Classical examples.

In c. 1839–40, when Fairbairn was contemplating his new house, Chantrell was the region's most eminent architect. True, Clark had achieved a degree of eminence for his distinguished public buildings in and around Leeds, but at a time when architects everywhere enjoyed a status somewhere between tradesmen and undisputed professionals, Chantrell's ecclesiastical work, his public lectures and archaeological publications brought him a prestige way above his fellow architects in the town.[31] And by c. 1840, Clark's career had peaked. It seems he was a difficult man with whom to deal and by the late-1830s he had fallen out with many of the leading townsmen; his fondness for writing vitriolic letters to the local newspapers when building committees failed to award him commissions can only have hastened his downfall.[32] Conversely, in 1840, Chantrell was absolutely at the top of his game: the rebuilding of Leeds Parish Church — completed to universal praise the following year — was rapidly approaching completion after three years of construction. Not only was it a source of immense local pride, but as the country's largest new church since St Paul's Cathedral, there was much national interest too. If Fairbairn wanted a big name to design his house, he need have looked no further than Chantrell. Furthermore, the two certainly knew each other, meeting on close to equal terms via several Leeds institutions. Fairbairn joined the Leeds Philosophical and Literary Society in November 1838,[33] a society that met in premises designed for it by Chantrell in 1819–22 and where he gratuitously supervised extensive alterations in 1839–40;[34] Chantrell himself was a member. Furthermore, Chantrell's status in the society was much enhanced by his annual lectures on architectural and archaeological subjects. The two also knew each other via the hugely successful Leeds Public Exhibition of 1839 — an event aimed, in part, at 'enabling the working classes to avail themselves of the instruction it affords' — where both Fairbairn and Chantrell were on its organising committee.[35] They also served on the committee for the second Public Exhibition on 1843. Around 1839–40 the two were involved with the Yorkshire Agricultural Society and possibly concurrently, they were shareholders and committee members of the Leeds Zoological and Botanic Gardens.[36] Perhaps most significantly, Fairbairn was a member of the Church of England.[37] He was buried at St John the Baptist, Adel, an exceptional Norman church some five miles north of Woodsley House, but it is not clear where he worshipped; if at Adel, then the Chantrell link is much strengthened as the latter supervised an important restoration there in 1838–39, followed by another in 1843. Chantrell and Adel's rector, the Revd George Lewthwaite, were good friends,[38] with both, subsequently, serving on the small committee of the Yorkshire Architectural Society. If Fairbairn needed a reference before employing an architect, Lewthwaite would certainly have provided one.

What are Chantrell's stylistic claims as the designer of Woodsley house? The entrance front does have a certain similarity to his sketches for remodelling Sibton, but as he was not that house's initial architect, we should not read too much into it. Indeed, Woodsley's principal front is not especially remarkable. Far more interesting are its side and rear elevations, both of which need some 'mental reconstruction' as there have been so many later additions to the house. So far as the sides are concerned, significant is the upper storey, concealed at the front behind the balustrade, but lit by side windows in the manner of Soane's 'bridge' lodge at

31 This statement is hard to quantify, but his frequent appearances in the Leeds newspapers were invariably accompanied with laudatory epithets; in contrast, Clark appears to have had no public role in Leeds, and his name rarely appeared in the papers. Sometimes, even the opening of one of Clark's own buildings failed to mention its designer's name.

32 Webster, as at note 30, pp. 132–33.

33 Leeds Mercury, 17 November 1838.

34 LPLS papers, Leeds University, Special Collections, MS 1975/1 including Report for the Year 1839–40, LPLS, 1840.

35 Fairbairn was the vice-president, chairing several of the planning meetings, e.g. 16 April 1839. (Leeds Mercury, 20 April 1839). Chantrell's involvement is noted in the Leeds Intelligencer, 13 May 1839. Chantrell also leant several 'curious' items to the exhibition.

36 Information is patchy, but it is known that Chantrell was involved at the garden's formation in 1837 as a shareholder, and in 1838 he served on its council (Leeds Intelligencer, 20 May 1837 and 23 December 1837). Fairbairn was recorded as a member of the committee in 1845 (Leeds Mercury, 3 May 1845). It is not clear whether they had any concurrent involvement in the gardens.

37 Taylor, as at note 20, p. 494.

38 Lewthwaite and his two clerical sons between them published a number of antiquarian articles in which Chantrell's work receives warm praise.

Tyringham, or the Lothbury façade of the Bank, and an unusual device Chantrell had earlier exploited in two houses at the beginning of his career.[39] Especially interesting are the chimneystacks with their semi-circular topped motif, subtly emphasised by their stone detailing (fig. 7). Certainly Soanian in general character, they are similar to Soane's Prince's Street entrance to the Bank, built in 1808 while Chantrell was his pupil, and even closer to the central chimneystack he proposed for Butterton Grange, Staffs, in 1815–16;[40] less literally, this type of semi-circular blank arch crops up regularly in Soane's designs.

Even more convincing is Soane's inspiration inside the house, principally in the magnificently decorated entrance hall and staircase. The two spaces are divided by a pair of fluted columns (fig. 8), taken directly from the Corinthian order found at the Temple of Vesta at Tivoli. This order was not unique to Soane, but it was his favourite. It differs from more 'orthodox' Corinthian in that the columns are squatter, and its capitals are enriched. 'It is striking and unusual in having a curly-leaved acanthus leaf, with the addition of long, fern-like leaves, two on each face, protruding above the second row of acanthus and curving with a corkscrew move-ment. The flowers are very large and consist of six petals, which stand out from the face of the capital.'[41] According to Margaret Richardson, 'Soane — in pursuit of the unorthodox — seized upon [this order] as the perfect exemplar.'[42] He believed that 'every part of this beautiful composition has never been surpassed',[43] he used the order in his own work extensively — perhaps most prominently in the Tivoli Corner of the Bank's exterior wall — he praised it in his RA lectures and even had a full-sized copy of the capital made for the *Pasticcio* which adorns the Monuments Court in Soane's London house. He chose it to form the background of the portrait of himself, painted by William Owen in 1804. Perhaps most significantly, drawing the capital was a regular part of the syllabus for Soane's pupils; indeed copying an illustration of the temple and its order was the very first exercise Soane set for his new pupil in June 1807, the fourteen-year-old Chantrell. And if, thirty-three years on, he needed reminding of its precise details and proportions, the order was faithfully reproduced in Desgodetz's *Les Edefices antiques de Rome*, 1682, readily available

39 These were Eastwood House, Keighley (c. 1818–19) and Forest House, Bacup, Lancs (c. 1816–21). For both see Webster, as at note 2, pp. 171–76.
40 Sir John Soane's Museum, drawing FO. V. 94.
41 M. Richardson, 'John Soane and the Temple of Vesta at Tivoli' in *Architectural History*, 46, 2003, p. 132.
42 *Ibid.*
43 Soane, RA Lecture II, quoted in *ibid.*, p. 135.

in a late eighteenth-century English translation, a book Chantrell probably owned along with most of the period's serious architects.[44]

At Woodsley House, the frieze that runs above these columns and around the hall is a Greek key, one of Soane's favourite motifs. Beyond, the Imperial staircase — precisely square in plan — is lit from above by a shallow glass dome, surrounded by another Greek key frieze (fig. 9). The base of this dome sits on shallow segmental arches, a development of the arrangement first exploited by Soane in his Stock Office at the Bank (1792) and subsequently used by him at Pitzhanger Manor (1800–03), the Breakfast Room at 13, Lincoln's Inn Fields (c. 1812) — constructed

44 The translation was published by George Marshall as *The Ancient Buildings of Rome*, 2 vols, London, 1771, 1795.

8. Woodsley, now Fairbairn House, Clarendon Road, Leeds, 1840–41, entrance hall with columns taken directly from the Corinthian order found in the Temple of Vesta at Tivoli (photo: author).

9. Woodsley, now Fairbairn House, Clarendon Road, Leeds, 1840–41, dome over the staircase resting on segmental arches in the manner of Soane's at the Bank of England and elsewhere (photo: author).

while Chantrell was a pupil there — in the Court of Common Pleas (1822–25) and elsewhere. What is also interesting about the staircase is that one imagines from its top lighting that it is in the centre of the house. However, only some shallow, minor service rooms separate it from the house's external west wall; the staircase could easily have been lit by conventional vertical windows had its architect so desired. One is left to conclude its designer was intent on lighting it from above. If Woodsley House really was by Chantrell, he might well have seen this as a unique opportunity to design a top-lit, domed space as the ultimate tribute to his esteemed master. Chantrell should at least be given serious consideration as the house's architect.

Acknowledgement

The writer wishes to record with gratitude, much valuable assistance from John K. A. Brooke, great-great-grandson of John William Brooke. Christopher Hammond and Susan Wrathmell also supplied helpful information.

Leeds Town Hall: a Design for the main Entrance Hall and Staircase

Derek Linstrum

This was one of Derek's last articles, dated 'December 2000' on the original typed copy. It was intended for the *Leeds Museums and Galleries Review*, but as that journal ceased publication, it has not appeared in print before.

According to one of Cuthbert Brodrick's biographers, in his younger days the architect of Leeds Town Hall was a tall, dashing-looking man, close-shaven save for sideburns like those worn by Prince Albert. His hair was brushed back from his forehead, and he affected an artistic negligence in his dress.[1] We can picture him lunching at the Leeds Club in Albion Place — where, apparently, he ate regularly — before returning to his office in nearby Park Place to don a smoking jacket and light up a Corona before settling down to work. Another writer assured us that he made his own perspective drawings and invariably smoked a cigar when colouring them.[2] It sounds like the Parisian world of George du Maurier's *Trilby*, and it is no surprise that after fewer than twenty years practice in Leeds Brodrick abandoned Yorkshire and took a lady companion to live, first in Paris and then in le Vesinet, a *ville-parc* close to the French capital where he enjoyed painting and gardening, let his beard grow, and took on the appearance of a *bon-viveur*.[3]

Unfortunately, too few of these smoke-impregnated, coloured perspective drawings survived but those that can be found in the Drawings Collection of the Royal Institute of British Architects, the Leeds City Art Gallery, the Ferens Gallery, Hull, and the Scarborough Public Library testify to his skill as a brilliant draughtsman and colourist. There was, therefore, some excitement when a large watercolour (343 × 280 mm) attributed to Brodrick and subsequently acquired for the Leeds collection, was displayed in a London gallery in December 2000 (fig. 1).[4] Although it is not signed and its early provenance has not been established, it appears to be by the same hand as the often-reproduced depiction of the royal opening of the Town Hall in 1858 (fig. 2) in the Leeds collection. It is a professionally rendered exhibition piece enlarged from a small, meticulously drawn sepia ink and wash drawing which, by happy coincidence, was already in the collection of the West Yorkshire Archives Service (fig. 3).[5] This came to the Archives with the material on the Town Hall from the Town Clerk's and Public Works Departments, and it is inscribed on the old mount to which it has been stuck 'View of the Staircase to Gallery of Leeds Town Hall'. It is almost certainly in Brodrick's hand, and it might have been submitted as part of his entry in the 1852 competition, but there is no corresponding plan to indicate how it could have been integrated in the available space, nor is there a sectional drawing to show how the upper level related to the Victoria Hall. Whether or not to build a gallery, and in what form, was discussed

1 D. Harbron, 'Cabbages at Salona', *Architectural Review*, 79, 1936, pp. 33–35.

2 T. Butler Wilson, *Two Leeds Architects*, Leeds, 1937, p. 33.

3 D. Linstrum, *Towers and Colonnades: the Architecture of Cuthbert Brodrick*, Leeds, 1999, pp. 137–41.

4 *Inside Out. Historic Watercolour Drawings, Oil Sketches and Paintings of Interiors and Exteriors, 1770–1870*, London, 2000, item 51. It was bought with a grant from the Re:source/V&A Purchase Grant Fund.

5 West Yorkshire Archives, Leeds, LC/Wks. Small Plans/Town Hall A.

1. Cuthbert Brodrick (attrib.), *Leeds Town Hall, Design for the main Entrance Hall and Staircase*, watercolour, n.d. (photo: Leeds Museums and Galleries).

6 One of the 1854 watercolours that had been exhibited in Paris in 1967 was seen again in a European context in Vienna in 1996–97 in the Council of Europe exhibition *Der Traum vom Gluck: die Kunst des Historismus in Europa*.

on several occasions, but the present one dates only from 1890, the work of W. H. Thorp. The design of the entrance hall was an integral part of the question of whether or not to build a tower and several versions of the entrance were recorded as having been made and discussed, although most are now lost.

The competition conditions of 1852 stipulated that only line and sepia wash could be used and coloured drawings would not be considered; that implies that the newly discovered watercolour belongs to a post-competition phase when Brodrick, who was a fine draughtsman and watercolourist, was indulging in *jeux brilliants* and making elaborate presentation drawings, firstly for the town council and then for exhibition purposes. In 1854 he had made two large watercolours of the Town Hall from the south-east, and these were hung at the Royal Academy in London in the same year; another was exhibited at the Paris Exposition of 1867, and there were others,[6] but few have survived. Leeds City Art Gallery possesses two of the exterior, and in 1936 Dudley Harbron illustrated an article about Brodrick with a view of the exterior of the Victoria Hall which cannot now be found;[7] when the latter was being made — no doubt with the inspiration of the inevitable cigar — Brodrick was intending that the large apse at the north end should be ribbed and segmentally panelled in a High Renaissance style, but the great organ case designed by Brodrick caused the proposed decoration of the apse to be eliminated. However, the newly discovered watercolour is of a much finer quality which suggests that it was intended for an important exhibition. Could it have been submitted to the old-established Paris Salon, to which exhibitions Brodrick is believed to have been a contributor?

7 Harbron, as in note 1, pl. 4, p. 34.

2. *Leeds Town Hall, the Victoria Hall on 7 September 1858*, with the royal party on the platform. This magnificent watercolour is not signed; it is generally attributed to Brodrick himself, but, although he was an accomplished watercolourist, the outstanding quality of this work suggests that a professional perspectivist, possibly Thomas Allom, might have been involved (photo: Leeds Museums and Galleries).

3. Cuthbert Brodrick, *Leeds Town Hall, design for the entrance hall and staircase,* probably produced as part if his competition entry, 1852 (photo: West Yorkshire Archives Service).

An especially interesting aspect of the staircase design is that it is closely based on Genoese palaces, in particular Gregorio Petondi's Classical Revival remodelling of the Palazzo Balbi of 1780. This contains a remarkable scenographic staircase[8] which, despite its seventeenth-century appearance, was only forty years older than Brodrick (fig. 4). Petondi made use of the characteristic Genoese coupled giant-order columns, and it obviously impressed itself on Brodrick's memory, so much so that if it were not for the inscription which declares that the sepia watercolour is a design for the Town Hall, one might wonder if the newly-acquired watercolour

8 A. Blunt (ed.), *Baroque and Rococo Architecture and Decoration,* Ware, 1988, p. 75, pl. 97.

4. Gregorio Petondi,
Palazzo Balbi, main
staircase, remodelled 1780
(photo: Derek Linstrum).

is a worked-up version is one of Brodrick's Grand Tour drawings. It is known that
Brodrick visited Genoa in 1844–45, as one of the drawings from his missing
sketchbook showed the staircase in Palazzo dell'Università;[9] this, like that in
Palazzo Balbi, has the characteristic Genoese coupled columns which Brodrick was
apparently proposing to use in the Town Hall staircase. There are, however, some
differences between the newly discovered watercolour and the sepia drawing. The
former shows a lower Tuscan order and an upper Ionic, while the sepia drawing
appears to have an upper Corinthian or Composite, but otherwise the two are

9 Linstrum, as at note 3,
fig. 13, p. 10.

almost identical except that the watercolour has elaborately decorated ceilings and walls, and the drawing has pilasters between the panels on the upper level walls. In the lower right-hand side there is an arched opening with flanking sunken panels similar to that in the entrance hall of Brodrick's 1852 Hull Royal Institution;[10] the latter probably derived from Palazzo Balbi. Finally, in noting how Brodrick made use of his studies as sources it must be remembered that he used coupled giant-order columns in the Victoria Hall,[11] to which the staircase would have been a prelude.

With the advent of John Gregory Crace[12] as designer and executant of the decorations in the Victoria Hall, the entrance vestibule, the courtrooms and the mayor's suite of rooms, Brodrick must have felt he had found a kindred spirit. Both loved France, both were outstanding draughtsmen and colourists, and that knowledge poses a question. How closely might they have collaborated both in the decoration in situ and/or over the drawing board? There are several similarities between the colours and decorative details in the watercolour of the staircase and the 1858 watercolour of the Victoria Hall such as the *rosso antico* of the columns, the repeated Greek-key pattern, the colouring of the entablature and the blue frieze at capital level. Should Brodrick and Crace share the credits? That must remain an open question, but one building for which Brodrick was responsible for the internal colour scheme was the 1861 Hull Town Hall.[13] A contemporary description refers to 'the grand staircase, where the *coup d'oeil* is such as is seldom seen in a building in a provincial town'.[14] One other design, unfortunately unexecuted like so many of Brodrick's buildings, that has relevance for the design which is the subject of this article is that for the Manchester Royal Exchange.[15] Although the original, doubtless highly-coloured view of the interior has been lost, the photograph taken from an old black and white slide shows that the decoration on the vaulted dome and ancillary spaces was intended to have been in a similar High Renaissance/Baroque taste to Brodrick's ambitious design for the staircase for the Leeds Town Hall; but like so many of his grand designs they were forgotten like the smoke from a cigar.

10 Illustrated in Linstrum, *ibid.*, figs 15 and 16, p. 10.
11 In that respect the Leeds building differs from St George's Hall, Liverpool, in which the columns in the similar basilican arrangement are single and less effective.
12 For an account of the work of J. G. Crace, see M. Aldrich (ed.), *The Craces: Royal Decorators 1768–1899*, exhibition catalogue, Royal Pavilion, Art Gallery and Museums, Brighton, 1990. For the decoration of the Town Hall, see Linstrum, as at note 3, pp. 29–38.
13 J. J. Sheahan, *History of the Town and Port of Kingston-upon-Hull*, Beverley, 1866, pp. 628–89.
14 The decoration in Hull Town Hall was executed by J. L. Coulton of London.
15 Linstrum, as at note 3, pp. 86–89, illustrated on p. 90.

Ghosts from the Castle of Love: Cliffe Castle in photographs

Daru Rooke

On 11 February 1910 retired wool spinner and worsted merchant Henry Isaac Butterfield died at his recently acquired Devonshire home Winterbourne. He was ninety years old.

The Devonshire newspapers were quick to produce obituaries for this important local benefactor. They retailed anecdotes of his discreet generosity to both Teignmouth and its people, remembering him as an infirm but energetic member of the local community.[1] In Yorkshire the obituaries were longer and more knowledgeable. After all it was here that he had been born, one of the famous Butterfield Brothers whose business was 'one of the largest and most important commercial establishments in the district' with trading links that stretched from China to America.[2]

It was also here in Keighley that Butterfield had created one of his greatest legacies, the vast 'modernised Tudor' mansion known as Cliffe Castle whose complex roof structure of towers and minarets greeted visitors to the town.[3] In some later assessments Butterfield's house building has been seen as characteristic of what mill-owner's brass could buy, a vulgar expression of *nouveau riche* taste that could be viewed as a 'monstrous fantasy'.[4] But this in no way sums up the complexity of either Butterfield or the house he created. As the *Keighley News* commented, Mr Butterfield was of 'a nature hostile to the prosaic and of a taste refined and artistic' and his homes were a vivid incarnation of this spirit.[5]

Cliffe Castle was one of several homes which Butterfield created. Retiring early from trade he had spent much of his formative years establishing the family business in Philadelphia, Paris and New York. In America he met Miss Mary (later Marie) Roosevelt Burke, the daughter of the Hon Michael Burke (who claimed descent from the Earls of County Mayo) and niece to the celebrated Judge Roosevelt. They were married by Cardinal McClusky and Archbishop Ireland in New York in 1854 and established homes in the rue Pressbourg, Paris and at the Villa Marianna, Nice. Mrs Butterfield also had extensive properties in New York.[6]

The couple were thought to be one of the most beautiful in Paris and through the Roosevelt family connections became well known members of the court of Napoleon III.[7] Surviving correspondence and *carte de visite* albums show them entertaining and being entertained by French and Russian nobility and taking a full part in the glamorous life of the imperial city. Sadly this was to end in 1867 with the sudden death of Marie Louise at just twenty-nine. Butterfield was left a widower with one son.

The following decade saw further family losses. Butterfield's eldest brother John had died in 1865. He was followed by Richard in 1868, Sarah Hannah in 1871 and

1 'Obituary', *Keighley News*, 19 Feb 1910.

2 *Keighley News*, 18 December 1865.

3 'Country Houses. No. 18. Cliffe Castle, Keighley', *Bradford Weekly Telegraph*, 7 July 1883.

4 Private Collection, Diary of Sir Albert Richardson, 21 September, 1953.

5 *Keighley News*, as at note 1.

6 *Keighley News*, as at note 1.

7 Cliffe Castle, Keighley, Butterfield Archive, Letter to Henry and Mary Butterfield from Emilie Schaumberg 31 March 1858.

William in 1874. With each death property and wealth were bequeathed to Henry Isaac Butterfield. With the death of William came the inheritance of Cliffe Hall in Keighley.

Cliffe Hall had been a significant place for all of the Butterfield family members. A smart Elizabethan revival villa by Webster's of Kendal, the house had been commissioned by Keighley solicitor and flax spinner Christopher Netherwood during the 1820s. It was completed by 1833. Trade difficulties made the house increasingly uneconomic for Netherwood and the house was initially leased to the Butterfields before being bought by them in 1848. Latterly it was lived in by Henry Isaac's unmarried siblings Sarah Hannah (an abolitionist, teetotaller and nonconformist) and William (worsted manufacturer) and it was to this house that Butterfield's own son Frederick was sent to be cared for after his mother's death.[8]

The inheritance of Cliffe Hall in 1874 presented an interesting opportunity to Butterfield. Wealthy, energetic, independent and cosmopolitan he took the decision to keep on the family home alongside his establishments in Paris and Nice. But the vision that developed was not the retention of the house solely as an untouchable shrine to family memory but rather as a Summer Palace in Keighley where he could dazzle the local inhabitants and celebrate his prestigious connections.

Any uncertainty about how to approach the property probably came to an end late in 1874 when a serious accident nearly destroyed the house. In November 1874 Henry Isaac, already in residence at Cliffe Hall, detected the smell of gas in the ground floor Breakfast Room. Calling one of the housemaids Butterfield inspected and tested the newly installed burners in the rise-and-fall gasolier that lit the room. Then the maid tested the water slide. As she lit a match, gas escaped from the slide and caused a massive explosion.

The *Keighley News* was quick to report Mr Butterfield's injuries and the tragic death of the maid Kate Campion.[9] Writing to a correspondent on the 28th December Henry Isaac's son Frederick described what happened to the building: 'the force of the explosion was such that five doors were blown off, the majority of the windows shattered and a conservatory entirely flattened and almost all the walls cracked'.[10] The scale of damage may well have decided Butterfield to rebuild the Hall.

The house that began to emerge in 1875 took almost a decade to complete, cost an alleged £130,000 and resulted in modest Cliffe Hall being renamed Cliffe Castle.[11] Initially work was entrusted to Keighley-born architect George Smith (1842–1900) but, following a series of disagreements and disappointments, the commission was passed over to the Bradford architect Wilson Bailey. Internally work was carried out by local and French craftspeople with a presiding genius in the form of French decorator Monsieur Gremand. Day to day supervision of both the work and the installation of objects with which Butterfield sought to fill the house, was given to his son Frederick and his steward (and local mill owner) James Wright. The task was not an easy one.

Surviving correspondence outlines disagreements about costs, damage to valuable fittings, rows with the local corporation about the new lodges and general dismay that Butterfield had been 'caught … by such sharks'.[12] His travels around Europe in search of fine fittings, furniture and paintings took him away from the scene of operations and regular reports had to be completed to keep him thoroughly informed. As Frederick Butterfield was to state in his memoirs: 'my best

8 Sir F. W. L. Butterfield, *My West Riding Experiences*, London, 1927, p. 20.

9 Anon., 'The Gas explosion at Cliffe Hall', *Keighley News*, 28 November 1874.

10 Cliffe Castle, Keighley, Butterfield Archive, Letter from F. W. L Butterfield to Neil 28 December 1874 , 'La force de l'explosion était telle que cinq portes ont été emporté, la plupart des fenêtres brisées et une grande serre entièrement jettée à bas et presque tous les murs craqués'

11 Cliffe Castle, Keighley, Butterfield Archive, Letter from Letter from H. I. Butterfield to F. W. L. Butterfield, 28 March 1878.

12 Cliffe Castle, Keighley, Butterfield Archive, Letter from H. I. Butterfield to J. Wright, 7 March 1878.

years for study were employed in representing my absent father and generally watching over his enormous expenditure at Cliffe ... when he turned the comparatively modest Cliffe Hall ... into the present elaborate Cliffe Castle and proceeded to fill the new building with every costly detail his Parisian experiences could suggest'.[13]

By 1884 work was largely complete and the new Cliffe Castle, whilst respecting and incorporating aspects of the Webster house, was very different. The building now boasted a series of towers in stone and glass, a conservatory and winter garden by the specialist company Messengers, a 70-foot long music room in the form of a baronial hall, a series of interconnected drawing rooms forming a French style enfilade, a grand staircase with genealogical glass by Powell Brothers of Leeds and a landscaped estate which had been enlarged from twenty to three-hundred acres.[14] In terms of technology the house was gas-lit, steam-heated, benefited from secondary double glazing, the latest kitchen fittings and 'telephonic communication' in key rooms.[15]

As one reviewer stated: 'Cliffe Castle is a castle in every sense of the word. It has been Mr Butterfield's idea to establish a modernised Tudor Castle in the Victorian era, to construct a building which while it maintained faithfully the external architectural characteristics of the Elizabethan period, should also present the elegance and delicacy of the modern architect combined with interior arrangements which for efficiency and splendour should not be surpassed'.[16] Unlike the more usual historicist solutions to a medieval style building, Cliffe Castle's antiquarian exterior in no way defined its comfortable and cosmopolitan interior.

In December 1884 Butterfield celebrated his success with a grand ball which epitomised his antipathy to the prosaic. Female guests were instructed to wear white; Butterfield and his Spanish confidential secretary, Signor Edo Eugster y de la Deheza wore hunting pink. Flowers were shipped in from the villa in Nice and the centrepiece of the ball was a cotillion in the French manner. The last dance, a ladies' *farandole*, ended the proceedings at four a.m. The local papers were quick to describe every detail of the finished house and its important company.[17] Several local poets including C. W. Craven and William Wright were also moved to publish romantic eulogies of what came to be termed 'the Castle of Love'.

The building was also celebrated in a series of large format photographs which recorded all the key rooms of the newly completed castle as well as sweeping shots of the landscaped grounds. None of the images illustrate the domestic quarters or service rooms of the house.

A selection of images were mounted in a leather and cloth bound volume marked 'Cliffe Castle'. Others were retained in a portfolio. They cover the period from the 1880s to the 1890s. Three of the images bear the impress of Alexander Jennings, Keighley. Jennings was a local photographer who moved from Skipton to Keighley in the late nineteenth century. By the time of his death in 1919 he had studios in Bingley and Keighley and was a well-respected Conservative and freemason.[18] His choice as photographer reflects Henry Isaac's continued patronage of local business and craftspeople when developing his home.

All the images remained in the ownership of Butterfield's direct descendants and were donated to Bradford Museums and Galleries during the 1980s through to the 2010s. They form a remarkable record of the house as completed. Their value is

13 Sir F. W. L. Butterfield, as at note 8, p. 25.
14 Anon., 'The Cliffe Castle Estate', Keighley News, 24 August 1878, p. 4.
15 Anon., Picturesque Views of Castles and Country Houses in Yorkshire, Bradford (Bradford Illustrated Weekly Telegraph), 1885, pp. 79–82.
16 Bradford Weekly Telegraph, as at note 3.
17 Anon., 'The Grand Ball at Cliffe Castle', Keighley News, 26 December 1884.
18 Anon., 'Obituary', Keighley News, 11 October 1919.

especially important as the twentieth century brought dramatic change to the house.

Following Butterfield's death in 1910 the Castle was occupied by his son Sir Frederick. During his period of tenure many of the decidedly Victorian interiors were removed, modified or given a Georgian gloss. The house was finally sold by Sir Frederick's daughter Countess Manvers. In June 1950 the original contents were the subject of a four-day auction. The building was purchased by Keighley-born philanthropist, hotelier and Lord Mayor of London, Sir Bracewell Smith. Using the President of the Royal Academy, Sir Albert Richardson, as his architect, Sir Bracewell initiated a dramatic re-modelling of the castle into a museum and art gallery. Important spaces were lost but Sir Albert, increasingly fascinated by Victorian architecture and decoration, was respectful of key features such as painted ceilings and decorative glass. The survival of any of Henry Isaac's 'Castle of Love' was due to his advanced sensitivity to an unfashionable period.[19] Work was completed in 1960.

The photographs have been infrequently published, with that of Butterfield sitting in the reception rooms being the most reproduced.[20] Largely the images aim to record the splendours of what the editor of Craven's *Commercial and General Directory* for 1884 described as one of the 'noblest mansions in the country'. Together they form a virtual tour of a building whose contents were dispersed in 1950 and whose decorative finishes and spaces were compromised in the 1950s and 60s.

For the present study the author proposes to present key images from the sequence with accompanying text outlining the genesis of the house.

Fig. 1. A. Jennings, *Cliffe Castle from the Flower Garden*, c. 1890

This unusual view from the rear of the castle gives a perspective on the building's new roofscape and garden context.

As part of the development of the castle grounds, the kitchen garden was relocated and the space converted into a flower garden. This new feature gave dramatic views out over the Aire Valley but was partially enclosed by an elaborate sequence of glasshouses. These (together with the house) blocked glimpses of 'the workshops, chimneys &c., which are utilised in the staple manufacture of the town' and which were clearly felt to be a threat to its picturesque setting.[21] The curving conservatory corridor on the right led down to the newly completed library which was filled with elaborately bound French volumes originally owned by Napoleon III's half-brother the Duc de Morny.

Each glasshouse in the sequence was devoted to a different plant type, those at the bottom having fuchsias, then heaths and further along, azaleas, roses and ferns. The glasshouses led up to a painted and gilded semi-circular showhouse which balanced the dome of the winter garden below.[22] The main flower bed was laid out with carpet bedding described in 1887 as 'gay and brilliant'.[23]

The upper terrace path also gave a good view of the Castle's final silhouette. To the left were the long walls and double chimneys of the new ballroom completed by W. Bailey in 1884, its roofline broken by ornamental ventilators for gas sunlights. Behind stood the nursery tower which later contained accommodation for Butterfield's great grand-children, a smoking room and retiring rooms. Beside this came the dome of the winter garden, then Smith's Minaret Tower of 1878 and finally (to the right) the Grand Tower which visually announced the entrance front.

19 Diary of Sir Albert Richardson, as at note 4.
20 P. Thornton, *Authentic Décor*, London, 1985, p. 338.
21 Anon., 'Cliffe Castle, Keighley', *The Gardening World*, 8 October 1887, p. 88.
22 *Bradford Weekly Telegraph*, as at note 3.
23 *The Gardening World*, as at note 21, p. 89.

1. A. Jennings, *Cliffe Castle from the Flower Garden*, c. 1890. Photograph.

In the centre of the photograph Butterfield (with homburg hat and mourning band) sits on a garden bench. To his left is confidential secretary and companion Signor Edo Eugster y de la Deheza who was noted for his operatic performances.[24]

Fig. 2. Anon. *The Breakfast Room, c. 1885*

The Breakfast Room was situated to the left of the Entrance Hall and was used for family dining. The redevelopment of the Castle included the creation of a conservatory which led out from this room. It was used for shade-loving plants such as camellias and could be viewed and accessed from two large French windows which can be seen on the left hand wall.[25] Behind the viewer was a bay window fronting an elaborate piece of grotto-work created by French craftsmen under the direction of Monsieur Aucante 'the artist in this especial class of work'.[26]

The decorative scheme took its lead from the main reception rooms along the garden front. Silk brocatelle woven with a pattern of peacocks and flowers was hung in the gilded wall compartments and used to form swagged curtains and furniture upholstery.

The furnishings of the room included an ebonised and gilded suite of French furniture (sideboard visible rear wall centre) decorated with the Butterfield crest.[27] Other furnishings included gilt chairs carved to simulate knotted rope work and an overmantel mirror thematically decorated with grapes. Both are listed in Butterfield's notebook as having been bought from Tradico of Milan in 1879.

Nineteenth-century writers commenting on the room drew attention to the decorated ceiling painted by M. Leroux which represented luxuriant flowers and foliage. They also commented on the room's most important feature, a portrait of Queen Victoria by Lowes Cato Dickinson (1819–1908) shown centre left. The c. 1870 work was based on a miniature commissioned by Queen Victoria from the artist F. A. Tilt as a gift for the American philanthropist George Peabody. The American link may well have had added resonance for Butterfield whose wife was an

24 Anon., 'La Colonie Etrangère en Angleterre', *La Colonie étrangère*, 31 July 1892. This Swiss publication was directed by Butterfield's friend, the musician Baron de Scriba.
25 *The Gardening World*, as at note 23.
26 *Keighley News*, as at note 14.
27 *Bradford Weekly Telegraph*, as at note 3.

2. Anon. *The Breakfast Room, c. 1885.* Photograph.

American and who came to believe himself an American citizen too. Both Butterfield and his wife are recorded as having been presented to the Queen at a royal levee.

Also in the room and positioned below Queen Victoria's portrait, were French silvered bronze statues of Queen Elizabeth I and Mary Queen of Scots. Butterfield seems to have appreciated the romance of Marie Stuart and visits to nearby Barden Tower (where she was once held prisoner) were part of the usual repertoire of Cliffe Castle house-party outings.[28]

On the walls were memorial portraits showing Butterfield's own family. They included images of his sister and brothers and nephew Freddie (visible in rear left corner).[29]

Fig. 3. Anon. *The Dining Room, c. 1890*

A sequence of reception rooms (of which the Dining Room formed the centre) was developed along the garden front of the castle. Each south-facing room took advantage of spectacular views across the landscaped park with its terraces, marble fountains and fishpond. The rooms incorporated sliding doors inset with bevelled mirrors said to have been imported from France. The doors allowed the reception rooms to be closed off for use as independent spaces. Opened up they formed a vast *enfilade* terminating in the winter garden. The flexibility of these spaces aided circulation during the grander parties held at the Castle and added to the drama of the house.

The individual compartments provided a Music Room and Music Drawing Room (appropriately decorated with ceiling panels of the Arts and fitted out with an ebony Steinway piano bought from one of the great European exhibitions in

28 *La Colonie étrangère*, as at note 24.
29 E. F. T., *The Haunted Castle*, Keighley, c. 1884, p. 14.

1885), a Dining Room and a Grand Drawing Room, the latter completed by Wilson Bailey.[30] The Dining Room (photographed *c.* 1890) shows the mirrored doors drawn back into the walls and the opening framed by an elaborate *portière* known to have been of crimson and gold brocatelle. On the left hand wall (out of view) was a French-made white 'demi statuary marble' chimneypiece surmounted by an Italian mirror decorated with vine leaves and grapes.[31]

The cornices were described as of antique work and included painted and gilded bands of moulded plaster fruit in a renaissance taste. The corners were emphasised by trophies of game birds. Here as elsewhere plasterwork was carried out by Benjamin Dixon of Bradford from French designs supplied by M. Gremand.[32]

Unlike the flanking rooms, where painted ceilings were preferred, Butterfield chose to use a tapestry to decorate the ceiling. This was said to be 'representative of various incidents in the building of Solomon's temple, and ... a rare antique

30 Cliffe Castle, Keighley, Butterfield Archive, Letter to H. I. Butterfield from Steinway Pianofortes, 3 December 1885.
31 Cliffe Castle, Keighley, Butterfield Archive, Letter from H. I. Butterfield to F. W. L. Butterfield, 27 August 1877.
32 *Keighley News* as at note 14.

3. Anon. *The Dining Room,* c. 1890. Photograph.

specimen of the … royal manufactury of Les Gobelins'.[33] Despite its rarity the centre of the tapestry had to be cut to allow the ventilator and fixings for the large French crystal chandelier originally supplied to the room. Additional lighting was provided by oriental vases fitted with gilded lilies and candle sconces positioned in the corners of the room.

The room was ornamented by a series of elaborately framed portraits by the Italian painter/sculptor Roberto Bompiani (1821–1908) all hung high on the crimson silk wall panels. The works included images of Butterfield's niece Jennie, Countess Montauban (d. 1878), here visible to the right of the doorway. Montauban was the son of French statesman and general, the Comte de Palikao (1798–1878). Palikao's bust and portrait were displayed elsewhere in the house. The Bompiani commission also included a posthumous portrait of Henry's wife Mrs Butterfield and a likeness of her close friend the American society beauty Miss Emilie Schaumberg, later to become famous as Mrs Hughes Hallett of Dinard. Both were displayed in this space.

Fig. 4. Anon. *The Great Drawing Room, c.* 1890

The last room in the sequence of Second Empire inspired reception rooms was the Great Drawing Room. An addition to the Webster house, the room was loftier than its counterparts and had an inlaid oak floor usually kept covered by a 'very luxurious French Carpet, specially manufactured for the purpose'.[34] Letters in the Butterfield archive confirm that the carpet (used for the whole suite of rooms) was recommended by the decorator M. Gremand in 1878.[35] Photographs show an unreformed design of putti and butterflies against naturalistic representations of trellis, flowers and ornamental balustrades. It was probably selected at one of the many European expositions which Butterfield attended. Oriental screens and a monumental conical pendulum clock were also acquired in this way in 1878.

Gremand was responsible for the design of the curtains and *portières* and the choice of silk brocatelle for the walls. Drawings for the former were approved in November 1878 and Butterfield's correspondence at this time show his concern that the novel ideas might be seen before the work was officially unveiled.[36] Writing to his steward J. Wright in December 1878 Butterfield advised 'don't let anyone see the rooms — so give the strictest orders to Elizabeth (Crabtree, the Cliffe Castle housekeeper) on the subject, the reason she can give is that the workmen can't be disturbed in their work'.[37]

The brocatelle for the wall hangings had also been a matter for debate. Here, as in the Music Room, Dining Room and Breakfast Room, a silk brocatelle of peacocks and flowers was chosen with a different colourway used in each room. Gremand had advised that the silk (here in white and gold) would cost 48/6d per yard. However Butterfield, ever conscious of mounting costs, discovered the same material at Maples for only 33/6d. This was the fabric chosen. As Butterfield stated 'The design is beautiful, most effective and quite superior' and was delighted to have triumphed over the specialist.[38]

Clearly the south facing character of the rooms put the hangings at risk from light damage despite French festoon blinds used as glass curtains. The photograph of *c.* 1890 shows striped floral cotton used to cover wall panels and furniture upholstery. Individual bags of the same material protected the lower sections of the curtains.

33 *Picturesque Views of Castles and Country Houses in Yorkshire*, as at note 15, pp. 80–81.
34 *Picturesque Views of Castles and Country Houses in Yorkshire*, as at note 15, p. 81.
35 Cliffe Castle, Keighley, Butterfield Archive, Letter from H. I. Butterfield to F. W. L. Butterfield, 15 November 1878.
36 Cliffe Castle, Keighley, Butterfield Archive, Letter from H. I. Butterfield to F. W. L. Butterfield 24 November 1878: 'Mr Gremaud has sent you the window curtain designs — which I have approved — but don't show them to everybody'.
37 Cliffe Castle, Keighley, Butterfield Archive, Letter from H. I. Butterfield to J. Wright, 1 December 1878.
38 Cliffe Castle, Keighley, Butterfield Archive, Letter from H. I. Butterfield to F. W. L. Butterfield, 11 November 1878.

Nineteenth-century visitors to the house were particularly interested in the associations of many of the furnishings chosen by Henry Isaac for this space. Newspaper reviewers were keen to point up the royal or literary links of so many of the original furnishings as well as their very foreignness. In the Great Drawing Room visitors remarked on the collection of Italian views by the American artist J. F. Cropsey (1823–1900) but the key attraction was the malachite chimneypiece seen to the right of the photograph.

As originally conceived the room was to have had a Louis XVI statuary marble chimney piece listed in a letter of August 27th 1877. Later Butterfield acquired the spectacular malachite and gilt bronze example from the Demidoff's Florentine villa of San Donato. This is shown in the record photographs of the 1880s and 90s and may have been bought at the 1880 sale of the palace contents arranged by Paul Demidoff.[39] It was used to display decorative lustres acquired from Lord Byron's

39 F. Haskell , 'Anatole
Demidoff and the Wallace
Collection', in *Anatole Demidoff,
Prince of San Donato*, Wallace
Collection, London, 1994,
pp. 27–29.

collection and was backed by an elaborate pier glass decorated with putto and portrait medallions. Its glamour in the context of Keighley was such that, well into the twentieth century, staff whispered that the gilt bronze mounts were of solid gold.[40]

Fig. 5. Anon. *The Ballroom or Music Room c. 1890*

Revealed to a select audience at the *bal blanc* held in December 1884, the Music Room marked the final phase of Butterfield's grand re-modelling of Cliffe Castle. Under Wilson Bailey's direction the chosen scheme was darker and more thematically appropriate to the Elizabethan character of the house, taking the form of a baronial hall. The furnishings however, reflected Butterfield's continuing passion for Second Empire taste and objects with royal provenance.

The room was intended for musical and dramatic performances and dances. It was approached by a long curving corridor which acted as a gallery for sculpture and paintings. Key works by Canaletto and van Dyck were shown here together with cabinets of porcelain once owned by Lord Byron and the French King Louis-Philippe.[41] The corridor ended with a highly unusual marble refreshment buffet.

Dominating the room itself was a stage, its proscenium arch described by the *Keighley News* in 1885 as 'a painting of [a] Shakespearean subject, representing the bard in the centre with drama and music represented allegorically on either side… The … drop scene is an artistical representation of Mr Butterfield's Italian seat at Nice, La villa Marianna, as seen from the Heights of Cimiez'.[42] This was the work of Frankfurt-born artist Friedrich Karl Otto Steinhardt (1844–94). Steinhardt was

40 Cliffe Castle, Keighley, Museum Archive, 'Reminiscences of Tom Foster', 20 August 1981. 'Emmott told Tom that the inside panels of the malachite fireplace were of gold and that it was worth £4,000. He said Henry Isaac Butterfield acquired it from an Italian count who lost heavily to him while playing at cards'.

41 *La Colonie étrangère*, as at note 24.

42 Anon., 'The Cliffe Castle Garden Party', *Keighley News*, 1885.

5. Anon. *The Ballroom or Music Room, c. 1890*. Photograph

a particular favourite of Butterfield, painting portraits of Henry Isaac and his son Frederick in 1883–84. He was a regular visitor to Butterfield's villa in Nice and is known to have decorated elaborate dinner party menus for the family's holiday retreat.

As completed the walls were given a painted and stencilled programme of decoration. Swags of painted pink drapery gathered by the Butterfield crest and monogram lay upon an olive green ground highlighted with gold. Photographs show that this scheme soon disappeared under Cliffe Castle's growing art collection. On the right hand wall the photograph shows a tapestry variously described as a seventeenth-century 'tapestry piece said to be Italian ... representing a Roman Battle' and, in the Cliffe Castle sale catalogue of 1950 (as lot 322), 'Flemish tapestry showing the 'Triumphs of Hannibal' ... signed I. Mander ... 1619'.[43] Early commentators also identified this as another purchase from San Donato. It went unsold in 1950 and was subsequently lost.

Flanking the tapestry and still on display at the Castle was a pair of equestrian portraits depicting Napoleon III and Empress Eugenie. These are by the French artist C. E. Boutibonne (1816–97) and are signed and dated 1857. These works reflect a similar pair in the Royal Collection commissioned by Queen Victoria in 1856 and emphasise Butterfield's ongoing passion for the French Imperial family.

Visible on the stage is a bronzed bust of Butterfield. This is by the Spanish sculptor Augustin Querol y Subirats (1860–1909) who completed the marble version in 1888. In front of the stage is one of a series of ebonized and gilt renaissance style chairs with velvet and applique upholstery also still at the Castle.

Artificial lighting was provided by gas brackets and two large gas sunlights installed by Harlands in January 1884.[44] Clearly gas lighting provided a relatively safe light source in a room with a varnished and gilded pitch pine ceiling. Evidence from the twentieth century suggests that the rafters above the ceiling were hung with patent liquid-filled fire bottles which would hopefully fall and put out a fire if required. Elsewhere iron shutters allowed the spaces to be cut off should fire break out.[45] Butterfield had experienced both house and mill fires and his correspondence reflects a constant concern about the risk of fire.

Fig. 6. Anon. *Henry Isaac Butterfield's Bedroom c. 1890*

Although perceived as private apartments, Butterfield's own suite of rooms featured regularly in descriptions of the house. Positioned off the Grand Landing at the top of the main staircase the suite included a Bedroom, Bathroom and lavishly appointed Boudoir. Both the Bedroom and the Boudoir were photographed in the 1880s–90s

The Bedroom itself was a modestly proportioned room with a white marble chimneypiece and decorative cornice. Unlike the Boudoir next door the walls seem to have been painted or papered rather than hung with silk damask.

Here, as in the Breakfast Room below, space was given to family portraits. To the right of the bed can be seen a portrait of Butterfield's sister Sarah Hannah. To the left of the bed was Norbert Schrodl's memorable portrait of the youthful Mrs Butterfield painted in 1866. The room's shrine-like quality is re-enforced by the painting of the *Madonna and Child* hung against the bed draperies and thought to be by Charles Signani.[46] To the right was *The Holy Family* after an original by Andrea del Sarto and bought from the Duke of Modena's collection in 1878.[47] Both works

43 Hollis and Webb, *Cliffe Castle Keighley*, Leeds, 1950.
44 Cliffe Castle, Keighley, Butterfield Archive, Letter from J. Wright to H. I. Butterfield, 1 January 1884.
45 Cliffe Castle, Keighley, Museum Archive, 'Reminiscences of Mr Slack, Cliffe Castle gardener', 1985.
46 M. Fisher Garside, 'The Art Collection of H. I. Butterfield', unpublished M.A. thesis, Leeds Polytechnic, 1989, p. 31.
47 Cliffe Castle, Keighley, Butterfield Archive, Letter from H.I. Butterfield to F. W. L. Butterfield, 8 May 1878.

6. Anon. *Henry Isaac Butterfield's Bedroom* c. 1890. Photograph

contributed to a programme of devotional images found throughout the house and reflect Butterfield's own conversion to Catholicism at the time of his marriage.

The bed and matching furnishings were of coromandel wood and were said to have been the property of the composer Rossini.[48] Other accounts claimed that the bed was in fact Rossini's death bed. The suite may have been bought by Butterfield at the sale of the composer's Paris house. Its choice emphasises Butterfield's ongoing and final hostility to the prosaic . . .

Afterword

Cliffe Castle is managed by Bradford Museums and Galleries and is the subject of a programme of research and restoration. Several key rooms together with repatriated original furnishings are now on public display

48 *The Haunted Castle*, as at note 29, p. 10.

Political Ambition, Civic Philanthropy and Public Sculpture, 1900: the City Square, Leeds

Melanie Hall

L eeds' City Square (fig. 1) is a notable example of late-Victorian civic pride in which the bronze equestrian statue of *Edward the Black Prince* (fig. 2) is accompanied by figures of four local worthies, and was originally encircled by four pairs of figure lamps representing *Morn* and *Even* (fig. 3). It was an allegory of Leeds' civic past and national importance, and celebrated its elevation from township to city. The statues were donated by wealthy manufacturer Alderman (Thomas) Walter Harding,[1] with contributions from Councillor Richard Boston, Richard Wainwright and Leeds City Council. However, several different sculptures were proposed for the centrepiece and the four worthies were not part of the original scheme. At first

1 For Harding see, M. Hall, 'Colonel Thomas Walter Harding', *Oxford Dictionary of National Biography*, Oxford, 2007.

1. City Square, *c.* 1917, showing the Post Office to the extreme left; Mill Hill Chapel to the right; and the *Black Prince* in the centre, surrounded by a circular balustrade at the four entrances to which are pairs of figure lamps representing *Morn* and *Even*. They carry incandescent orbs, suspended from electroliers. Four figures stand on another balustrade looking towards the Post Office: *James Watt*, *John Harrison*, *Dean Hook* and *Joseph Priestley* (from left to right, if facing them). In the lower left-hand corner of the image, the entrances to the public lavatories are illuminated by lamps based on the monumental mace (photo: Leeds Library and Information Service).

2. Thomas Brock, *Edward the Black Prince*, 1896–1903, bronze (photo: Charlotte Winn).

glance, the ensemble was a somewhat puzzling choice. This essay outlines the various proposals and considers how City Square took form in the context of local political rivalries, Harding's political and artistic ambitions, and his desire to create a new, enhanced civic identity for Leeds.

Three Schemes for City Square

In 1889 Birmingham became the first municipality without an Anglican cathedral to be elevated to city status; Leeds was the second, in 1893, the promotion granted on the basis of its 'population and municipal importance'.[2] The Council wanted to celebrate Leeds' ascent from borough to city with the creation of a new 'city

2 J. V. Beckett, *City Status in the British Isles, 1830–2002*, Aldershot, 2005, pp. 54–57.

3. Alfred Drury, Even, 1896–1903, bronze (photo: Charlotte Winn).

square'. A square adorned with an equestrian statue of the young Queen Victoria had been proposed for Leeds in the 1850s as Cuthbert Broderick's Town Hall was being built; that suggestion remained in civic memory.[3] Successive council administrations strove to combine public prestige and utility, constructing a civic identity through municipal buildings including the Library (1871–72) and Art Gallery (1887–88). In addition, the Yorkshire College (1874) and Grand Theatre (1876–78) were founded with municipal co-operation.[4] These underlined the Council's leadership in providing for the education and leisure of the growing middle and artisanal classes. The Hardings, whose wealth came from steel pin manufacturing in Leeds and in Lille, France, supported these institutions. Walter Harding sought

3 R. Barnett, 'Frampton's Monument to Queen Victoria', *Leeds Arts Calendar*, 81, 1977, pp. 19–26.
4 A. Briggs, *Victorian Cities*, London, 1990, pp. 139–83.

election to Leeds' Council to help establish the Art Gallery, to which he subsequently donated numerous art works.[5]

Urban redevelopment in the city centre provided the opportunity for a public project to mark Leeds' city status. Following the demolition of the eighteenth-century Mixed Cloth Hall, an area in front of the Midland, the North-Eastern, and the London and North-Western railway stations — Leeds's transport hub — awaited re-development. Part of the site was earmarked for a new Post Office, eventually completed to the designs of Sir Henry Tanner in 1896 (fig. 1). The Corporation purchased the site in 1889 for £66,000, planning to improve it as the Post Office neared completion.[6] Naming the space City Square was an inexpensive acknowledgement of city status and implied little more than a pragmatic solution to a problem area; the Corporate Property Committee proposed an open, asphalted space with ornamental lamps to improve pedestrian access to the stations in the face of increasing traffic and to provide somewhere for businessmen to congregate during work breaks without blocking the pavements.[7]

A proposal to move the statue of *Sir Robert Peel* (William Behnes, 1852), Conservative prime minister, to the square from its site in front of the old Post Office (originally the Court House), brought the debate into the local political arena by triggering campaigns from rival parties for influence over town planning decisions, use of space, and the civic image. Leeds' bronze of Peel, depicted in modern suit rather than classical toga, had been the first monument erected to the statesman's memory and the first to be cast in a single piece. As such it was a progressive civic symbol embodying innovative technology, celebrating the clothing industry and Leeds's modernity as well as Peel's ministerial record, notably as the founder of the modern police force.[8] The banker, William Beckett (Conservative MP for Leeds in the 1840s), had led an all-party subscription campaign for the statue, but it was not until 1895 that the Conservatives managed to wrest control of Leeds City Council by one vote from the Liberals who had held power for over sixty years. Positioning Peel in City Square would affirm this modest victory.[9]

The Leeds and Yorkshire Architectural Society offered an unsolicited proposal addressing the use, layout and imagery of the new square. It comprised an open space combining easy pedestrian access with a new architectural and sculptural feature at its centre — a bronze 'pack-horse ridden by an old Leeds clothier in costume of the last century', mounted on an elevated architectural composition with *bas relief* panels on the plinth.[10] At the plinth's corners, four bronze figures would represent civic life: Leeds's first mayor, John Harrison (1576–1656), had endowed St John's Church (1632–34), Leeds Grammar School and almshouses, and had had his lands sequestered by Cromwell for his support of Charles I; Ralph Thoresby (1657–1725) was Leeds's principal local historian and chronicler; John Smeaton (1724–92), engineer, was shown holding a model of the Eddystone Lighthouse; finally, there was Joseph Priestley (1733–1804), Leeds's famous Unitarian minister and scientist whose place of ministry, Mill Hill Chapel, bordered the Square.

This sculptural statement of civic identity would celebrate Leeds's growth through the textile trade and affirm its historic status as a centre for cloth-making, while placing the grouped figures within a clear architectural framework. The square would represent an allegorical and actual crossing-point for regional travel and history; the clothier symbolized travel from country to town and, in its

5 A. Summerfield, 'Regional Collections of Twentieth Century British Art', in G. Waterfield (ed.), *Art Treasures of England in the Regional Collections*, London, 1998, pp. 74–77.

6 *Leeds, the Industrial Capital of the North*, Leeds, Yorkshire Post, 1947–48, pp. 41–43; G. Black, 'City Square and Colonel Harding,' *Transactions of the Thoresby Society*, 16, 1974, pp. 106–12.

7 *Yorkshire Post*, 18 January 1896, p. 10; 21 November 1896, p. 7.

8 M. Stafford (Hall), 'Peel's Statue in Leeds – a first for town and country,' *Leeds Arts Calendar*, 90, 1982, pp. 4–11.

9 In 1897 Peel was repositioned outside the Town Hall, *Yorkshire Post*, 20 March 1897, p. 7.

10 *Yorkshire Post*, 24 Mar. 1896, p. 4; *Builder*, 28 March 1896; *Leeds Corporate Property Committee Minutes*, [henceforth LCPCM] 17 April 1896.

entirety, the scheme signalled Leeds' transition from past to present, from horse to rail, from town to city. Its central image represented a collective citizenry linked through artisanal work, trade, the professions, philanthropy, scientific innovation and religious toleration. However, by omitting the city's recent association with heavy engineering, it monumentalized the regionally prominent Anglican and Dissenter, pre-Industrial Revolution establishment, while suggesting a complementary relationship between the working trades and the professions.[11] How best to represent the civic community was not simply an aesthetic debate; issues of citizenship and representation were topical in Leeds politics as the growing labour movement sought access to the city's Conservative/Liberal Council, and workers' marches turned city streets into negotiating grounds.[12]

Liberal Unionist Alderman, City Art Gallery chairman, committed art patron, and aspirant lord mayor, Walter Harding swiftly proffered his own proposal. Harding had already embellished Leeds' skyline with the three Renaissance-style campaniles of his steel pin manufactory, Tower Works, and had national and international horizons for his artistic, as well as his political, ambitions. The Corporate Property Committee had begun discussing the square while Harding was on vacation in northern Italy. Receiving news that either Peel or an elderly clothier astride a packhorse with a group of old-time local worthies might soon occupy City Square, Harding headed home to press for his own vision.[13] He understood the Architectural Society's aim to create a sculptural entrance to the city but his outlook was markedly more ambitious, less historicist and parochial. He saw Leeds as an international city, part of a manufacturing empire that exported products and exhibited art treasures throughout Europe and America, most recently at the Chicago World's Fair (1893) where both Leeds Art Gallery's collection and those of Yorkshire industrialists were represented.[14] When Henry Trueman Wood, Secretary to the Royal Commission for the British Section, praised Chicago as a 'wonderful city', more interesting than 'London, or Manchester, or Leeds', he had apparently laid down a challenge that Harding accepted.[15] The imagery of the City Square should celebrate loyalty to the Crown, national ambition and an ideal of service.

Harding's scheme

Harding commissioned William Bakewell — whom he had previously employed to design Tower Works — to produce a design that would transform City Square from an open space into an outdoor place.[16] Quadrant granite balustrades would encircle a platform with a central equestrian statue. As the site sloped, the platform would be approached by steps on three sides, the fourth being level with the street. Bronze female nudes bearing lamps would illuminate the enclosure's four entrances, a commission intended for Alfred Drury, a prominent representative of the 'New Sculpture' trend, noted for bringing high art to everyday objects.[17] As a centrepiece Bakewell included (Sir) Hamo Thornycroft's model for an equestrian statue of Edward I; originally entered for London's ill-fated Blackfriars Bridge competition (1881), the highly-regarded model was shown at the Chicago World's Fair, at the Royal Academy, and at Leeds Art Gallery's 1895 Spring Exhibition.[18]

Models and plans for the Architectural Society's and Bakewell's schemes were exhibited at the Art Gallery in May 1896.[19] In June, the Corporate Property Committee approved the Harding/Bakewell scheme, 'with the exception of the central figure and the bronze ornaments on [the] balustrade.'[20] These were left 'to the

11 See D. Fraser (ed.), *A History of Modern Leeds*, Manchester, 1980, especially A. J. Taylor, 'Victorian Leeds: an overview', pp. 389–409.

12 T. Woodhouse, 'The working class', in Fraser, as at note 11, pp. 353–88.

13 T. W. Harding, *Memoirs of the Harding Family*, 4, c. 1920, pp. 19–20. Mss, Butler Collection.

14 Leeds lent Francis Walker, 'The Convent Garden', cat. 474, *Royal Commission for the Chicago Exhibition*, 1893. *Official Catalogue of the British Section*, London, 1893. I am grateful to the late Derek Linstrum for information about local businessmen who attended the fair.

15 H. T. Wood in the *Fortnightly Review*, quoted in Briggs, as at note 4, p. 83.

16 B. Lewis, 'The Black Prince in City Square', *Leeds Arts Calendar*, 84, 1979, p. 27. For a distinction between place and space see, for example, Yi-Fu Tuan, *Space and Place: The Perception of Experience*, London, 1977, esp. pp. 54, 202; Henri Lefebvre, *The Production of Space*, Oxford and Cambridge, MA, 1991, esp. pp. 68–168.

17 S. Beattie, *The New Sculpture*, New Haven and London, 1983, pp. 5–6.

18 Lewis, as at note 16, pp. 21–28. The scheme, which aimed to place equestrian statues of medieval English kings on the plinths along the bridge, was abandoned, *The Builder*, 23 April 1881; *Royal Commission for the Chicago Exhibition*, 1893, Hamo Thornycroft, 'Edward I', cat. 45; *Catalogue of Spring Exhibition*, Leeds, 1895.

19 *Yorkshire Post*, 11 June 1896, p. 4; LCPCM, 19 May 1896.

20 Ibid., 12 June 1896; 1 July 1896.

21 Harding, as at note 13, p. 21.

generosity of private donors.'[21] The Corporation would pay for the balustrade, electrical supply, and for gated, underground lavatories with an attendant.[22] By late 1896, Harding had offered to fund 'ornamental work' costing some £10,000.[23] However, subsequent alterations and additions to his scheme suggest local tensions and party patronage.

Harding had joined Leeds Municipal Council in 1883 as a Liberal but, following the party split over Home Rule, he joined the Liberal Unionists. By 1895, a Conservative-led coalition with the Unionists formed the national government; in Leeds, Harding was elected alderman in acknowledgement of this allegiance.[24] When Harding offered to contribute a centrepiece to the Square in December 1896, he specified a new subject and 'interviewed' several sculptors choosing, in place of Thornycroft, the much younger Thomas Brock, to produce Edward the Black Prince, a subject Harding regarded as 'a type of high chivalry and public service'.[25] Models of the Black Prince and Drury's figure lamps were exhibited in the Art Gallery.[26]

Public sculpture was a favoured tool of politicians. A high profile contemporary controversy in London gives an insight into Harding's politically motivated decision to alter his scheme and chose a different sculptor to execute it. During the same period Thornycroft was commissioned by the serving Liberal prime minister, Lord Rosebery, to provide a memorial statue to his famous Liberal predecessor, W. E. Gladstone (proposed 1898, erected 1905 in the Strand); he was also completing a statue of Oliver Cromwell to stand outside the House of Commons (proposed 1895, erected 1899). One of Harding's local opponents, Gladstone's son, Herbert, Liberal MP for West Leeds, was an active supporter.[27] Oliver Cromwell was intended to provide a counterpart to Baron Carlo Marochetti's equestrian Richard the Lion Heart, erected (controversially) outside the House of Lords in 1860.[28] However, Cromwell's suitability as an icon of parliamentary democracy was so contentious that the statue was placed in a sunken garden behind high railings and unveiled at dawn during the parliamentary recess. Although it had begun as a party commission, ultimately the Liberal prime minister, Lord Rosebery personally paid for it but the brouhaha contributed to his resignation (1895).[29] Cromwell had not been the only suggestion for this site. Marochetti had planned, but not executed, an equestrian statue of the Black Prince as the appropriate companion to Richard I.[30] Thus, commissioning a Black Prince for Leeds represented the completion in the provinces of a sculpture scheme planned for London.[31] To the romantic royalist Harding, the Prince was both a military leader and a symbol of constitutional democracy; Edward's role in the so-called 'Good Parliament' of 1330–76 is prominently recorded on a plaque on the pedestal where he is described as, 'the flower of England's chivalry' and 'the upholder of the rights of the people'.

Opposition to the scheme

At least thirty-three equestrian statues to heroes of the medieval and early modern periods were erected in Europe, and at least thirty-seven in America to founding fathers and Civil War heroes during the Victorian and Edwardian period. Despite the international currency of his proposal Harding's scheme encountered opposition from local inhabitants and within the Council, notwithstanding its subsequent unanimous acceptance of his funding offer.[32] Former 'mayor of the masses', Liberal Alderman Archie Scarr, a vocal opponent of civic extravagance,

22 LCPCM, 6 April 1898; 9 September 1898; 18 March 1904.
23 Ibid., 18 December 1896; 6 January 1897; Harding, as at note 13, p. 67. Yorkshire Evening Post, 8 December 1896, p. 4.
24 Archival material now in the possession of Mr and Mrs Edmund Butler, pp. xi–xii.
25 Harding to Chairman, 15 December 1896, LCPCM, 18 December 1896, pp. 176–77. The Black Prince had been proposed for Blackfriar's Bridge. See, 'Edward the Black Prince, A City Square Souvenir', Official Programme, Leeds, 1903 and Lewis, as at note 16. Harding claimed to have considered: the Duke of Marlborough, Henry V, Simon de Montfort, St George and Elizabeth I, Harding, as at note 13, p. 22. For Victorians and the Black Prince see, M. Girouard, The Return to Camelot, Chivalry and the English Gentleman, New Haven and London, 1981, p. 18. For Harding's discussions with Thornycroft see, Leeds, Henry Moore Institute, Centre for the Study of Sculpture, Thornycroft Papers, A2, Hamo Thornycroft, 'Diary', 26 February; 5, 13, 19 July 1898; 30 April 1902.
26 LCPCM, 19 May 1896; Yorkshire Post, 11 June 1896, p. 4.
27 Thornycroft Papers, ibid., C283, Herbert Gladstone to Thornycroft, 23 March 1895.
28 J. Physick, The Wellington Monument, London, 1970, p. 26.
29 E. Manning, Marble and Bronze: the Life and Work of Hamo Thornycroft, London, 1982, pp. 129, 137–38. Thornycroft Papers, as at note 26, C544; C583, C641, Rosebery to Thornycroft, 13 December 1899.
30 Physick, as at note 28, p. 26.
31 Harding, as at note 13, p. 22.
32 Ibid.

objected that one person alone had 'the power to say what should and what should not be placed' in the Square. He offered to contribute a fountain.[33] His suggestion was referred to a sub-committee on which Harding sat but, when Scarr refused a fountain designed by Drury as an addition to Harding's monumental plan, the proposal was dropped.[34] Liberal Councillor Joseph Henry questioned Harding's selection of events and interpretation of the past, deemed his vision of civic patriotism imperialist, and challenged his conception of democracy before complaining that Harding had, 'gone back 550 years and fished out of history a character of whom nobody knew anything.'[35] Henry's references to 'the masses of the English people ... in a state of serfdom' during the Prince's lifetime echoed current struggles to widen the franchise.[36] Although there was no real synthesis between the Labour movement and progressive Liberalism in Leeds, Herbert Gladstone supported a tactical alliance with Labour's leaders in 1892. Henry, the 'watchdog of Liberal interests in their stronghold of West Leeds', opposed a Tory-Liberal alliance as a means of countering Labour's political challenge.[37] In 1891, three candidates representing Labour parties fielded candidates in Leeds' local elections; for Harding, Henry's criticism showed lack of patriotism and 'socialist' tendencies.[38] Labour won its first ward in 1903, the year of the Square's inauguration.

The local press aired further suggestions for the Square including one for a utilitarian tramway junction. Local antiquarian, Walter Rowley F.S.A., sardonically suggested an equestrian statue of the Abbot of Kirkstall, 'whoever he may be', possibly prompted by the recent gift to the city of the medieval ruins of Kirkstall Abbey as a public park[39], but surely targeting Harding himself. Harding, who enjoyed antiquarian pursuits, lived in Abbey House, the extended and modernized gatehouse to Kirkstall Abbey, reputed home of the last Abbot, where he staged medieval costumed balls. At his mayoral ball, 'most of the guests were attired as sovereign princes, knights, barons, abbots of the Cistercian order, or ladies and gentlemen of the Court of King Henry II'; Harding appeared as the king.[40] Rowley also called for local figures to be represented: Thomas Wade (philanthropist), William Sheffield (founder of Leeds Grammar School), William Pickering (engineer of the Aire and Calder Navigation and clothier), Richard Oastler (campaigner for reduced factory working hours), and William Hey (founder-surgeon of Leeds General Infirmary). Rowley's proposals echoed the Architectural Society's in representing local and regional liberal values and a more progressive view of a collective, voluntaristic citizenry.

Additions and Alterations

Harding's civic philanthropy was acknowledged in 1898 when he was elected lord mayor. Surprisingly, he then decided to add four bronze figures together with six more bronze lamps by Drury, designed by Harding's son, Ambrose, and based on the municipal mace, for the lavatory entrances.[41] Gift-giving is rarely entirely disinterested and can have a spiralling effect; once the process of giving and receiving has taken place, a further round of benefits and obligations may recommence.[42] Harding had set his sights on challenging Herbert Gladstone for his West Leeds seat in the 1900 general election, the year he anticipated the Square's completion.[43]

Harding considered five candidates for the four 'worthies' in the square — Harrison, Priestley and Thoresby, the Rev. Walter Hook and — a late addition —

33 D. Fraser, 'Politics and Society in the Nineteenth Century,' in Fraser, as at note 11, pp. 294, 296. Yorkshire Post, 7 January 1897, p. 6.
34 LCPCM, 18 December 1896, p. 177; Harding, as at note 13, p. 22.
35 Yorkshire Post, 7 January 1897, p. 6.
36 Ibid.
37 T. Woodhouse, 'The Working Class,' in Fraser, as at note 11, pp. 360–63.
38 Harding, as at note 13, p. 30. Leeds Mercury, 3 November 1891, pp. 4, 6.
39 Yorkshire Post, 28 November 1896, p. 8; C. Dellheim, The Face of the Past: the preservation of the medieval inheritance in Victorian England, Cambridge, 1982, pp. 103, 109.
40 Harding, as at note 13, p. 29.
41 Ibid., p. 63; Yorkshire Post, 23 February 1901, p. 7; LCPCM, 3, 25, May 1898. Leeds's civic mace dates from 1694.
42 See, 'Introduction', Alan Schrift (ed.), The Logic of the Gift, Towards an Ethic of Generosity, New York, 1997, p. 10.
43 T. W. Harding, 'Letter to the Electors of the West Leeds Parliamentary Division', Yorkshire Post, 2 October 1900.

4. (left)   Henry Charles Fehr, *John Harrison*, 1898–1903, bronze (photo: Charlotte Winn).

5. (right)   Alfred Drury, *Joseph Priestley*, 1898–1903, bronze (photo: Charlotte Winn).

44 R. V. Taylor, *The Biographia Leodiensis, or Biographical Sketches of the Worthies of Leeds …* London, 1865, pp. 91–97.
45 *LCPCM*, 3 May 1898, p. 5; Harding, as at note 13, p. 59.
46 E. D. Steele, 'Imperialism and Leeds Politics, c. 1850–1914,' in Fraser, as at note 11, pp. 335–37.
47 See, M. H. Spielmann, *British Sculpture and Sculptors of To-Day*, London, 1901, p. 112; Harding, as at note 13, p. 23.

James Watt (fig. 7). Three, Harrison (fig. 4), Priestley (fig. 5) and Thoresby — echoed the Architectural Society's proposal. Harrison's inclusion suggests an anti-Cromwellian vision of democracy, while affirming Anglican and philanthropic traditions.[44] Fehr's figure of Harrison was donated by the Corporate Property Committee chairman, Conservative Councillor Richard Boston.[45]

Priestley's inclusion acknowledged Leeds's powerful Nonconformist community. As Mill Hill Chapel (rebuilt since Priestley's time) fronts the Square, his omission would have been pointed, particularly as the Chapel was the spiritual home of James Kitson (later Baron Airedale) MP (Lib., Colne Valley), Harding's successor as lord mayor in 1899, scion of the 'aristocracy of Dissent', and a power broker in regional Liberal politics.[46] Priestley is depicted as a scientist, with magnifying glass, mortar and pestle.[47] Though Drury's figure received critical praise, Harding had reservations about its inclusion on account of Priestley's support for the French Revolution, his radicalism culminating in his emigration to the young United States in 1793. In his anonymous account of Priestley's life in the *Yorkshire Post*'s 'Sketches of the Statuary', Harding warned against Priestley's radicalism, blaming Priestley's

6. (left) Frederick William Pomeroy, *Rev. Walter Farquhar Hook*, 1898–1903, bronze (photo: Charlotte Winn).

7. (right) Henry Charles Fehr, *James Watt*, 1898–1903, bronze (photo: Charlotte Winn).

links with the Constitutional Society of Birmingham for the burning by a mob of 'his house ... books, manuscripts and apparatus' in the Priestley riot of 1791.[48] Anxieties about civil disturbance caused Harding to join the Leeds Volunteers, of which he became honorary colonel on his retirement. Harding feared a repeat of the 1890 gas workers' riot (in which he had acted as an intermediary) and noted with relief that no rioting had taken place during his mayoralty.[49]

For the remaining figures, Harding had F. W. Pomeroy make a model of Hook, and Fehr of Thoresby.[50] Pomeroy's statue of the Rev. Walter Farquhar Hook (1798–1875) (fig. 6), who, 'created a new standard of duty for every parish priest who has come after him', was the only figure in living memory to be included.[51] His Leeds ministry (1837–60) oversaw twenty-one new churches, thirty schools, and twenty-three parsonages, Woodhouse Moor's dedication as a public park, and the Parish Church's rebuilding. Using public sculpture to encourage civic responsibility and provide reassurance was not new;[52] Hook's presence reinforced Anglicanism, civic philanthropy and reform; he provided a reassuring symbol to counter any fears of the unrest associated with Priestley.

48 *Official Programme*, as at note 25, p. 54.
49 Harding, as at note 13, p. 29.
50 Harding, as at note 13, p. 23.
51 G. M. Young, *Victorian England, Portrait of an Age*, Oxford, 1974, p. 71; *Yorkshire Post.*, 1 Mar. 1900, p. 7; 4 May 1900, p. 6; *Black and White*, Handbook to the Royal Academy and New Gallery, London, 1901, p. 49 and Spielmann, as at note 48, p. 120.
52 See, D. Bindman, 'Roubiliac's Statue of Handel and the Keeping of Order in Vauxhall Gardens in the Early Eighteenth Century', *Sculpture Journal*, 1, 1997, pp. 22–31.

53 *Yorkshire Post*, 29 April 1899, p. 7; 17 September 1903, p. 9. Thoresby was a double loser, since he had been also a candidate, proposed by the Architectural Society, for inclusion in a proposed gallery of local worthies in the Town Hall (1858), *Leeds Mercury*, 14 August 1858, Supplement p. 1.

54 Harding, as at note 13, p. 22.

55 LCPCM, 3 May, 1898, p. 5, Walter Wainwright to the Leeds Town Clerk, offering the statue on his father's behalf, n.d.; Harding, as at note 13, pp. 59–60.

56 The pedestal features a shallow-relief bronze scroll with names of men from the Prince's era.

57 Harding, as at note 13, p. 60. *Yorkshire Post*, 29 April 1899, p. 7; 17 September 1903, p. 9. Harding, as at note 13, p. 22.

58 *Yorkshire Post*, 7 January 1897, p. 6.

59 Harding, as at note 13, p. 30, The South African War took place during his mayoralty. *Yorkshire Post*, 3 September 1903.

60 See, C. Tacke, 'National Symbols in France and Germany in the Nineteenth Century', in H-G. Haupt, M. Müller and S. Woolf (eds.), *Regional and National Identities in Europe in the Nineteenth and Twentieth Centuries*, The Hague, 1998, pp. 411–36.

61 *Art Journal*, 1891, p. 131 (illus.).

62 London, Victoria and Albert Museum, Brock Papers, MS L 9–1986, Anon, 'The Life and Works of Thomas Brock', pp. 82, 122–23; Harding, as at note 13, pp. 61–62.

63 *Yorkshire Evening Post*, 8 December 1896, p. 4.

64 A French campaign for Joan of Arc's canonisation, stimulated by the clerical party, received papal approval, 1894 with beatification, 1908. L. Tickner, 'The Political Imagery of the British Women's Suffrage Movement', in J. Beckett and D. Cherry (eds), *The Edwardian Era*, London, 1987, pp. 100–16; L. Tickner, *The Spectacle of Women: Imagery of the Suffrage Campaign 1907–14*, Chicago, 1988, pp. 205–13; B. Caine, *English Feminism*, Oxford, 1997, pp. 131–72.

65 E. J. Evans, *Parliamentary Reform, c. 1770–1918*, Harlow, 2000, pp. 75–82.

A surprising deathbed offer from former engineer, Richard Wainwright (d. 1898), to contribute a statue of the inventor and engineer James Watt (Fig. 7) finally displaced the local antiquarian, Ralph Thoresby, from the fourth plinth.[53] Harding had Fehr make a model of Watt and himself took it to the dying engineer for approval.[54] Watt was not local, but his developments to the steam engine had enabled Leeds (and Harding's) industries to thrive.[55] Harding's and Wainwright's relationship is unclear; Wainwright was not among Leeds's wealthy elite but his donation enabled the imagery of the modern city to win out over the old town.

Harding's more nationally-orientated scheme emphasized a tradition of constitutional monarchy and unity against a common foe, republican France. It bridged national and local interests, while stressing civic philanthropy, Anglicanism, Nonconformity and engineering.[56] However, his chances of success as a Liberal Unionist against the popular, sitting MP, Herbert Gladstone, were limited and the promised additions to the Square failed sufficiently to boost Harding's campaign. He regarded his defeat as the greatest disappointment of his career.[57] Yet Harding's ambition was unabated. Perhaps he hoped for an alternative form of recognition as he determined to enhance the equestrian statue.

The Black Prince, seven years in preparation, spoke to topical Anglo-French rivalry. Britain was poised for war with France when the commission commenced, and engaged in the South African War from 1899–1902, when the French openly sympathised with the Boers. During the fourteenth century, as Councillor Henry had observed, 'England was at war with France on French territory — a war in which the Black Prince was engaged for the greater part of his life, and which was undertaken for the purpose of winning the French crown.'[58] Harding, wishing to 'stir patriotic feeling of the citizens, in those exciting times', added relief panels to the pedestal, purportedly depicting the battles of Crécy (which gave England control of the seas) and Poitiers.[59]

Medievalising equestrian monuments provided popular national symbols during the late nineteenth century.[60] As it neared completion in 1900, Harding insisted that Brock significantly rework the *Black Prince* to compete with a specific French icon; Emmanuel Fremiet's equestrian statue of *Joan of Arc*, in the Place des Pyramides, Paris (1874; improved version, 1889), had recently received positive coverage in the British art press.[61] Lamenting that Brock's 'horse was not satisfactory and the figure of the prince lacked spirit and was inferior by much to the original model', he insisted the sculptor bore the cost of a second full-scale model.[62] Brock's first model, illustrated in the *Yorkshire Evening Post*, was indebted to Thornycroft's maquette of Edward I, notably in the motif of the shield on his back.[63] Subsequently added details, including the Prince's flourishing sash and the horse's tied tail, directly reference Fremiet's *Joan of Arc*. Sophisticated audiences were, presumably, intended to judge the *Black Prince* in an international equestrian parade.

Joan of Arc was an iconic national figure in France where activists campaigned for her canonisation; in Britain, where enfranchisement was a topical concern, she was an icon for the militant women's movement.[64] Debates about women's rights had political significance in Leeds, which hosted the 1884 Conference of the National Liberal Federation where a motion supporting women's enfranchisement was carried.[65] The Boer War gave this issue greater prominence, raising questions 'about the relationship of feminism to nationalism and militarism on the one hand, and to internationalism and pacifism on the other.'[66] For Harding, the two equestrian figures and the code of chivalry they embodied were in direct competition. He explained at the inauguration that the Prince's 'manly virtues' had led to good governance, while the French saint's heroine-ism had instead been driven by 'frenzy'.[67] Harding juxtaposed British parliamentary democracy and French republicanism, implicitly suggesting Joan of Arc (and who knows what else) was out of control.[68]

The Black Prince failed to satisfy as either a work of art or manufacture. Brock's second version, too, caused disappointment. Harding thought it 'not equal to' the French in artistry. He had sought verisimilitude, insisting that the sculptor model the figure on the Prince's effigy in Canterbury Cathedral which also inspired the leopard masks around the pedestal.[69] In Victorian public sculpture, antiquarian authenticity rarely extended to the medieval warhorse. Although Chaucer inspired the bronze steed's 'amble' pose, Brock's model was a serving cavalry horse.[70] Spirited models posed hazards for sculptors and 'each time (Brock) showed himself … the horse started to snort and quiver, to display its teeth and perform an unpleasantly suggestive kind of dance.'[71] The sculptor was not helped when the horse seemingly mistook his spatula for a carrot. This was one of the largest equestrian statues yet attempted; a British casting would have affirmed national industrial prowess. Although Singers of Frome cast most of City Square's statuary, an equestrian this size was beyond their capabilities.[72] The Société des Bronzes of Belgium, which had cast Godfroy de Bouillon (1848) by Eugène Simonis for the Place Royale in Brussels (the first of this medieval revival genre) 'and many other equestrian statues', cast the work, apparently the largest they had yet attempted.[73] The statue's components arrived for assembly in Leeds, carried by barge along the Aire and Calder Navigation, transported free of charge by a company from Hull.[74]

Inauguration and reception

The day of the inauguration, 11 September 1903, was declared a local holiday. Harding had hoped that his election set-back might be countered by royal approval. Edward VII, Prince of Wales when the Square was planned, had been crowned in 1901, so Harding invited the current Prince of Wales, George (later George V) to inaugurate the statues. He declined, having too recently visited Leeds.[75] Lord Rosebery (who frequently performed such unveilings), was then approached but also declined.[76] Nevertheless, crowds lined the streets to view an orchestrated piece of civic theatre. The band of Harding's 'own regiment', the Leeds Volunteers, played as civic dignitaries in official robes processed from the Town Hall to the Square, led by the mace bearer.[77] Former mayor, Lord Allerton and former lord mayor, Sir James Kitson, MP, occupied a podium within the granite walls with regional leaders, members of the local business community and the sculptors. Sir Henry Irving, who was in town performing at Leeds Grand Theatre, presided, perhaps fittingly as the Yorkshire Post had already deemed the Black Prince 'the most impressive equestrian statue in England' despite 'just a touch of the stage heroics.'[78]

Morn and Even attracted most comments. Combining classical allegories of time and life-span with famous symbols of liberty, they were modelled on French precedents which encircle the Paris Opera House, Felix Chabaud's L'Étoile du Matin and L'Étoile du Soir (1876).[79] Whereas Chabaud's females stand next to lamp stands, Drury's are transfigured into carriers of light; showcasing new technology, they

66 Caine, as at note 64, p. 133.
67 Yorkshire Post, 3 September 1903, p. 9.
68 Evans, Parliamentary Reform, pp. 76–77.
69 Harding, as at note 13, p. 62.
70 Chaucer, The Tale of Sir Topas.
71 'Life', as at note 62, pp. 76–77, 122–23.
72 Harding, as at note 13, p. 63. The statues are stamped, 'J. W. Singer and Sons Ltd. Founders.'
73 Ibid.; Butler Collection, City Square Album, p. 52. It was cast in two sections, the horse and Prince's legs and the torso. Yorkshire Post, 3 and 17 September 1903, both p. 9.
74 Yorkshire Post, 1 September 1903, p. 9. 'Black Prince' boots enjoyed a brief popularity, and 'Black Prince' barges once again float along the canal.
75 Harding, as at note 13, p. 64.
76 Ibid.
77 Yorkshire Post, 17 September 1903, p. 9.
78 Ibid., 3 May 1902, p. 9. R.A. no. 1726.
79 Harding, as at note 13, p. 23; Album, as at note 73, pp. 1, 3.

80 B. J. Barber, 'Aspects of Municipal Government, 1835–1914', in Fraser, as at note 11, pp. 322–23.

81 For photographs of the figure-lamps carrying municipal light fittings see, *Official Programme*, as at note 25, That the figure-lamps were fitted with torches c. 1960 was coincidental. I am grateful to the late Robert Rowe, former Director of Leeds City Art Galleries, for his recollections of the 1960s rearrangement.

82 *Yorkshire Post*, 20 August 1903, p. 4.

83 Beattie, as at note 17, p. 114.

84 Harding, as at note 13, p. 63.

85 For example, *Leeds Mercury*, 1, 2, 3, 5, 7, 9, September 1903, 29 October 1904, 21 October 1905.

86 *Leeds Municipal Journal*, 18 September 1903.

87 Council Minutes, 2 September 1903, p. 2.

88 1898, No. 1961; 1899, No 90, 1882; 1900, No. 1922; 1901, No. 1705; 1902, No. 1726. (A. Graves, *The Royal Academy of Arts ... Contributors ...*, London, 1905–06). The Prince, too large to be brought inside, occupied the outer quadrangle, *Studio*, 26, Spring, 1902, p. 41.

89 Spielmann, as at note 47, pp. 112, 120. *Studio*, 30, 1903, p. 135; *Illustrated London News*, 26 September 1903, p. 445.

90 'Life', as at note 62, p. 121.

91 T. P. B., 'The Monuments of our Provincial Towns, 3: Leeds', *The Builder*, 10 November 1916, p. 296; K. Parkes, *Sculpture of To-day*, London, 1921, vol. 1, pp. 80–81; C. R. Post, *History of English and American Sculpture*, Cambridge, MA., 1921, pp. 209, 212.

92 LCPCM, 19 June, 21 August, 18 September 1903.

93 Black, as at note 6, pp. 106–12.

94 *Yorkshire Post*, 27 May 1901, p. 8.

95 Ibid.

96 *Yorkshire Post*, 15 October 1922, p. 1; 24 August 1933, p. 1.

97 *Town Planning and Improvement Committee Minutes*, 3 November, 1 December, 1959, 31 May 1960. *Official Programme*, as at note 26, p. 33 (illus.).

celebrated Leeds Council's introduction of electric street lighting (1891) nine years after the Electric Lighting Act.[80] The civic purse, rather than technology, was unequal to the sculptor's original design in which the figures carried torches fitted with 'incandescent orbs'; instead they held cumbersome municipal electroliers.[81]

Duty and productivity combined in the anonymous (Harding's?) praise in the local press of *Morn*, bearing flowers, and *Even* which though weary, 'steadfastly holds aloft the light-giving globe'.[82] The art press, represented by Marion Spielmann and the *Yorkshire Post*'s anonymous art critic, was enthusiastic. *Even*'s head, modelled on twelve-year-old Clarrie Doncaster, was cast as a separate work as *Spirit of the Night*.[83] However, Harding recorded that, 'before the inauguration two of the figure lamps ... were uncovered for some hours and at once some letters appeared in the papers declaring them to be most undecently [sic] nude, abusing me as a perverter of public morals and even calling upon the magistrates to have the statues forthwith removed!'[84] A slew of letters and cartoons ensued.[85] The *Leeds Municipal Journal* responded that, 'the contemplation of Works of Art of the highest order is not only brought within the reach of the citizens, but it is brought into their streets, and if their souls are not lifted up thereby it but proves there are amongst them those "fit for spoils, the emotions of whose spirits are as dull as lead."'[86]

Harding was granted the freedom of the city for his 'public spirit ... in the furtherance of the culture of Art in the City', an honour Joe Henry proposed.[87] Individually and collectively the statues received national coverage; the plaster models were exhibited at the Royal Academy from 1898 to 1902.[88] Spielmann (a friend of Brock) endorsed the scheme throughout, including photographs of three plaster models in his *British Sculpture and Sculptors of To-Day* (1901), and covering the inauguration for *The Studio* magazine.[89] Thornycroft warmly endorsed Brock's work declaring of the *Black Prince*, 'There is nothing grander in England and I am proud it has been done by an Englishman.'[90] The statues continued to feature in specialist publications, including *The Builder*'s 1911 series on monuments of provincial towns and cities.[91]

Postscript

How people originally used the Square remains unclear, though a policeman patrolled its entrances.[92] *The Black Prince* soon became a Leeds icon and a popular post card subject, though his significance became a puzzle. Popular memory soon concluded that Harding had erroneously thought Leeds Castle, the place of the Prince's birth, had been in Leeds, not Kent.[93] The Architectural Society questioned the piecemeal process of street improvements, decrying the 'incongruity' of placing a sculpture garden in the midst of a grimy tramway junction.[94] Their most trenchant criticism was directed to 'the circular balustrade' which, while 'enclosing and cutting off the view of the base of the new buildings', was 'an absolute waste of money.'[95] City Square found use as an outdoor civic theatre on two further occasions; at the inauguration of the First World War Memorial, originally sited on the edge of the Square (1922), and during George V and Queen Mary's 1933 visit.[96]

By 1959–60, traffic congestion around City Square was so acute that its granite balustrade and figures of *Morn* and *Even*, together with the mace lamps and underground lavatories, were removed and the four worthies rearranged.[97] As Victorian sculpture regained recognition, Sir John Betjeman, poet laureate, led a popular campaign for the return of Drury's female figure lamps. Sculptor Mitzi

Cunliffe, working on a frieze for Leeds University, suggested an arrangement in which the figure lamps formed parallel lines, lighting a route for pedestrians under the Prince's pointed finger and averted gaze.[98] City Square was thoughtfully rearranged in 2002 by the Civic Architect, John Thorp, to include some retrieved balustrading and a fashionable fountain. When the weather permits, City Square is a thriving piazza with open-air dining reminiscent perhaps of the Italian squares and French pavements that inspired Harding.

Acknowledgements

I am grateful to Terry Friedman who introduced me to Leeds public sculpture while I was a research assistant at the Henry Moore Centre for the Study of Sculpture, Leeds. Thanks are due to Mr and Mrs Edmund Butler for providing access to archival material relating to Harding; to the Friends of the Courtauld Institute; and the Leeds Philosophical and Literary Society for financial assistance for preparatory research.

I am also grateful to Charlotte Winn, a former student on the University/Temple Newsam course, who kindly took all the modern photographs for this essay. She has fond memories of Terry as her teacher. In a second career she has worked as a garden designer and is grateful for Terry's help when she was working on period gardens.

98 I am grateful to the late Mitzi Cunliffe for information about this rearrangement.

'The chant of the higher art': artists and designers in the early Garden City

Rosamond Allwood

'I am an arty party,
He is an arty party,
We are an arty party,
And our art is extremely high.'

(Chorus from 'The Chant of the Higher Art')

On 22 January 1910 residents of the new Garden City of Letchworth, Hertfordshire, enjoyed their second annual pantomime. Actors playing members of a 'Higher Arts Club' intoned 'The Chant of the Higher Art', whilst performing a 'mystic dance'.[1] The cast included artist William Ratcliffe, a founder member of the Camden Town Group, and friend of Harold Gilman and Spencer Gore; landscape painter C. J. Fox, and Newlyn School member Edward Docker. The 'Spirit of the Place' was played by Percy Gossop, studio manager of W. H. Smith, and later first Art Director of *Vogue* magazine. As well as taking a leading role, Gossop designed the posters and the scenery, while his wife designed the costumes (figs 1 and 2). The pantomime was a knowing and affectionate skit on the preoccupations of many of the early residents of the Garden City; including the importance of Art ('Art with a capital A') in everyday life, as well as suffrage, class-consciousness and the freedoms of childhood. Although it poked fun at the way local artists attempted to mould the taste of the inhabitants — 'you see, we're engaged in a kind of mission work: spreading culture among the middle and lower classes' — the pantomime gives clear evidence about the way these artists saw themselves and their central place in the new town.

Although much has been published on the planning and architecture of Letchworth, there have been relatively few studies of the artists, designers and craft workers attracted to the town.[2] This essay will argue that in its first ten years the fledgling Garden City appealed to a large number of creative artists as an ideal place to live and work. It examines the importance of the artistic life in the town, and records the various artists and designers who moved to Letchworth. The best-known of them are the Camden Town Group painters Harold Gilman, Spencer Gore (fig. 3) and William Ratcliffe (fig. 4), but other artists, included C. J. Fox and Edward Docker, both mentioned above; portrait and genre painter Frank S. Ogilvie; artist and etcher Louis Weirter; and artists Margaret Thomas (fig. 5) and A. J. Bamford. Designers and makers working in the Letchworth book and printing trades included Percy Gossop, bookbinder Douglas Cockerell, lettering artist Eleni Zompolides, and typographer Bernard Newdigate. Craftsmen included weaver

1 C. Lee and C. B. Purdom, *The Garden City Pantomime 1910: Book of the Words*, London, 1910, p. 18. Copy in Letchworth Public Library. This, the second of three annual pantomimes, was held at the Pixmore Institute, with eight performances between 22 January and 5 February 1910.

2 See P. R. Meldrum, 'Letchworth — a town of artistic heritage', *Hertfordshire Countryside*, March 1983, pp. 14–17. The standard history of the Garden City is Mervyn Miller, *Letchworth The First Garden City*, Chichester, second ed. 2002. Also see A. W. Brunt, *A Pageant of Letchworth*, Letchworth, 1942. The following more recent works all contain chapters on Letchworth: Standish Meacham, *Regaining Paradise. Englishness and the Early Garden City Movement*, New Haven and London, 1999; Dennis Hardy, *Utopian England. Community Experiments 1900–1945*, London, 2000; and M. Miller, *English Garden Cities, An Introduction*, Swindon, 2010.

MR R. P. GOSSOP as the "SPIRIT OF THE PLACE"
THE GARDEN CITY PANTOMIME, 1910

1. Percy Gossop, Advertisement for the second Garden City Pantomime, 1910. This image, which was also used as a large poster, shows the artist as 'The Spirit of the Place', Notice the typical Garden City houses in the background (photo: Garden City Collection, Letchworth Garden City).

2. Photograph of Percy Gossop taken from the Letchworth Theatre Calendar, 1913 (photo: Garden City Collection, Letchworth Garden City, LBM3001.245).

3 Ebenezer Howard, 'The Land Question at Letchworth', *The City*, no. 7, July 1909, pp. 153–57.

Edmund Hunter; potter (and architect) W. H. Cowlishaw, founder of the Iceni Pottery (fig. 6); woodworker Stanley Parker (brother of architect Barry Parker) (fig. 7); and sculptor and silversmith Onslow Whiting. In the early days there were also jewellers, a mosaic artist, another weaver, a stained-glass designer and two sandal-makers.

Letchworth Garden City was founded in 1903, five years after the publication of Ebenezer Howard's seminal work *Tomorrow: A Peaceful Path to Real Reform* (1898) republished in 1902 as *Garden Cities of Tomorrow*. Howard saw garden cities as the solution to the pressing problems of urban over-crowding and rural depopulation, giving residents the best of both town and country. He hoped 'to unite people of good will, irrespective of creed or party, in a worthy purpose — the building of a City on juster, saner, healthier and more efficient lines than cities of the old order.'[3] A new company, First Garden City Ltd, purchased 3,800 acres in northern Hertfordshire in 1903 and building began the following year. The competition for the town plan was won by Barry Parker and Raymond Unwin, architects strongly influenced by the ideas of Ruskin and William Morris. As socialists they were as concerned with the design of workers' cottages as with large private houses, and their strong Arts and Crafts background gave the new town its distinctive look: cottages and houses with sweeping red-tiled roofs, dormer windows and white rendered walls,

3. Spencer Gore, *House on Wilbury Road, Letchworth*, 1912, oil on panel, 15.2 × 31 cm. This small work shows the view from the front garden of Harold Gilman's house, in typical Camden Town colours. Private Collection.

4. William Ratcliffe, *The Window*, 1913, oil on canvas, 50.8 × 40.7 cm. This work belonged to Lewis Falk, whose uncle was inspired to move his embroidery business to Letchworth after hearing Ebenezer Howard talk of how 'This new town was to be a Utopia of clean, pure air, flowers and perpetual sunshine.' (photo: North Hertfordshire Museum Service, ref. LM 2004.15).

5. Margaret Thomas, *Danish Child*, c. 1901, oil on canvas, 31.5 × 29.4 cm. (photo: North Hertfordshire Museum Service, ref. LM 5529).

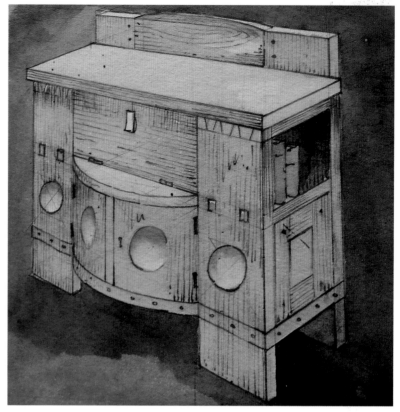

6. (above)   W. H. Cowlishaw, Iceni Pottery hanging lamp, pierced earthenware with lustre glaze, 9.8 × diam. 18.8 cm, 1907–14 (photo: Garden City Collection, Letchworth Garden City).

7. (right)   Stanley Parker, design for an Arts and Crafts side cabinet, ink and wash on paper, early twentieth century. Private Collection.

4 Bill Furmston, landlord of the non-alcoholic Skittles Inn recorded that before his move to Letchworth many interested friends tried their best to dissuade him. He visited in 1904 with a party of 200 from Ruskin College and South Place Ethical Society. See W. G. Furmston, *Ancestral Jottings, an Autobiography*, Letchworth, n.d. (post-1941), p. 719.

5 'The Garden City and its "Cranks"', article in *The Christian World*, 14 Feb. 1907, reprinted in *The Citizen*, 23 February 1907, p. 6.

and each with its all-important garden. Thomas Adams, the first Company Secretary, was a master of marketing and publicity, ensuring that Garden City, as it was called, remained in the public eye. This enabled the project to attract the industry that it needed to survive and grow, as well as enticing growing numbers of 'Pioneers', as the first residents were soon known. These individuals each made a conscious and life-changing choice to become part of the new community, often against the advice of friends and family, many making an exploratory visit after hearing Ebenezer Howard lecture on the pure air, flowers and perpetual sunshine of this Utopia only thirty-five miles north of London.[4] In the early years the town was more of a muddy building site than the promised paradise, but this guaranteed that many of the self-selected group who arrived in the decade before the First War were resilient optimists, inspired by Howard's vision, and keen to play their part in building a new and better future.

Very soon Letchworth gained a reputation for also attracting cranks and free-thinkers: 'It is diverting to speculate whether the man who has just come from town as a "settler" and sits next to you in the railway carriage is a Theosophist, or a Tolstoyan, or a William-Morrisian, or a Wallaceite, or a vegetarian, or a fruitarian, or a general food-reformer, or a woman's-righter, or a Socialist, or a back-to-the-lander, or a Christian-Scientist, or just a common Christian', as one commentator wrote in 1907.[5] The First Garden City Company always played down this aspect of the town to avoid frightening potential industrialists — Letchworth was, after all, intended to be a working, self-sufficient town — considering relocation to a cleaner, healthier and more spacious environment, but evidence shows that the lure of the Simple Life was for many a real attraction. One of the main (teetotal vegetarian) hotels was even called The Simple Life Hotel. The Garden City was described as having made

the simple life practicable and even fashionable. Bachelors — artists and literary men, some of them — live in their own or rented cottages, bake their own unleavened bread and jam-tarts and porridge, and the problem of how to live on sixpence a day presents no difficulty at all. [6]

This quotation could have been written to describe artist William Ratcliffe, for most of his life virtually penniless, and remembered by many as living on porridge or boiled onions. Although the Garden City was planned as a town with enough industry to support the workforce, the factories grew relatively slowly. In the first few years the smaller houses gained a reputation as weekend cottages, not helped by the fact that many of the workers for whom they were intended found the rents too high, and disliked the designs, with 'doors and latches like chicken houses.'[7] Artists and writers found the town far more congenial; a reporter for the *Dundee Courier* visiting in 1906 described Letchworth at this time (before the industries had really developed) as a home of choice for 'artists, both men and women, and possibly also of literary folk and journalists, for as we drove slowly past the already pretty little gardens we saw ... both men and women working hard with both brushes and pallets [sic] or scribbling busily at desks or in notebooks.'[8]

By 1910, six years after the first houses were built, Letchworth was described by a resident as 'essentially a place where Art should predominate over the prosaic side of life, and not a few actively engaged in Art are attracted to the place thereby'.[9] These artists, architects and craft workers, the 'small brother hood of enthusiasts come out from the world to build a New Jerusalem in the desert, [for whom] the artistic view of life was very much in evidence',[10] formed what Standish Meacham has described as one of three classes in Letchworth before the First World War. They did not belong to the working class which grew in tandem with the new industry, nor the middle class of businessmen and factory owners, but a second idealistic middle class 'or rather, a first — those who had been among the city's original settlers and whose commitment to Letchworth stemmed from commitment as well to the ideals of Howard, Parker, Unwin, and their ilk.'[11] It was this group which defined the town in the national press, out of proportion to their numbers; even in 1914 the general artistic nature of the inhabitants was still worthy of notice. *Punch* magazine published a cartoon showing a typical Letchworth washing day, with a sensitive (male) artist sitting in a deck chair insisting that clothes be hung in a harmonious colour scheme on his washing line (fig. 8).

The national media found an easy target in Letchworth's Simple Lifers, with articles such as 'On the track of the Sandal in Garden City' (*Gloucester Citizen*, 1907), which also described how women wore embroidered linen smocks in 'art' colours, free from whalebone stays or corsets. A schoolboy's postcard to a friend the same year shows how the Simple Life concept was well understood, and confirms the shockingly modern clothing of the inhabitants: 'Letchworth is a very pretty place not far from Royston and is quite new. All the people are enjoying the simple life and they go about with no stockings on.'[12] The local paper told the same story, noting that the town is 'a veritable hotbed of simple-lifers', but could not satisfactorily answer the question 'What is this Simple Life?' It described women dressed

6 Ibid.,
7 The City, No 2, February 1909, p. 35.
8 'The Garden City. Its Houses and Inhabitants', *Dundee Courier*, 23 August 1906, p. 4.
9 'Proposed Life Classes', *The Citizen*, 10 September 1910, p. 3.
10 Allen Foxley, *The City*, No. 11, Nov. 1909, quoted in Brunt, as at note 2, p. 105.
11 Meacham, as at note 2, p. 140.
12 Postcard written and sent on 9 August 1907. Private Collection.

GARDEN CITY WASHING-DAY.

OUR SENSITIVE ARTIST INSISTS ON A HARMONIOUS COLOUR-SCHEME.

8. 'Garden City Washing-Day', cartoon, Punch, 1 July 1914, p. 107 (photo: courtesy of Frank Foy).

'in a somewhat primitive style'; hatless, flannel-collared men; 'deep-breathers', the 'no salt, thanks', 'bare walls' and 'ever-open door and window' crusade, as well as the fruitarians and vegetarians, but came to no distinct conclusion.[13] The classified advertisements of the same paper provide more evidence of the Simple Life: 'MARRIED COUPLE would like to share their "simple life" cottage with another couple, or with one or two ladies of sympathetic views.'[14] This free-thinking atmosphere must have resonated with many of the artists and designers who moved to the town; F. S. Ogilvie was on the Executive Committee of the Healthy & Artistic Dress Union, so for him Letchworth's acceptance of rational dress would have been extremely welcome.[15]

From the start the appearance of the town was important to its artistic residents. The first copy of the local paper, The Citizen, contained a piece by artist Frank Ogilvie entitled 'Suggestions for Artistic Improvements in Garden City.'[16] This was a plea for picturesque planting to overcome the barren appearance of the town, proposing '... arches over gateways, doorways and elsewhere, a curved pathway or two in each garden, as straight [ones] are stiff and inartistic, and also creepers over arches and on the walls.' In these early years the state of the public realm was a source of constant tension between the First Garden City Company on one side, and artists and architects on the other, down to the colours used on hoardings. The conversation below, from 1909, between an imagined 'Mr First Garden City Limited' and a 'Mr Letchworth' shows how the latter is automatically assumed to be 'artistic':

'The new hoarding in East Cheap — why did you put that up?' asks Mr Letchworth. 'Don't you like it?' he [Mr Garden City] cried in obvious astonishment. 'Come, you can't deny it gives colour and interest to a rather bare piece of road? I thought you artistic people liked colour.' 'So we do,' I said; 'but ... I am afraid it would take a long time to explain to you.' ... I came away wondering whether Mr Limited could be brought to believe that there is such a thing attainable as good taste, at least in architectural matters. For today the hoarding is an architectural feature of Garden City of which we 'artistic people' scarcely feel proud.[17]

13 'The Artfulness of Simplicity', The Citizen, 17 September 1910, p. 2.
14 The Citizen, 3 September 1910, p. 4.
15 See http://peasant-arts. blogspot.co.uk/2011/02/walter-crane-and-peasants.
16 The Citizen, 22 September 1906, p. 8.
17 The City, No. 9, September 1909, p. 200.

A complaint of a more serious nature was the accusation that artists drove up the price of workers' housing in Letchworth, with their aesthetic objections to slate roofs:

'Heaven preserve us from such horrors' says 'Mr Artist' in favour of more expensive red tiles, picturesque dormer windows and wide frontages. 'Is it not this aim after artistic effect which makes the problem of housing the poor in Garden City so difficult?' asked 'A Social Reformer' in 1910, arguing that although artists are right to demand beautiful homes, they should not be so prescriptive.[18] However, the insistence on red roof tiles, and no more than twelve houses per acre, came from the Parker & Unwin practice, as consulting architects to the First Garden City Company, rather than individual artists. This tension between art and utility in the design of Garden City housing remained a perennial source of conflict.

The year 1907 saw the opening of a new building called The Cloisters or 'Adult School', which added greatly to the Garden City's appeal to more spiritual and esoteric thinkers. This was, and remains, an extraordinary structure, designed by architect and potter W. H. Cowlishaw as an open-air adult school for the study of psychology and philosophy. Residential summer schools on theosophical subjects were held at The Cloisters, as well as numerous lectures, recitals and craft classes. It became an integral part of the young Garden City, attracting many enthusiasts to the town. Those staying on site slept in hammocks, lowered between polished green marble columns, the sexes divided by a hanging curtain. Other students advertised for congenial lodgings: 'WANTED by Lady (Vegetarian). Board [in] Letchworth during summer months, including Summer School; Christian Scientists or Theosophists preferred.'[19]

This spiritual side of Letchworth almost certainly helped attract the designer and craftsman Edmund Hunter when he relocated the St Edmundsbury Weavers from Haslemere around 1908. Hunter founded the firm in an effort to rescue the traditional silk hand-weaving industry from decline, and by the time of the move to Letchworth it was already known for high-quality textiles, including hangings for the private chapels at Buckingham Palace and Windsor Castle. Hunter exhibited annually at the Arts & Crafts Exhibition Society and at the Home Arts & Industries Association exhibitions. However hand-weaving of silk, particularly using real metallic threads, was prohibitively expensive, and Hunter realised that to keep the business going, he would also have to use power looms. The availability of suitable premises in Letchworth, as well as low ground rent and rates, and good quality housing for his workers, persuaded him to move to the town. However the fact that it was a magnet for esoteric thinkers must also have appealed, as Hunter and his wife Dorothea shared an interest in theosophy. The family soon became immersed in Garden City life, Edmund Hunter regularly lecturing on subjects such as 'Mysticism in Art' at the Adult School.[20] Artist Spencer Gore, who borrowed Harold Gilman's house during the summer of 1912, may also have been attracted by this aspect of the town, as he is known to have had a copy of the works of Madame Blavatsky, a founder of the Theosophical Society.[21]

One attraction of Letchworth for artists was the ability to commission a new house with a studio. These studios are generally an integral part of the house, sometimes double-height rooms with large windows. Edward Docker's 1905 house by Baillie Scott had a studio of this type, and C. J. Fox designed his own house completely around a main double-height studio room. Harold Gilman's house was

18 'Homes for the Workers in Garden City', The Citizen, 11 June 1910, p. 2.
19 The Citizen, 11 June 1910, p. 4.
20 The Citizen, 10 Nov. 1910, p. 4.
21 Y. Holt, 'An Ideal Modernity: Spencer Gore at Letchworth', in D. P. Corbett, Y. Holt and F. Russell (eds), The Geographies of Englishness: Landscape and the National Past 1880–1940, New Haven & London, 2002, no. 9, p. 111.

designed by Parker & Unwin in 1908–09 with a large studio; sculptor, Onslow Whiting had a one-storey studio, designed by Randall Wells, which may be seen in paintings by William Ratcliffe, and Percy Gossop soon added a large north-facing studio to his house. The availability of houses with studios was known outside the town, as an advertisement from the local paper makes clear:

WANTED, at Lady-day, by an artist, a small detached HOUSE in Letchworth, one with studio preferred, three or four bedrooms, bathroom, etc. Address L. Gay, Ightham, Kent.[22]

After Harold Gilman's wife Grace left him in 1909, returning to her native United States with their children, Gilman moved to London. He rented out his Letchworth house for some years, the advertisement mentioning the studio, and making it clear that it was 'An Artist's furnished HOUSE'.[23]

In addition to their primary function as workrooms, the studios acted as social spaces. The obituary of Signe Parker, widow of craftsman Stanley, remembered that: 'Many older Letchworthians have delightful recollections of the house in Wilbury Road, the rendezvous of artists and musicians, and many an evening was spent in the company of the band of interesting people whom she and her husband gathered around them. Amongst them would be Harold Gilman, the now famous painter, Onslow Whiting, the sculptor C. J. Fox, Fitzwater Wray … and William Ratcliffe. As more residents joined the group larger studios were used, such as Fox's and Whiting's, where Signe instructed her guests in the art of Swedish folk-dancing.'[24] Edward Docker offered his large studio to the Letchworth Arts Club for their evening lectures.

In February 1907, three years after the first residents had moved in, an Applied Arts Club was formed, 'with the intention of sharing a studio for handicraft-work, pottery and modelling, metal and wood-work, enamelling, etc.' The committee included architects as well as designers and makers, and the Club offered pottery classes, supported by Miss Annie Lawrence, founder of The Cloisters.[25] This interest in the applied arts may have been the impetus behind the foundation the following month of the Letchworth Guild of Handicraft; a group 'Formed to assist Craftsmen by training and co-operation to produce work true and beautiful.' The idea of a craft co-operative, modelled on medieval guilds, was not a new one. Mackmurdo's Century Guild of 1882 was followed closely by the Art Workers' Guild in 1884, and Ashbee's Guild of Handicraft in 1888. During the later years of the nineteenth and early twentieth centuries, community craft workshops were formed across the country, from Newlyn in Cornwall to Keswick in the Lake District. Together with the countrywide Home Arts & Industries Association, they were seen as a way of reviving traditional crafts, particularly in rural areas. The village of Ickleford, just two miles from Letchworth, had its own version, the Ickleford Art Industries. This was started by art teacher Walter Witter and his wife Marie, who moved from London in 1900. Walter taught local boys metalworking, while Marie taught fine needlework and embroidery, and by 1908 their products won prizes at the Franco-British Exhibition. Formal links between the Witters and the Letchworth craft workers have not been traced, but many Garden City houses had beaten copper trays from the Ickleford workshops. The Letchworth Guild took orders for embroidery and metalwork, and organised a lecture programme. Its first lecture, on bookbinding, was given by Douglas Cockerell at the Mrs Howard Hall in April 1907. By 1909 the Guild was attracting speakers from outside the town, including

22 The Citizen, 21 January 1911, p. 4. Lydia Gay moved to Letchworth later that year.
23 The Citizen, 24 September 1910 and 1 October 1910, p. 4.
24 Signe Parker's obituary, The Citizen, 9 May 1947, p. 4.
25 Letters from Annie Lawrence and Andrew Muir, The Citizen, 2 February 1907, p. 5.

artists Frederic Yates and, a couple of years later, Henry Holiday. The town held an Art Workers' Market shortly before Christmas 1909, the stallholders almost certainly including members of the Guild, advertising their wares as ideal Christmas presents.

By this date the Applied Arts Club seems to have become a more general Letchworth Arts Club, meeting in rooms above Nott's Restaurant in the middle of the town. The Arts Club was described by its secretary, architect Allan Foxley, as 'the natural rendezvous for artists, and the centre of the art life of the city', but with the additional aim of exercising 'a very useful influence in urging the recognition of beauty as one of the necessary aims in the development of Letchworth.'[26] Twice-weekly life drawing classes began in 1910. The Arts Club, together with the Art Workers' Market, Embroidery School and the Iceni Pottery, were singled out by the local paper in December 1910 as having 'contributed handsomely' to the town's artistic output over the previous year. In autumn 1913, the Arts Club organised an exhibition of fine and applied art 'principally to spread the teaching of men like William Morris and Walter Crane', with sponsored prizes for designs for furniture, embroidery, book cover, posters and decorative illustration. The following year the Club put on 'The Garden of the Leech; a Masque of Letchworth'; Letchworth being a town where 'Art finds ... a place in national and civic life; for Art is not a mere matter of djibbahs and ingle-nooks, but of giving worthy forms of expression to our best selves, so that we may be incited to still better performance.' The references are to djibbahs, long collarless coats presumably worn by at least one of the town's arty set, and to the ingle-nook fireplaces which were such a feature of the larger houses.

As well as exhibitions at the Arts Club, there were at least four annual exhibitions of 'artistic craftsmanship, the work of Garden Citizens' organised by Juliet Branson, in her Baillie Scott designed house, Tanglewood. These included mosaics and jewellery by Mrs Branson, St Edmundsbury woven textiles, leatherwork by Miss Bartholemew, calligraphy by Eleni Zompolides, Wicksteed's revised edition of Blake's *Vision of the Book of Job* (1910) — the most important critical work on Blake to date, interpreting Blake's symbolism — oak furniture by Reginald Gardner and examples of Iceni pottery. Many of these designers also exhibited in London with the Arts & Crafts Exhibition Society; the 1910 exhibition displayed at least four pieces of Iceni pottery, gold and opal jewellery by Florence Cockerell, a stained glass cartoon of the *Madonna and Child* by P. R. Edwards, and a letter plate by Onslow Whiting. There were also examples of fine printing by Bernard Newdigate for the Arden Press, and bookbinding by Eleni Zompolides and others exhibited by W. H. Smith.[27]

The majority of these Letchworth artists, architects and designers had close links with London and the wider early-twentieth-century art world, particularly with other Arts and Crafts designers. Both Onslow Whiting and Douglas Cockerell taught at the Central School of Art while living in Letchworth, Cockerell having been appointed by Lethaby. His brother, Sydney, was secretary to William Morris (later Director of the Fitzwilliam Museum). The Cockerells also had connections with C. R. Ashbee and the Cotswold School. Walter Crane was a supporter of the Garden City Movement; his son Lionel designed a cottage in the 1905 Cheap Cottages Exhibition in the town (furnished by Heal & Son). Crane senior may well have come across both Stanley Parker and William Ratcliffe while he was Director of

26 Letter from Allen Foxley, Hon. Sec. Letchworth Arts Club; *The Citizen*, 27 November 1909, p. 7.
27 'Local Exhibitors at the Arts & Crafts Exhibition Society', *The Citizen*, 15 January 1910, p. 8.

Manchester School of Art; at the Royal College of Art he taught Eleni Zompolides. Both he and portrait painter Frank Ogilvie were on the committee of the Rational Dress Association. Crane designed the cover of the *Garden Cities & Town Planning* journal and in 1912 was 'Chief Tree Planter' at Letchworth's Arbor Day. Percy Gossop knew all these people, and exchanged Christmas cards with the Cockerells, the Dents and the Heal family; he designed posters for Heals, and for the London Underground. Although Harold Gilman did not live long in Letchworth, returning to London after his wife left him in 1909, he painted two striking portraits of Garden City women: Signe Parker (*Meditation*, Leicester Arts & Museums Service) and Eleni Zompolides (*The Blue Blouse*, Leeds City Art Gallery). There were other connections through Bedales, the progressive school attended by friends Stanley Parker and Robert Bennett, the latter articled to Parker & Unwin in Buxton from 1898. Bennett later set up an architectural practice with Wilson Bidwell, who had also worked in Buxton, designing many of Letchworth's domestic houses and major buildings. Parker spent some time with Charles Voysey and both he, and his partner Unwin, were known nationally through their own publications and in magazines like *The Studio*.

By 1913 the town was already beginning to lose some of its initial Arts & Crafts idealism, as an article that year made clear, 'In the past some artists have been disappointed with Letchworth. They were hoping that it might be possible to establish such a town as, for instance, William Morris would have been delighted to see, in which everything might be considered from the standpoint of the artist.' The author thought this an impossible aim, given that Letchworth was founded as a working town, like Rotherham or Bolton, and even though 'aesthetic ideas do not permeate every nook and corner of Letchworth, it is remarkable rather, under all the circumstances, that so much has been accomplished as we see in Garden City today.'[28]

Those who were disappointed left. In 1923 it was said 'Great expectations have their reverses in great disappointments; and a thin stream of pioneers passed out of the city, which proved either too celestial for them or not celestial enough.'[29]

The artistic community of Letchworth was never the same after the First World War. A short satirical play, *Lenin in Letchworth*, performed by the Independent Labour Party in 1921 for the Unemployment Fund, had a lament for the early days:

> Gone is the Garden City we knew!
> The mud, the artists, the cranks.
> Its populace now is a sordid crew
> Of money-grabbers and swanks.
> Gone are the vegetarians;
> Of djibbahs we're almost bereft,
> No stockingless sandal-arians;
> Hardly an anarchist left.

The ditty continues in the same vein, finishing:

> Ideals are dissolved in the clouds!
> The people eat fried fish and ham!
> They go to the pictures in crowds!
> What thought for art? Not a —— [damn][30]

With the coming of the war, the Iceni Pottery closed and Cowlishaw later became an architect for the War Graves Commission. Founder Ebenezer Howard moved on to the second garden city at Welwyn. Some artists, like C. J. Fox, moved away from

28 'Arts & Crafts in Letchworth', *The Citizen*, 23 May 1913, p. 5.
29 Harold E. Hare 'The City's Legend. Some Recollections of Letchworth Life', *Garden Cities & Town Planning*, XIII, No. 6, June 1923, p. 98.
30 Cutting entitled 'A Letchworth Play' in Lawson Thomson scrapbook, vol. 3A, p. 64, item B, North Herts. Museums, from an unnamed newspaper, the cutting dated 'Jan.1921', in ink. This play may be the origin of a persistent, but unverified, rumour that Lenin visited Letchworth.

the town; others died. The St Edmundsbury Weavers moved to Edinburgh in 1927, to set up Edinburgh Weavers with Morton Sundour. A. W. Brunt, editor of *The Citizen*, chose to concentrate on the years 1905–14 when writing his *Pageant of Letchworth*, as he described the period as one of great constructive activity, completely cut through by World War I. The tradition of fine printing continued, and a number of artists remained in the town, but the pioneering spirit of the early years could never be reproduced: 'Nor do I think', wrote Truda Fitzwater-Wray for Letchworth's Golden Jubilee in 1953, 'that ever again will there be collected in one small town such a brilliant circle of artists, medieval craftsmen, writers and musicians — innate bohemians all — who had time and leisure to meet, to talk, to create beautiful things, to make music for the sheer joy and love of it.'[31]

Alphabetical list of Garden City artists, designers and makers

(Information taken mainly from local *Directories*, newspapers, obituaries and the 1911 census). Space has not allowed discussion of the town's architects — they are merely grouped at the end of the list below — nor of others like Father Adrian Fortescue whose principal employment was outside that of art or craft.

George Adams (1857–1910)
Sandal-maker, potter, painter in watercolour, jeweller. Trained at Sheffield School of Art. Lived with his family at Millthorpe with Edward Carpenter before moving to Croft Lane, Letchworth.

Revd Alfred J. Bamford (1849–1929)
Artist 'whose brush was used more for personal pleasure than the outside recognition it deserves' (A. W. Brunt, *Pageant of Letchworth*, Letchworth, 1942, p. 103). Exhibition of his work at Letchworth Museum in 1931.

Juliet Branson (1851–1938)
Lived at Tanglewood, Sollershott West, a Baillie Scott house. Made mosaics and jewellery, also watercolours and pastels. Listed in directories as 'Artist'. Pre-WWI held annual exhibitions of Letchworth art and design at her home. A friend of John Singer-Sargent.

Douglas B. Cockerell (1870–1945)
Studied under Cobden-Sanderson at Dove's Bindery, where he repaired William Morris's books. Set up own bindery 1897. Controller of W. H. Smith bindery 1905, moved to Letchworth 1906. Lived at Elm Tree House (1907–10), Pixmore Farm (1911–13), 298 Norton Way South (post-1913). Pre-eminent British bookbinder of the early twentieth century, rebound many important books including the Codex Sinaiticus for the British Museum.
Son: Sydney Morris Cockerell, b. 1906; worked as D. Cockerell & Son until firm's move to Grantchester, 1964

Florence Cockerell (1868–1912)
Silversmith; exhibited silver, gold and opal jewellery. Exhibited at the Arts & Crafts Exhibition Society. Mother of jeweller 'Casty' Cobb (1903–95), friend of block-printer Joyce Clissold.

William Harrrison Cowlishaw (1869–1957)
Architect of The Cloisters, founder of the Iceni Pottery 1907–14, where he worked with George Adams and G. A. Hodgkinson. After the war designed cemeteries and

31 Truda Fitzwater-Wray ('Klossie'), 'Joyous Memories', *Town & Country Planning*, September 1953 (cutting in Letchworth Library, Local History Guide, Wop-Z, Wray). 'Klossie' was the widow of well-known cycling journalist 'Kuklos', William Fitzwater-Wray.

memorials for the Commonwealth War Graves Commission. For the Iceni Pottery, see R. Allwood and Y. Jones, *Lustre Ceramics from British Art Potteries*, Wolverhampton Art Gallery, 1980, p. 35.

Hugo Dick (dates not known)
Handweaver and teacher, loom maker, sandal maker (1913).

Edward Docker (1858–1932)
Genre painter, associated with the Newlyn School and St Ives Arts Club before moving to Letchworth. Commissioned Baillie Scott to build his house, Thornleigh (later called Springwood), in 1905. In the 1911 census he is described as 'Painter (Artist)'. The first four of his six children were born in France, the later children in Letchworth.

Philip Robert Edwards (1867–?)
Stained glass designer. Lived at Elspeth Cottage, 106 Wilbury Road and 28 Leys Avenue (1909). 'Artist' in stained glass, who exhibited with the Arts and Crafts Exhibition Society.

Charles James Fox (1861–1937)
'Landscape painter and Restorer of Old Pictures' (1911 census). 'Many residents will remember the Sunday evening gatherings at "The Den" Croft Lane (which Mr Fox designed and built himself) where many of the artistic colony of Letchworth would meet for music and good talk.' (obit., *The Citizen*). Exhibited at the RA and New Water Colour Society from 1883. Left Letchworth for Bishop's Tawton near Barnstaple, and later Watergate near Looe, which Ratcliffe, Gossop and Onslow Whiting all visited.

Lydia Gay (1855–1949)
'Artist-Sculptor' (1911 census), of 139 Wilbury Road, Letchworth. Later listed as a photographer, of 9 Norton Way South.

Harold Gilman (1876–1919)
Founder member of the Camden Town Group. Moved to Letchworth 1908, left following the breakdown of his marriage the following year. While waiting for his house to be built, he rented a cottage on Eastholm Green with William Ratcliffe and Stanley Parker as neighbours, and became Ratcliffe's mentor.

Spencer Gore (1878–1914)
Founder member of the Camden Town Group, moved to Letchworth 1912, borrowing Gilman's house. Made some of his most progressive works during this period. See R. Allwood, *Spencer Gore in Letchworth*, North Hertfordshire Museum Service, Letchworth, 2006.

Edmund Hunter (1866–1937)
Designer and weaver. Founded the St Edmundsbury Weaving Works in Haslemere *c.* 1902, moving to Letchworth *c.* 1908. His Letchworth factory and house were designed by Barry Parker. At Letchworth both hand and power-loom weaving was used, producing high-quality ecclesiastical textiles, as well as more commercial work. Hunter's personal interests appeared in his designs; tarot cards, theosophy, heraldry, birds and animals. Hunter's son, Alec, also designed for the firm. In 1927 the Hunters help set up Edinburgh Weavers for Morton Sundour, and Alec later

joined Warner & Sons at Braintree. The family shared an interest in the revival of folk and Morris dancing. See: *The St Edmundsbury Weaving Works*, Stevenage & Letchworth Museums, 1981.

Robert Percy Gossop (1876–1951)
Artist, working with print companies. Gossop, with his wife, moved to Letchworth in 1905 as studio manager for W. H. Smith; designed the WHS logo in 1913. Founder member of the Letchworth Dramatic Society in 1907, designing the scenery and posters, with his wife designing the costumes. Designed adverts for Heals and for London Transport. Became first Art Editor of British *Vogue*, and co-founded the COID with Milner Gray. Described himself as an eager student of the Arts & Crafts Exhibition Society's work. In 1927 published *Advertisement Design*.

John Scott Lamb (c. 1843–1913)
Lived in a Baillie Scott house, Corrie Wood, Hitchin Road. In 1911 was described as a 'Decorative Artist' born in Elgin, c. 1843.

James Lee (c. 1850–?)
'Painter (Artist).' Moved to Letchworth 1907. Lived with author son Charles (1870–1956) and family at 113 Wilbury Road. Charles wrote the Garden City pantomimes with C. B. Purdom; was proof-reader at Dents.

Bernard Newdigate (1869–1944)
'Designer to Printers', typographer, scholar of the art of the book. Born in Derby. Residence: Astley Cottage, Hitchin Road. Worked for the Arden Press, which was bought up by W. H. Smith. See John Scruby 'Bernard Newdigate 1869–1944', *Journal of the Letchworth Garden City Society*, 64, March 1996, p. 4.

Frank S. Ogilvie RA (c. 1857–1937)
Portrait painter. Residence: Airlie, Sollershott West. Worked for seven years as an architect, before training as an artist in Italy and then with Herkomer at Bushey. Successful portrait painter, whose sitters included Annie Besant, many civic dignitaries, and various local figures. Committee member of the Healthy & Artistic Dress Union and through this knew Walter Crane.

(Frederick) Stanley Parker (1876–1946)
Lived at 102, Wilbury Road. Brother of Barry Parker. Attended Bedales School 1894–95, then trained at Goodall's Cabinet Works and Manchester School of Art, returning to Bedales to help in the Carpentry Department. Worked with Simpson of Kendal 1897–98, then assistant to Voysey 1899. Worked again at Bedales before moving to Letchworth. In 1911 he described himself as an 'Artist (painter), working on own account at home' but later became craft teacher at St Christopher School. Parker was an extremely skilled wood- and metal-worker, see *Studio Yearbook*, 1923, pp. 88–89. He exhibited furniture at Letchworth Museum in the 1950s. He was a great friend of William Ratcliffe, who lived in his house on and off throughout his life. The three Parker daughters, Brynhild, Phyllis and Lisa all trained as artists.

William Ratcliffe (1870–1955)
Trained at Manchester School of Art, worked as a wallpaper designer before moving to Letchworth around 1907 as a graphic designer for the Garden City Press. By 1911 was a full-time artist, living in Letchworth on and off throughout his life. Founder member with Gilman and Gore of the Camden Town Group, and later member of

the London Group. See Rosamond Allwood, *William Ratcliffe, Paintings, Prints and Drawings*, Letchworth, North Hertfordshire District Council, 2011.

Robert J. Salter (1875–?)

'Artist, Portrait Painter' (1911 census) of 2 Hillshott. From 1912–23 is listed as a photographer, with 'The Studio' or 'Salter Studio' on Station Road.

Margaret Thomas (1842–1929)

Sculptor and painter, exhibited International Exhibition 1862, RA 1868–77. From the 1880s onwards travelled with companion Henrietta Pilkington in Europe, North Africa and the Middle East, writing three travel books, and illustrating two more. Wrote *How to judge pictures* (1906) and *How to understand sculpture* (1911). Moved to Countryside, Croft Lane, Letchworth in 1911. See: Samantha Clarkson, *Oil Paintings by Margaret Thomas*, North Hertfordshire Museums Service, Letchworth, 2007.

Louis Weirter (also known as Louis Whirter) (1873–1932)

Scottish artist, ex-RA and Paris Salon. Etcher and illustrator, who painted various views of Letchworth which Norton and Willian published as picture postcards. Published a series of twelve cartoons in *The Citizen* (1909). Lived at Tudor Cottage, Norton Way (1907), then moved to Baldock. Brother-in-law of Thomas Adams, the first Secretary of First Garden City Co. Ltd. Served on the Somme in WW1, and executed a number of war paintings. Later designed posters for London Transport.

Onslow Whiting (1872–1937)

Silversmith and sculptor. 'Art Master, London County Council, Central School of Art, Silversmith Dept.' 1911. Taught there 1901–27. Residence: Southernwood, 1 Norton Road with his mother and two sisters, designed for him by Randall Wells; later lived on the Wilbury Road, and finally 27 Souberie Avenue. Designed Letchworth's War Memorial.

Eleni Zompolides (1880–1958)

Trained in design under Walter Crane at Royal College of Art, then studied lettering and calligraphy under Edward Johnston at the Central School. Worked with Douglas Cockerell as artist/designer for W. H. Smith, and moved with the firm to Letchworth in 1908, working at the bindery and associated Arden Press. Until her marriage to Charles Townsend in 1912 she lodged at 69 Norton Road. Later lived at Stotfold Bury, and worked freelance. See John Scruby, 'Eleni Zompolides: 1880–1958, Lettering Artist and Designer' in *Albion*, vol. 33, reprinted in the *Journal of the Letchworth Garden City Society*, 65, June 1996, p. 4.

Letchworth architects included Robert Bennett, Wilson Bidwell, Aylwin Cave, H. Cowlishaw, Courtney Crickmer, Barry Parker, Allen Foxley, Cecil Highnett, Clapham Lander, Joseph Cedric Swallow, Raymond Unwin. Many of these architects were also artists or craftsmen in the Arts & Crafts tradition; Barry Parker was an accomplished watercolour painter, and Wilson Bidwell designed furniture and jewellery.

The Triangle Mystery: a new source for Gaudier-Brzeska's Vorticist sculpture

Evelyn Silber

Writing in 1916, within a year of the sculptor's death on the Western Front at twenty-three, Ezra Pound acclaimed Henri Gaudier-Brzeska's 'amazing faculty for synthesis', exemplified in his three-page history of world sculpture, 'Gaudier-Brzeska Vortex'.[1] It is equally apparent in Gaudier's creative assimilation of sources, as diverse as any Pop artist, and his rapid development during a career lasting only from 1911 to 1915. His interest in material culture and popular imagery outside the canon of western high art, which then formed the staple of academic art education, encompassed natural history, architectural and satirical prints, newspaper cartoons, posters, Japanese prints and netsuke, early Chinese bronzes and brush calligraphy, as well as African and Oceanic artefacts of the kind already attracting the attention of other modernist contemporaries, notably Derain, Picasso, Modigliani and Epstein. To that creative brew, I propose to add horse brass designs, probably culled from the pages of trade catalogues.

The pinnacle of Henri Gaudier-Brzeska's brief career was his role as one of the leading figures, with Ezra Pound and Wyndham Lewis, in Vorticism, and as a member of the rather larger group of artists, poets and thinkers who identified with Wyndham Lewis's Rebel Art Centre during 1913–14. Gaudier was one of the eleven signatories of the Vorticist Manifesto, flamboyantly launched with the publication of Blast in June 1914.[2] Together with his influential short essays in Blast, his critical writing in The Egoist, and the stylistically varied, but always experimental, drawings and sculpture he produced during winter 1913 to autumn 1914, these rapidly established him within a select group of advanced artists of the London, pre-War avant-garde — the Bloomsburies, the Camden Town artists and, most radical of all, the circle around Wyndham Lewis, Jacob Epstein, Edward Wadsworth, William Roberts, David Bomberg and the dissident Futurist, Christopher Nevinson.[3] They are also the basis of his catalytic and enduring influence on subsequent artists, notably Henry Moore.[4]

Redstone Dancer (fig. 1), carved towards the end of 1913 and first exhibited in January 1914 at the Grafton Group exhibition at the Alpine Club, is widely seen as his breakthrough work, a startlingly unconventional figure, which gyrates to a primitivist erotic pulse. Notwithstanding the eclecticism of its underlying sources, it embodied a new sculptural aesthetic based on mass, line and rhythm, a sculptural doppelganger to Stravinsky's contemporary Rite of Spring.[5] It can be seen as the dynamic counterpart to the more hieratic, serpentine figures of pregnancy and

Note: (S*) refers to sculpture catalogue entries in E. Silber, Gaudier-Brzeska: Life and Art, London, 1996.

1 E. Pound, Gaudier-Brzeska. A Memoir, 1916 (Hessle, Marvell Press edition, 1960), pp. 20–24.

2 'Vortex Gaudier-Brzeska', Blast,1, 1914 (reprinted Santa Barbara, Black Sparrow Press, 1981), p. 43 and ibid.

3 All these writings are reproduced in E. Pound, Gaudier-Brzeska. A Memoir, 1916. On Gaudier-Brzeska's life and work see also H. S. Ede, Savage Messiah, London, 1931; H. Brodzky, Henri Gaudier-Brzeska, London, 1932; M. Levy, Gaudier-Brzeska; Sculpture and Drawings, London, 1965; R. Cork, Vorticism and Abstract Art in the First Machine Age, 2 vols, London, 1976; R. Cole, Burning to Speak; the Life and Art of Henri Gaudier-Brzeska, Oxford, 1978; R. Cole, Gaudier-Brzeska; Artist and Myth, Bristol, 1995; E. Silber, Gaudier-Brzeska, Life and Art, London, 1996; P. O'Keefe, Gaudier-Brzeska. An Absolute Case of Genius, London, 2004.

4 A. Garrould, T. Friedman and D. Mitchinson, Henry Moore Early Carvings 1920–1940 (exh. cat.), Leeds City Art Galleries, 1982, pp. 19, 23–24.

5 M. Levy, as in note 3, p. 16; R. Cork as in note 3, I, p. 175; R. Cole, 1995, as in note 3, p. 76; E. Silber, as in note 3, cat. no. 69, p. 267, figs 94–99. Gaudier sculpture catalogue references to be abbreviated =S69.

1. Henri Gaudier-Brzeska, *Red Stone Dancer*, 1913, red Mansfield stone, H: 43.2 cm. Tate (photo: ©Tate).

2. (opposite page)   Henri Gaudier-Brzeska, *Designs for elephant horse brasses*, pencil and pen on invoice paper, 1908–09, 25.4 × 20 cm. Private Collection.

6 *Flenite Figure*, 1913 (Minneapolis Institute of Art) and *Female Figure in Flenite*, 1913 (Tate). On 7 October 1913 Gaudier visited Epstein's London studio and saw these works in progress, reporting to Sophie Brzeska, 'he is doing the most extraordinary statues, absolute copies of Polynesian work with Brancusi-like noses.' Letter from Gaudier-Brzeska to S. Brzeska, 8.10.13, Essex University Library, reproduced in Ede, as in note 3, p. 247.

7 Pound, as at note 3, pp. 137–38.

birth then being carved by Jacob Epstein, such as *Figure in Flenite* and *Female Figure in Flenite*.[6]

In this sculpture, related drawings and many subsequent drawings and sculptures, a discrete triangle metonymically represents the facial features or the entire head. The motif is usually interpreted as integral to Gaudier's espousal of the geometrically based modernist aesthetic articulated by the philosopher, T. E. Hulme, and contextualized by reference to the contemporary work by Lewis and others. In his introduction to Gaudier's Memorial Exhibition at the Leicester Galleries, London, in June 1918, Ezra Pound identified the triangle, circle and oval as keys to the overall composition of *Red Stone Dancer* (fig. 1) which he characterised as

almost a thesis of his ideas upon the use of pure form. We have the triangle and circle asserted, *labled* [sic] almost, upon the face and right breast. Into these so-called 'abstractions' life flows, the circle moves and elongates into the oval, it increases and takes volume in the sphere or hemisphere of the breast. The triangle moves towards organism it becomes a spherical triangle (the central life-form common to both Brzeska and Lewis). These two developed motifs work as themes in a fugue … The 'abstract' or mathematical bareness of the triangle and circle are fully incarnate, made flesh, full of vitality and of energy.[7]

3 (above). Henri Gaudier-Brzeska,
Designs for horse brasses, 1908–09, pencil
and pen on invoice paper,
16.6 × 20.5 cm. Private Collection.

4. (right) Henri Gaudier-Brzeska,
Designs for door knockers, 1908–09, pencil
and pen on invoice paper, 32 × 19.8 cm
(sight). Private Collection.

Pound's commentary pays verbal homage to the exuberant lapidary prose of 'Gaudier-Brzeska Vortex', published in *Blast* in June 1914.[8] The clearly defined, solid triangle, circle and oval, in his reading, render the inanimate animate, generating a new vital, formal synthesis in this pivotal work.

The recent emergence of a group of Gaudier's youthful drawings (figs 2–4) suggests that, in facing the *Red Stone Dancer* with a large low relief, soft-edged triangle, the sculptor may have been recalling, reinventing and applying a piece of crafted, industrially produced design he had encountered during his time as a French state scholarship winner studying, ostensibly for a business career, in Bristol and Cardiff in 1907–09. This small group of previously undocumented and un-exhibited drawings, all from a Cardiff source, are now in a Yorkshire private collection. Judging from shared elements of technique, approach and layout four of these were produced over a brief period, possibly a single session:

1. Eight horse brass designs of elephants (fig. 2). 25.4 × 20 cm, paper creased and marked from folding in eight. Verso invoice dated 30.6.1902 from Durie & Co., Bristol outfitters and tailors, made out to H[enr]y Downs, 10 White Ladies Road, Bristol.

2. Six horse brass designs with shell and triangle motifs (fig. 3). 16.6 × 20.5 cm, paper creased from folding in eight. Verso invoice dated 31.12.1902, from Durie & Co, Bristol, made out to Henry Downs, 105 Hampton Road, Bristol.

3. Four doorknocker designs — clown's head, lion's head and two non-figurative. (fig. 4). Inscribed in Gaudier's hand 'Door Brass' and 'Study of Horse Brass HG', 32 × 19.8 cm (sight), paper creased from folding in eight. Verso invoice dated 1.4.1904. from Dunlop Mackie & Co., spirit merchants, made out to H. Downs, 105 Hampton Road, Bristol.[9]

4. Four designs for doorknockers — one owl and three fox-head motifs. Invoice paper, 19.8 × 32 cm, paper creased from folding in eight. Verso invoice dated 1.1.1906 from Dunlop, Mackie & Co. made out to H. Downs, 105 Hampton Road, Bristol.

With these were two further documents of significance in identifying the original invoice recipient, Henry Downs, and supporting the Bristol or Cardiff provenance and date of the drawings. The first is a letter on the headed paper of W. Smith & Co., 34 Corn Street, Bristol, dated 24.5.1900, announcing that, following the decease of William Smith and on the basis of over thirty years' involvement with the business, Henry Downs would be continuing it under the same name. The company's primary interests seem to have been trade with the Colonies, William Smith being described as a Colonial broker.[10] In 1893–94, Henry Downs is recorded as resident at 'Enderleigh', 6 Meridian Street in Lower Cotham Park, just round the corner from Gaudier's Bristol hosts, the (presumably unconnected) Smith family, at 'Penleigh', 24 Cotham Grove.[11] One may conjecture a neighbourhood acquaintance. From other sources we learn that Henry Downs was 'a splendid specimen of a Scot' whose 'fresh complexion, snow-white hair and commanding figure reminded people of Thackeray as represented in pictures'. A kindly man with an extensive friendship and business network, he may have seemed an improvement on his former boss; Smith, a JP and former Alderman, was considered shrewd but 'rather brusque and outspoken in business and other matters.'[12] Henry Downs

8 Ibid., pp. 20–24.
9 The initials 'HG' are closely comparable to the colophon on the December 1908 *Study of a Heron* (Musée National d'Art Moderne, Paris AM 3376D (1)); Silber, as at note 3, fig. 4; B. Fauquembergue, 'Les signatures de Gaudier-Brzeska', in *Henri Gaudier-Brzeska* (exh. cat.), Orléans, Musée des Beaux Arts and Toulouse, Musée d'Art Moderne, 1993, pp. 178–79.
10 Described simply as 'merchants' in J. Wright & Co., *Bristol Directory*, 1902, the company's interests appear to have been primarily in colonial trade and land. 1893–94 *Bristol Mercury* identifies William Smith as one of the directors of a Bristol and West Canadian Land Mortgage and Investment Company with interests in Ontario. .
11 Wright's *Bristol Directory*, 1893–94; see also O'Keefe, as at note 3, p. 13.
12 On Henry Downs, *Bristol Times and Mercury*, 14.1.1908, p. 5. On William Smith, *Bristol Worthies*, 2nd series, Bristol, 1909, p. 101.

13 Recorded addresses: 105 Hampton Street, Bristol and Prudential Buildings, 19 Clare Street. *England & Wales, FreeBMD Death Index, 1837–1915* , p. 30. Probate on estate £6916 11s 7d granted to James Downs, engineer and Alfred John Downs, chartered accountant, *England & Wales, National Probate Calendar (Index of Wills and Administrations)*, 1858–1966, p. 82. [accessed via www.ancestry. co.uk 7.4.14].

14 P. O'Keefe, as at note 3, pp. 10–22.

15 Fifoot Ching & Co. is listed in J. Wright & Co. *Cardiff Directories* from 1902 to 1918, occupying room 112, on the 2nd floor of the Exchange. One partner, William Fifoot (1856–1939) was also partner in stockbroker and share dealer Matthews, Fifoot & Angel, based in 1929 at 24 Mount Stuart Square, and two of his brothers, Sydney and Frank, also spent a lifetime in the coal industry in Cardiff; *Western Mail* 29.2.28, p. 11 records Sydney Fifoot's 63 years' employment in the coal industry; *Western Mail* 3.1.1931, p. 8 obituary of Frank Fifoot, proprietor of J. P. Hacquoil & Co., shipbrokers and coal exporters. See also William Fifoot in the 1871 Census (Cardiff) (www.ancestry. co.uk accessed 30.4.14). A Mrs Ching was in 1902 resident at 23 Claude Road, Roath a few doors from George Brace, Gaudier's landlord at no. 29; J. Wright & Co., *Cardiff Directory*, 1902, p. 104.

16 Mr Ching to H. S. Ede, 9.1.1929, Kettle's Yard, Cambridge; Ede, as at note 3, pp. 28–29 (misremembered as 1928). Another Fifoot, Ching employee, Alfred Hazell, stated Gaudier was the third French student hosted there, R. Cole, 1978, as at note 3, p. 10.

17 The principal sketches are bird studies from life and from mounted specimens in a sketchbook containing work made in Cardiff and Nuremberg; Paris, Museé National d'Art Moderne AM3376D, a selection reproduced in C. Briend, D. Lemny et al., *Henri Gaudier-Brzeska dans les collections du Centre Pompidou, Musée national d'art moderne* (exh. cat.), Paris and Orléans, 2009–10, pp. 56–59. .

soon moved to grander premises, to 10 White Ladies Road sometime before 1902 and, late in 1902, to 105 Hampton Road, Bristol, which was still his home on 12 January 1908 when he died aged 69, leaving a substantial estate.[13] Downs is not recorded as a member of the Society of Merchant Venturers but may nevertheless have had some connections which brought this senior businessman into contact with the young French boursier attending Merchant Venturers' Technical College.[14]

The second suggestive piece of evidence is a letter dated 24 July 1908 from John Slater Ltd of Berry Hill Collieries, Stoke on Trent to H. Downs, at Fifoot, Ching & Co., Exchange Buildings, Mount Stuart Square, Cardiff, concerning the price and scheduled August delivery of a consignment of coal.[15] Though not the same Henry Downs, the connection is surely more than wildly coincidental, and could have had a bearing on that company's employment of Gaudier and other scholarship students. Gaudier worked for Fifoot, Ching from the beginning of October 1908 to the end of March 1909, after the completion of his studies in Bristol. Taken together the documentary and circumstantial evidence indicates that Gaudier, with his insatiable appetite for sketching paper (he regularly appropriated paper from his London employers, Wulfsberg & Co., for drawings during 1911–13) was given or procured these old papers in Bristol or, more likely, Cardiff and recycled them while working there.

In an often quoted passage Mr Ching recalled in 1929 that

'[Gaudier] was one of several students who came to us, and while he excellently fulfilled the duties allotted to him, one could easily notice that his mind was not altogether in his work. Art undoubtedly occupied the greater part of it, and in his spare moments he was everlastingly, pencil or pen in hand, sketching some little incident that appealed to him. During his lunch hours he periodically walked across to the Docks, and brought back with him a small sketch of, perhaps, the bow of a boat, or the elevation of a crane or tip, all of which showed genius.'[16]

The relatively few drawings definitely originating from his Cardiff sojourn are of boats and birds, notably painstaking fine pen drawings of mounted bird specimens from Welsh Museum of Natural History, Arts and Antiquities, modelled on natural history engravings and presented with an eye to effect, with elaborate captions as if they too were engraved illustrations.[17]

The schematic layout and heavy contours of Gaudier's designs for horse brasses and doorknockers are, by comparison, boldly direct in their unhesitating linear clarity, and less self-conscious, capturing and exploring design ideas rather than mimicking a technical effect. What was their appeal? Today a niche collecting area and rare nostalgic sight in a heavy horse display, brasses have figured within the parameters of agricultural and social rather than art history. Like heraldic symbols the coarse emblems manufactured in a sturdy, easily replicable medium, sold by saddlers and ironmongers for the tack room, have not attracted much academic attention. Their status seems to have been rather different around 1910 when they were becoming collectors' items. Contemporary interest in the Arts and Crafts Movement and in vernacular craft traditions dwindling in the face of industrialisation contributed to their appeal. The abstract beauty of many of the pierced patterns and clever combinations of symbols were praised in the pages of the *Connoisseur*, the craftsmanship of the sand-cast, high quality, smoothed and polished brass was appreciated and recommended as fashionable domestic decoration for the hall and

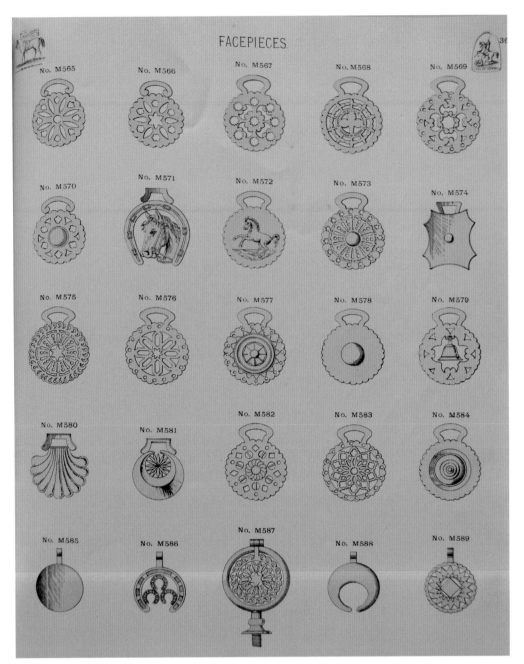

FACEPIECES.

No. M565 | No. M566 | No. M567 | No. M568 | No. M569
No. M570 | No. M571 | No. M572 | No. M573 | No. M574
No. M575 | No. M576 | No. M577 | No. M578 | No. M579
No. M580 | No. M581 | No. M582 | No. M583 | No. M584
No. M585 | No. M586 | No. M587 | No. M588 | No. M589

5. D. Mason & Sons of Walsall, *Universal Saddlery Album* 1912, Walsall Leather Museum. Note the shell and crescent designs.

18 E. V. Alison, 'Brass Amulets', *The Connoisseur*, XXXI, 1911, pp. 89–96, emphasises the antiquity of the animal decorative symbols, and recommends them to collectors as 'very decorative in a hall or round an inglenook fire'. H. R. Carter, 'English Horse Amulets', *The Connoisseur*, XLV, 1916, pp. 143–51, recommends brasses as a new field of collecting for those of modest means; old brasses are at risk of being melted down but these are the most desirable because of their superior design, metal quality and craftsmanship.
19 *The Equine Album of Hampson & Scott*, Wholesale Saddlery Manufacturers, Walsall, *c.* 1900 and *Matthew Harvey & Co.,Walsall, manufacturers of Harness Furniture, Spurs and Stirrups, c.* 1905, were two of the most extensively illustrated. A Bristol manufacturer, Marsh & Co., catalogue, *c.* 1905 is also well illustrated.
20 One of the most important interwar collectors was A. H. Tod, a teacher at Charterhouse School, who lived in Clifton, Bristol. His collection of about 1,000 brasses was photographed before its dispersal after his death in 1943; P. Brears, *Horse Brasses*, London, 1981, p. 42 and illustrations of part of the wall-hung collection, pp. 43–44, include elephant, heart and shell brasses. It is not known when he began collecting or whether this was a collection Gaudier might conceivably have seen.

inglenook.[18] The bored, creatively frustrated prentice clerk, obsessed with drawing, would have found in them and the trade catalogues in which large numbers were illustrated, a profusion of designs, including many animals, to explore, analyse and conjure with.

The layout of Gaudier's designs within a grid, pre-formed by folding the paper, mimics the schematic layout typical of the trade catalogues of those companies, mostly clustered in Walsall and Birmingham, which specialised in leatherwork, harness and the associated ironmongery (fig. 5).[19] This is a much more likely source than a museum or private collection display since brass collecting was still in its infancy and neither Bristol nor Cardiff Museums, for instance, seem to have owned brasses at this date.[20] The wares displayed in an 'equine album' ranged from the most functional buckles, links and bits, carefully smoothed and rounded to avoid injury in use, to decorative face-pieces, bradoons, swingers, flyers, terrets, bells and other arcane items for the adornment of prized cart-horses and their turnouts on high days and holidays. Designs exclusive to a particular manufacturer were rare since pirating was easy. Common motifs included abstract pierced patterns, where the brass showed especially well against dark polished leather, circular bosses, heraldically simplified horseshoe, crescent, star, sun and moon shapes, playing card suits, as well as animals and birds — horse, dog, fox, stag, cock, bear, lion, eagle, elephant and so on. Some images, such as the sun, crescent moon and stars, were then believed to have ancient origins associated by early enthusiasts with pre-Christian beliefs and cultural practices that endowed specific emblems with amuletic and talismanic properties, though it is debatable how far Gaudier would have been aware of such conjectures. Their production and use in Britain reached its height in the second half of the nineteenth century when company badges and commemorative images were added to the repertoire.[21]

The unmodulated shapes of Gaudier's drawings echo the impersonal precision of trade catalogue illustrations which provided accurate scale drawings of the profusion of manufactured fittings, most of which were purely functional (fig. 5). While the drawings have not so far yielded an exact match to any single catalogue, one would expect such catalogues to have been knocking around business premises, especially around the Coal Exchange in Mount Stuart Square, Cardiff. This was the heart of the Welsh coal export industry, at its height in 1900–10 with over 10.5 m tons of coal being exported annually from Cardiff Docks alone. The hub of this trade was the Coal Exchange Building, where mining and freight companies and many other associated trades and professions, including exporters Fifoot Ching & Co., had their offices.[22]

While stereotypical, these patterns offered ample scope not only for copying but for playful doodling and re-design. Gaudier's elephant designs (fig. 2, top left, bottom right and left) follow existing models, inspired by London Zoo's famous 'Jumbo', later the star of Barnum & Bailey's Circus.[23] The crescent and scallop shell (fig. 4, top left) are also common types which he replicates.[24] Lion-headed doorknockers (fig. 5) abound now, as then; alternatively, he may have adapted the design from another horse brass. The clown-headed design may be Gaudier's invention, foreshadowing his later relish in caricaturing friends and enemies alike. However, the most intriguing metamorphosis takes place in the remaining designs (fig. 4) which are variants on an established motif of hearts, used singly or in combinations of three or, as here, six (fig. 6).[25] Gaudier has stripped the emblem of any lingering sentimental or gaming associations by converting it into a plain inverted hollow triangle, very like a triangular metal link designed to connect harness straps at an angle.[26] The top right design has a humanoid shape, six triangles forming the torso, the curved flange the head, an inverted U-form for legs and the surrounding circular frame reading as hugely extended arms. Judging from the carefully added shading this was the design that engaged him most closely. It is a small step from this to read the completely abstract forms of the two lower doorknockers (fig. 5) as figures, the stirrup-shaped knocker reading as arms which hold an ovoid form that can strike the second stirrup/legs form below.

Given away or left behind when Gaudier moved on to Germany in April 1909, these sketches could be dismissed as mere juvenilia but for their remarkable prefiguration of the formal abstraction of his Vorticist work. The soft angled metallic

21 Alison, as in note 18, considered that 300 brasses would make for a 'complete collection' while Carter, as at note 16, considered there could be as many as 1500 different designs. Brears, ibid., pp. 43–44.
22 Delivery by horse and cart was limited to the domestic trade by 1908–09, but carthorses were still a frequent sight serving a wide variety of businesses; Alison as in note 16. A single face-piece brass might be worn daily but the full panoply was reserved for high days and holidays, e.g. rare film footage of a 1907 May Day parade including heavy horses in Llandudno by Mitchell and Kenyon; www.screenonline.org. uk/film/id/1311464/ (accessed 20.2.14).
23 G. Hartfield, *Horse Brasses*, London, Abelard-Schuman, 1965, plate II; Brears, as in note 19, plate on p. 62.
24 Hartfield, ibid., pl. VIII; an example in York, Castle Museum. A similarly presented real scallop shell on the wall of Gaudier's bedroom in St Jean de Braye is visible in a sketch, c. 1906–07; Silber, as in note 3, fig. 7.
25 A single heart in a plain circular frame (Hull Museums KINCM 1984 1 85) and a three heart composition unframed (Hull Museums KINCM 1984 1 90). See also H. S. Richards, *Horse Brass Collections*, Birmingham, Henry Devonshire, 1944, vol. 2, p. 34 where no. 235 is close to Gaudier's top centre design. Carter, as in note 18, p. 147, pl. XI, illustrates a hollow heart brass, commenting upon its rarity, and p. 148, pl. II, nos. 4,17,18, traces the origin of the heart motif to a bull's head.

triangle of these designs seems directly recycled in *Redstone Dancer* and becomes a distinctive element in his 1913–14 drawings and carvings, now changed in character and fully integrated into his modernist sculptural and graphic practice. Further, horse brasses and doorknockers provide another example of the kind of small, decorative utilitarian objects — medallions, Japanese netsuke, tsuba, Maori *hei-tiki* — that continued to fascinate him and which he made into a new genre with small carvings such as *Torpedo Fish*, *Doorknocker*, *Fish*, *Duck*. *Charm*, *Toy* and *Knuckleduster* carved in 1914.[27]

As Gaudier developed an autonomous artistic language that simplified and depersonalised figures without losing expressive vitality, he experimented with several means of suggesting facial features. Eyes, nose and mouth are reduced to brief linear curves and ridges in 1913 carvings *Wrestlers Relief*, *The Embracers* (*Samson and Delilah*), *Imp* and *Boy with Coney* and related drawings.[28] In *Red Stone Dancer* the 'spherical triangle', to use Pound's phrase, seems to make its debut. It then recurs, less successfully, as a faint line incised on the head of the maternal figure in *Caritas* (Orléans, Musée des Beaux Arts), which dates from early 1914.[29] The related drawings for both works show Gaudier exploring compact, powerful female figures, some with reductive oval and wedge features, while other faces are triangular glyphs superimposed on Brancusian egg-heads.[30]

The *Doorknocker* (S 81) is the work which most obviously references these drawings. In several bold preparatory studies (fig. 7), the technique of which also

26 The hollowed triangle is also nearly identical to a plain triangular harness link illustrated in, for instance, *Equine Album of Hampson & Scott*, p. 66 (Gear Buckles, Spring Hooks etc.) no. 326.

27 Silber, as in note 3, cat. nos. 80–82, 84–93, 95; J. Wood, 'Ornaments, Talisman and Toys: The Hand-held Sculptures of Henri Gaudier-Brzeska', in J. Black, C. Adams, M. J. K. Walsh and J. Wood, *Blasting the Future! Vorticism in Britain 1910–1920* (exh. cat.) London, 2004, pp. 40–48.

28 S 57, 66, 76 and 78.

29 *Red Stone Dancer* (S 69) first exhibited at the Grafton Group show held at the Alpine Club Gallery in January 1914 and *Caritas* (S 75) at the London Group in May 1914.

30 Silber, as in note 3, figs 94–96, 106–09.

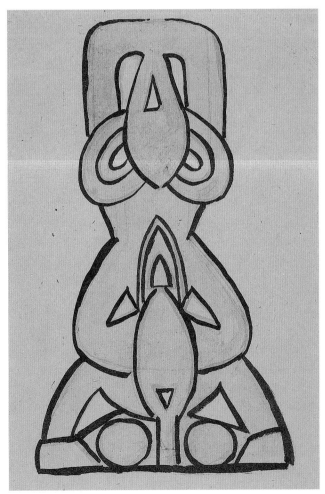

6. (above)   Horse brass: six hearts in a triangle, late nineteenth century, 123 × 91 mm, Hull Museums KINCM 1984 1 86 (photo: Streetlife Museum: Hull Museums).

7. (right)   *Study for Doorknocker*, c. 1914, 33 × 21 cm, brush and Indian ink on paper, Kettle's Yard, University of Cambridge HGB 63 (photo: Kettle's Yard, University of Cambridge).

recalls the early drawings, triangular forms recur singly as incised or relief elements down the centre, and in pairs as pierced voids.[31] In the finished sculpture the single central triangles have been omitted and replaced by a copulating couple reminiscent of Epstein *Totem*, 1913–14 (London, British Museum) and the birth depicted in *Flenite Relief* (see Wood figs 1–2), the smooth low relief elements played off more strongly against the triangular and oval voids. Here the continuously rounded tactile surfaces are reminiscent of the effect of the smooth, polished surfaces of the cast horse brass but, equally, illustrate sculpture as 'the relation of masses' even within the confines of what is essentially a thin metal plaque.

The triangle ceases to be an applied motif and acquires its own formal rationale and momentum in the other small sculptures of 1914. With its inherent strength and balance, it morphs to become not only the 'face glyph' in many pencil, pen and brush drawings, but also a fundamental element in the small carved pieces produced in 1914, notably *Torpedo Fish* and *Fish* (fig. 8), *Toy* and the hammer-like little marble *Duck*. These objects — without plinth or base and thus without any predetermined orientation, readily handled and pocketed — were both novel and ambiguous. Most carry more than one title underlining the formal and functional pun between decorative object and tool, human or animal figure and functional object. In *Torpedo Fish (Toy)* the triangular forms create a play in depth — low relief, facetted and pierced — and the whole piece is reversible to give different readings of a standing human figure — the triangular masses forming head/feet. In the intricate tool-like *Fish*, the reiterated sharp-angled triangles of the 'head' flip between fish, weapon, tool and decoration, seeming to signify in whatever function, 'danger! handle with care!' In *Toy* repeated triangular facets and pyramidal volumes dominate the composition in a masterly demonstration of the relation of masses in a miniature form.

Many of these pocketable little carvings in stone and brass were acquired by members of Gaudier's circle; the philosopher T. E. Hulme was the first owner of *Torpedo Fish, Ornament* and *Knuckleduster* – according to Pound he commissioned *Torpedo Fish* — Pound himself, the paperweight/*Fawn in brown stone*, the combative Wyndham Lewis the other *Knuckleduster*, Mrs Ethel Kibblewhite, *Fish* and Gaudier himself, the *Green stone Charm* which he famously wore on a cord around his neck. As Jon Wood has persuasively argued, these can be seen as talismanic pieces for fellow artists similarly committed to creating new modernist forms in art and literature. Semi-abstract, their *fainéant* utilitarian character and abstracted, often sharp-edged forms with their allusion to industrial processes and precision, were powerful embodiments of the machine aesthetic and anti-humanistic character of Vorticism. By adding in the likely back reference to his early brass designs, Wood's emphasis on the multi-layered meanings of these pieces acquires yet more depth. They are redolent of craftsmanship, objects made by and for the hand. Lucid in form, they are nevertheless laden with associations and emotions — desire and aggression, affection, unspoken gratitude, ambivalent feelings about city and country, machined tools and the 'primitive peoples of the earth'. Like many small art forms made by migrant, sophisticated cultures they were also works that, however, precious, were designed to function as an art of every day, beyond the gallery close to the heart and hand of the owner.[32]

31 See also *Study for Doorknocker* (Orléans, Musée des Beaux Arts, MO107), reproduced E. Silber, as in note 3, fig. 127.
32 Wood, as in note 27, pp. 40–48.

8.   Henri Gaudier-Brzeska, Fish and *Torpedo Fish* (Toy), 1914 from Ezra Pound, *Gaudier-Brzeska. A Memoir*, 1916, pl. 28. *Torpedo Fish* is normally shown inverted. (Photo: author)

Acknowledgements

My grateful thanks to the owners of the drawings and to Peter Brears, Roger Cole, the staff at Birmingham Central Library (Reference), Sarah Taylor (Bristol Record Office), Jane Bradley (Bristol Central Library), Gareth Salway and Helen McConnell (Bristol Museums and Galleries), Oliver Fairclough and David Jenkins (National Museum of Wales, Cardiff), Katrina Cooper (Cardiff Central Library), Caroline Rhodes (Hull Maritime Museum), Mary Moylett (National Screen and Sound Archive of Wales), and David Mills (Walsall, Leather Museum) for their help during the preparation of this article.

Jacob Epstein's Flenite Relief (1913)

Jon Wood

As we look back at sculpture in Britain one hundred years ago, the question 'What was "Vorticist sculpture?"' is still one worth asking, as our understanding of 'Vorticism' itself is reconsidered and reassessed. This short essay raises the question of Epstein's emerging 'Vorticist' sculpture through the example of a lesser-known work, now commonly known as *Flenite Relief*, which was executed in 1913 when Epstein was thirty-three years old. (figs 1 and 2). Since 2006 this sculpture has been in the collection of Leeds Museums and Galleries, thanks to the endeavours of the late Terry Friedman and Evelyn Silber and, subsequently, through the successful campaign led by Penelope Curtis at the Henry Moore Institute to acquire the work for the Leeds sculpture collections. *Flenite Relief* strengthened a collection which already had a good representation of sculpture and work on paper by Jacob Epstein (1880–1959), including his three *Baby Asleep* pieces (1904), *Maternity* (1910) and thirteen busts, as well as archive material documenting his work, life and career.

In 2007 the sculpture was presented in an exhibition I curated called *Creation Myths: Epstein's 'Flenite Relief' of 1913 in focus*.[1] This exhibition made the most of the intimate viewing conditions of the Henry Moore Institute's smallest gallery to enable visitors to take a close look at this remarkable two-sided sculpture and to see what it actually portrays. In so doing, it clarified a new reading of the work which literally turned the sculpture on its head. Rather than displaying two quite separate scenes, this piece in fact represents a single figure of a woman stretched out over its two faces, and delineates a different scene from the one implied by its previous title, *Flenite Relief: Woman Clasping a Phallus*, with which the work was provided when it was exhibited in 1987.[2] It is in this extraordinary and overlooked work that the complex and simultaneous sculptural renditions of birth and death — central to Epstein's emerging Vorticism — are to be found. *Flenite Relief* is also one of Epstein's most complex and enigmatic early images of women, additionally striking given the dominance of his *Rock Drill* (1913–15) in the established literature on his sculptural contribution to Vorticism and to avant-garde sculpture more generally.

Long out of sight in a North American private collection, the sculpture now commonly known as *Flenite Relief* has not received much art historical attention in the literature on Epstein, Vorticism or modern sculpture generally. It was regarded as a 'technical experiment' by Richard Buckle, a work of slight and experimental status.[3] This reading was later echoed by Richard Cork and Evelyn Silber, both viewing it as the 'least ambitious of flenite carvings'.[4] In 1987, when it was shown in the Epstein retrospective it acquired the title *Flenite Relief: Woman Clasping a Phallus*, a reading which privileged one side of the stone and that highlighted one possible aspect of this formally complicated sculpture's meaning, at the same time as it

1 *Creation Myths: Epstein's 'Flenite Relief' of 1913 in focus*, 3 November 2007 – 11 February 2012, Henry Moore Institute. It was also included in a larger exhibition I curated in 2012 called *1913: The Shape of Time*, Henry Moore Institute, Leeds, 22 November – 17 February 2013.

2 The image captions call one side 'Flenite Relief: Woman Clasping a Phallus' and the other side 'Flenite Relief: Birth', T. Friedman, 'Love and Birth' in T. Friedman and E. Silber, *Jacob Epstein: Sculpture and Drawings*, Leeds and London, 1987, pp. 157–59.

3 R. Buckle, *Jacob Epstein Sculptor*, London, 1963, p. 69.

4 R. Cork, *Vorticism and Abstract Art in the First Machine Age, Vol. 1: Origins and Development*, Berkeley, 1976, and Evelyn Silber, *The Sculpture of Jacob Epstein*, Oxford, 1986, p. 133.

Jacob Epstein (1880–1959), *Flenite Relief*, 1913, serpentine stone, Leeds Museums and Galleries (Leeds Art Gallery).

misread the overall figurative composition of the work.[5] It was also a reading that no doubt drew on an awareness of the phallic imagery that featured in much of Epstein's work at that time.

Despite these readings, the work is nevertheless a highly sophisticated and conceptually ambitious sculpture that portrays a mother bent over backwards, her arms crossed above her inverted head, in the act of giving birth, with a male baby emerging from between her legs. Radical now and even more so in the years before the First World War, this image of birth however has a darker meaning: the overall form of the stone is reminiscent of a gravestone so we are faced with an image of childbirth carved into the very shape of death.

Because both sides of the sculpture have infrequently been reproduced together it has not been subjected to close or extended scrutiny in the past and, when it has been discussed, one side has tended to have been given more attention than the other. This is partly because the sculpture does not photograph well. It is a challenging work to capture with a camera, not just because of its faceted and abstracted character, but also because the low relief is carved — across its five sides — into a dark, shiny serpentine. Legs in profile are etched into the thin upright sides, and on the very top Epstein has carved a belly button, utilising the upper, less visible side of the stone, much as Brancusi had done in his sculpture *The Kiss* (in this case to delineate his initials 'CB' in the hair of both lovers). The articulation of the bodies and body parts is, thus, subtle and obscure, etched in shallow relief as much as carved. Thus, the components as well as the overall composition are difficult to read. Putting this single sculpture in the spotlight reveals it to be a work that repays prolonged attention. It sheds light on many issues, some of which we may think

5 T. Friedman and E. Silber, as in note 2, pp. 158–59.

have been settled within art history — from what we might mean by 'Vorticist sculpture' and how memorial and commemorative sculpture was taken up within avant-garde circles in the years before the First World War, to how sculpture can be carved to carry a narrative not just in the round, but also, more unusually, 'on the loop' up and over a block of stone.

Epstein carved the sculpture while living in Pett Level on the Sussex coast, where he stayed on returning from Paris after the high-profile installation of his *Tomb of Oscar Wilde* in the cemetery of Père Lachaise. In Paris he made contact with many sculptors, including Modigliani and Brancusi, who shared his interest in carving directly into stone, unaided by assistants and with limited technical support. Their sculpture was meant to look as if it was made by an ancient, prehistoric maker, as much as by a modern artist. Rather than compete with the physical dimensions of the stone block, Epstein worked it in low relief, allowing each side to play a key role in the sculpture's meaning. The stay in Pett Level was highly productive period, as Epstein recalled to Richard Buckle: 'I could look out to the sea and carve away to my heart's content .... It was here that I carved the 'Venus', the three groups of doves, the two flenite carvings and the marble 'Mother and Child' .... This was a period of intense activity and were it not for the war and the impossibility of living in the country and making a living, I would have stayed there forever.'[6] This reminds us that Epstein's gaze was across the Channel towards France, not back inland: that the exciting developments in modern sculpture were occurring in Paris and not London.

The stone used by Epstein is a type of soft, dark green-black flecked serpentine, which gets its name from the snake skin look that the various mineral infusions give this stone. He renamed it 'flenite', a term which he invented, suggesting both 'granite' and 'flint'. It also implies an ancient function, as if the stone were a pre-historic tool or had some mythical symbolic purpose. This word was clearly important to Epstein in evoking an idea of 'primitive' creativity and labour as he used it in the title of two other sculptures during 1913–14. These include *Female Figure in Flenite* of the same year. The menacing quality of the black-ish serpentine stone is particularly powerful in relation to this sculpture, giving the pregnant figure a funerary quality which might also relate to the function of the Fang sculpture it quietly references.

There are connections with contemporary sculpture in London in these years too and, whilst Henri Gaudier-Brzeska's *Imp* of the following year comes closest to a response to Epstein's flenites, the figurative tool sculptures that Gaudier made in 1914 also relate to this side of the 'flenite' meaning. These small scale sculptures and the 'manual thinking' that charged them shed interesting light on the orientation of 'Vorticist sculpture'. As with Futurism, the hand is again an important motif of agency, but one that reaches across a wider and less secular range of references. The 'Vorticist hand' was a historical and highly interdisciplinary one which embraced not only the mechanised objects and processes of technological modernity (the machine, the gun, the drill), but also notions of craftsmanship (the artisan, the carver, the worker), ideas of magic, animism and 'primitive' agency (talismans, charms, amulets and totemic animalia), physical violence and sport (knuckle-dusters, boxing, wrestling) and erotica and sexual symbolism (fertility symbols, genital imagery, sex toys). This group of Gaudier's small-scale objects reflect all of these Vorticist preoccupations, often in the same piece.

6 R. Buckle, *Jacob Epstein Sculptor*, London, 1963, p. 65.

This is the case with Gaudier's *Doorknocker* (see the related drawing Silber, fig. 8) of 1914, a characteristically difficult work to read. In his preview of the Allied Artists' Association exhibition at Holland Park in June 1914, Gaudier himself reiterated something of this position: 'The sculpture I admire is the work of master craftsmen. Every inch of the surface is won at the point of the chisel — every stroke of the hammer is physical and mental effort.'[7] He went on to comment on his own exhibited work and focussed in particular on *Doorknocker* (1914), stating: 'The doorknocker is an instance of an abstract design serving to amplify the value of an object as such. No more cupids riding mermaids, garlands, curtains — stuck anywhere! The technique is unusual; the object is not cast but carved direct out of solid brass. The forms gain in sharpness and rigidity.'[8]

Gaudier's comments are very interesting in the light of the kind of object *Doorknocker* is and how difficult its asymmetrical forms are to read. Looking across the various studies for doorknockers he executed, it appears that the iconography of *Doorknocker* is sexual showing the forms of a copulating couple. This entirely tallies with Gaudier's rejection of polite, decorative subjects (which he complained could be randomly 'stuck anywhere'): the message here is that sexual intercourse is analogous to knocking on the door and entering a house. Thus, the sexual iconography of 'abstract design' 'amplifies', to use Gaudier's term, the object's meaning. His language is telling: since *Doorknocker* was also an object that moved and made a noise — it could be activated and thus functioned literally as well as metaphorically. Moreover, and as with Gaudier's *Red Stone Dancer* (Silber, fig. 1) (which seems to have one hand too many), there is a deliberate ambiguity between body parts in *Doorknocker*: hands, for example, double up as breasts. Gaudier's *Doorknocker* was a household object but, unlike the products that he made for Fry's Omega workshop, it was mischievously loaded with sexual resonance. If Gaudier's group of small-scale works cocked a snook at the ornaments, trinkets and paraphernalia of the luxury goods market, *Doorknocker* itself brought new challenges and a new sensibility to the threshold of the bourgeois residence itself. Through such works we are reminded of the sensibility at stake in a sculpture such as Epstein's *Flenite Relief* and the kind of associations in play. It was a work aimed at communicating raw power and dark agency, as bold and unflinching in emotion as it is magical and syncretic in form, as if it was an object that might hold some unknown or mysterious ritualistic function.

The 'mother and child' subject was popular in the sculpture of the period but Epstein reacted against this often sentimentalised genre by representing a woman not with a baby in her arms, but in the act of giving birth. His other sculptural renditions of this subject are known through the Ontario *Birth* and, more tantalisingly, through the studio photograph of the large, later destroyed granite *Mother and Child* (c. 1915–17) briefly owned by the great American collector, John Quinn. In these works the bold schematic articulation of birth can be gauged against the subtler and more slippery figuration of the more finished *Flenite Relief*. The use of non-Western figuration is striking, although the upside down posture — a feature that is also found in the *Flenite Relief* — is unusual in both Western and non-Western sculpture. The non-Western look, the brutal realism of its subject and non-Christian message of these works are all clearly pronounced when viewed alongside the more typical and sentimental formulations of 'mother and child' in late nineteenth century and Edwardian sculpture. The passage from one mode of repre-

7 Henri Gaudier-Brzeska, 'Allied Artists' Association Ltd, Holland Park Hall', *The Egoist*, 15 June 1914.
8 Henri Gaudier-Brzeska, 'Allied Artists' Association Ltd, Holland Park Hall', *The Egoist*, 15 June 1914.

sentation of womanhood to the other was a gradual one, subtly developed over a number of works. By the time Epstein carved *Flenite Relief* he had already (three years earlier) succeeded in producing a larger-than-life, full length pregnant female figure in Hoptonwood stone and in modelling *Standing Mother and Child* (1911) with the child turned to face the mother's body. In Gaudier's work the passage from one to the other is less gradual, as can be noted in his *Maternity* and mother and child sculptures and works on paper across 1913 and 1914. In such works we can discern a shift in these years from the depictions of tender, loving naturalistic embraces to a geometrically shaped and more animalistic piggybacking of child by the mother.

However, arguably one of the most radical aspects of Epstein's *Flenite Relief* — namely the image of a baby being born — would only later be followed up by sculptors with works that took this idea one stage back and into sculptures that depict foetuses. Leon Underwood's carving *Foetus* of 1924–25 offers a combination of figuration and design that chimes with Heinz Henghes' 1939 sculpture *The Unborn* and takes us, again through the medium of serpentine, into a far more compelling and visceral terrain, utilising the stone's polish to suggest the wetness and fluidity of its subject, as we are also left wondering whether this foetus is alive or dead, premature and/or still born.

Though an image of 'mother and child', *Flenite Relief* is neither a comfortable and reassuring nor a traditional rendition of the maternal relationship — whether sacred or broadly secular Nor is it a stone carving evocative of vitalism and regeneration. Birth and death are caught in the same sculptural moment, although it is not clear whether this is the death of both the mother and child together through childbirth, or the death of the mother or infant alone. Epstein's then current preoccupations with both death and commemoration (*Tomb of Oscar Wilde* of 1909–12) and in birth and creativity (*Rock Drill* of 1913–15) in a sense straddle this 1913 sculpture. They are also echoed in the creation myths of early sculpture in the displays at the British Museum which Epstein would regularly visit. In these ethnographic displays, distinctions between images of death and life, between commemorations of living rulers and dead ones, were always notoriously difficult for contemporary artists visiting the museum to draw and they maximised this ambiguity in their borrowings and appropriations. The rich and compelling contribution to modern sculpture and Vorticism that *Flenite Relief* made resides in its synthesis of these associations and in its blending of the deathly with images of sexuality, reproduction and fecundity.

Gaudier's *Hieratic Head of Ezra Pound* (1914) is a good example of this compressed and multivalent imagery, of the kind found in Epstein's *Flenite Relief*. As I have argued elsewhere, when viewed accumulatively over three sections (through the three dimensions of bust, phallus, torso) the sculpture can be seen as a much richer and less secular one than it has previously been considered.[9] A sculpture that comprises images of both life and death: a portrait, a fertility symbol and a funerary statue. Its narrative is articulated as a sequence of moments revealed to a viewer exploring the sculpture's forms in the round. This is a strategy we find in Epstein's *Flenite Relief* (1913): using all sides of the serpentine stone Epstein had also articulated a multiple image, comprising two faces, a couple in embrace and a female figure giving birth. Sculpted in the form of a headstone, the overall work thus had an elliptical narrative structure. The *Hieratic Head* does not mourn the 'dead' artist as an androgynous martyr and immortalise him as a heroic victim in flight (as Epstein's

9 J. Wood, 'Heads and tales: Gaudier-Brzeska's *Hieratic Head of Ezra Pound* and the making of an avant-garde homage', in David J. Getsy (ed.), *Sculpture and the Pursuit of a Modern Ideal in Britain*, c. 1880–1930, Aldershot, 2004, pp. 191–208.

did Wilde), but articulates a tripartite process of syncretic return which imaginatively restores the artist-subject to eternal creative life.

To grasp the unusual figuration of *Flenite Relief* the sculpture needs to be viewed in the round, revealing a narrative that is carved up and over the two main sides of the stone. It is the story of a body in action: one side shows the upper torso of a woman, her hands and arms folded above her head, and the other a male baby emerging from between her legs. The outlines of this image are articulated in a stylised way that reflects Epstein's knowledge of *The Kiss* by Brancusi, a funerary sculpture which he would have seen in Montparnasse cemetery in Paris and a work whose funerary associations, never taken up in later art historical appreciations of Epstein's *Flenite Relief* despite frequent stylistic comparison with Brancusi's sculpture, would have no doubt impacted much on his reading of Brancusi's two figures' loving embrace.[10] Formally and conceptually, Epstein compressed a lot into *Flenite Relief*: creating a complex image of mythic creativity, as well as birth and death simultaneously and 'on a loop', that aims at being both ancient and modern at once. Love and sex were a familiar double trope for Epstein and others, but the attempt to render the complete cycle of birth, life and death in a single stone is, of course, less so which is what makes this complicated little sculpture so interesting. Shaping these ideas in the form of a gravestone gives this sculpture further power as social mores and codes of decency and decorum are compellingly flouted by this carved, quasi-functional object. *Flenite Relief* was, and is, an extraordinary sculpture and one that still has extraordinary power today, just over a hundred years after it was made.

10 E. Silber, *The Sculpture of Jacob Epstein*, Oxford, 1986, p. 133, and most recently, R. Cork, *Wild Thing: Epstein, Gaudier-Brzeska, Gill*, London, 2010, pp. 104–11.

Rescuing Laurence Bradshaw's *Maternity* at the Radcliffe Infirmary: an object lesson from the archive

Katharine Eustace

'Sculptural reliefs from the existing Maternity Hospital and Nurses Home should be preserved and incorporated within the new buildings or public spaces.'

This commitment, made in the 2007 Public Consultation document on the development of the Radcliffe Infirmary site in Oxford,[1] prompted an exhaustive search through local libraries and archives in Oxford, and the compilation of my report to the University of Oxford. This established conclusively that the four reliefs referred to are by Laurence Bradshaw (1899–1978) (figs 1, 2 a–c).[2] Perhaps because of a fear that the reception of the earliest of the four figures, the polistone *Maternity* in 1931, might be controversial, there is a dearth of reference to the commission, the sculpture and sculptor in the Oxford sources.

1 *The University of Oxford's Radcliffe Infirmary Site and Science Area Masterplans for Public Consultation*, under 'Further Considerations Public Art', Oxford, University of Oxford Estates Department March 2007, p. 15; Oxfordshire History Centre, St Luke's, Cowley (PA pamphlet OXFO/362.1/RADC).

2 K. Eustace, 'Report on Sculpture from the Radcliffe Maternity Department (1931), later the Nuffield Maternity Home, and Nurses' Residence (1932/3), Radcliffe Infirmary', April 2013 (unpublished). The sculpture was subsequently the subject of a conservation report: M. Norman, 'Comments on the sculptures by Lawrence Bradshaw from the Nurses Residence and Radcliffe Maternity Dept/Nuffield Maternity Home', 4 July 2013 (unpublished). Laurence Henderson Bradshaw', *Mapping the Practice and Profession of Sculpture in Britain and Ireland 1851–1951*, University of Glasgow History of Art and HATII, online database 2011; http://sculpture.gla.ac.uk/view/person.php?id=ann_1269000135, accessed 29.04.2014.

1. Laurence Bradshaw (1899–1978), *Maternity*, Portland stone, 1931, in situ on the front elevation of the Nuffield Maternity Home before demolition in 2008 (photo: courtesy Modus Operandi art consultants).

3 Bradshaw archive, Henry
Moore Institute, Leeds
(hereafter HMI), BR/MA-C
(ref no. 53.1994).

4 A scheme was discussed at
Executive Committee meetings
in October 1926; 13 and
27 October 1926; Executive
Committee Minutes Book, May
1926 – September 1930,
ff. 18–19, 20; 7 July 1926; ibid.,
f. 7; Oxfordshire Health Archives
(hereafter OHA), RI I E I/2.

5 R. J. Overy, 'Morris, William
Richard, Viscount Nuffield',
Oxford Dictionary of National Biography
(henceforth ODNB), 2004;
P. Andrews and E. Brunner, The
Life of Lord Nuffield, A Study in
Enterprise and Benevolence, Oxford,
1955; M. Adeney, Nuffield A
Biography, London, 1993; and
P. Hull, An Illustrated Life of William
Richard Morris, Viscount Nuffield,
1877–1963, 1977.

6 An unidentified
architectural critic, quoted in
Anon., (A. Sanctuary?), The
Radcliffe Infirmary 1921–48, privately
printed, p. 8; Nuffield College
Archive, Oxford (Nuffield Ms
Box 53, 53/24/1–18).

7 A. H. T. Robb-Smith, A Short
History of the Radcliffe Infirmary,
Oxford, Oxford, 1970, p. 145.

8 Wednesdays, 20 April,
11 May, and 3 August 1927; as
note 4, ff. 44–45, 48, 57.

9 26 October 1927; as note 4,
f. 68.

10 Thomas Edward Collcutt
(1840–1924) was the senior
partner when Hamp joined in
1906; Architecture, July–August
1928, pp. 110–11, vol. VI, no. 33;
Architecture, July–August 1929,
vol. VII, no. 39, pp. 90–107; The
Times, 24 February 1928, p. 22;
designs by Hamp
www.liveauctioneers.com/item/
13888074; accessed 30.01.2013.

11 The Times, 18 April 1968,
obituary, p. 12.

12 Ibid.; for Hamp's campaigns
with Sir John Betjeman and
others see The Times, 13 March
1956, p. 6; 20 October 1959,
p. 13; 24 August 1959, p. 5;
3 September 1959, p. 6.

Photographs presented by the sculptor's widow, Eileen Bradshaw to the Henry Moore Institute Archive in 1994, however, provide the answers.[3] What follows is a narrative account of an exploratory trawl through primary sources in search of evidence.

The first inter-war development at the Radcliffe Infirmary was the Maternity Department, completed in 1931. It hinged entirely on the acquisition from the Radcliffe Trustees of the Observatory and its ten acres, but negotiations between the two bodies were slow and intractable.[4] However, on the intervention of the Oxford-born, motor-manufacturing pioneer, William Morris (1877–1963, later Viscount Nuffield),[5] the development, described as 'a brilliant piece of architectural surgery', proceeded at speed.[6] Morris proved both the catalyst and the driving energy behind the development. His first engagement with the Radcliffe Management Committee had been in 1924, when he paid off the Infirmary's overdraft of £9,000 with an Oxford Motor Ballot.[7] Subsequently he was invited onto the Management Board and, by 1927, was its President. In April 1927 a fund was established and the following month an offer to purchase the entire Observatory site was made to the Radcliffe Trustees.[8] In October 'Mr Hamp's plans for the extension of the Hospital were examined' (fig. 3), and he was requested to provide costings.[9]

Stanley Hinge Hamp (1877–1968) was in 1927 the surviving partner in the architectural practice Collcutt and Hamp.[10] He appears to have been a larger than life character, 'a lovable red-faced, walrus-moustached man with short bobbed hair and a large bow-tie [...] in his later years he wore hairy tweeds with long cut coats'.[11] Hamp was an advocate of architectural sculpture and conducted a 'lifelong campaign for a greater integration of the arts and architecture'.[12] Eclectic in style, his

2. Laurence Bradshaw figures on the Nurses' Residence, Radcliffe Infirmary, Oxford, 1932.

a. (facing page left) *Aesculapius* or *Hippocrates*, a bearded figure with a scroll, and a serpent encircling a column; 155 × 40 × 20 cm (approx.).

b. (facing page right) Female figure with scroll and goat-horned lyre; 160 × 40 × 20 cm.

c. (right) *Hygieia* or *Prudence*, female figure with serpent entwined in a tree and drinking from a vessel; 147 × 40 × 20 cm.

Cast, cement-based aggregate (photos: Polly Holbrook, 2007).

13 For the Liebig Extract of Meat Company, manufacturers of the Oxo Cube; P. Ward-Jackson, *Public Sculpture of the City of London*, Liverpool, 2003, pp. 306–08.
14 S. Bradley and N. Pevsner, *London 6:Westminster, Buildings of England*, New Haven and London, 2003. The sculptors included Bainbridge Copnall, Gilbert Ledward, and Newbury Trent, the latter responsible for a low relief plaque on the Odeon Cinema, George Street, Oxford.
15 Dr Ernest Mallam (1870–1946) a leading dermatologist with a private practice in the Banbury Road, was a member and regular Chairman of the Honorary Medical Staff Committee 1904–38; (A. Sanctuary?), as note 6; Committee of Management, 17 August 1927, 22 November 1927, 25 April 1928; OHA, RI 1 C1/23, Register No. 23, ff. 204, 207–08, 218.
16 Ibid., Extension Fund Committee, 24 May 1928, f. 97.
17 Ibid., f. 219.
18 Building Committee; OHA, Executive Committee Minutes, I E 1/2, f. 113. Andrew Walsh of Herbert Gowers, Oxford, Lord Nuffield's solicitors, became Chairman of Nuffield's Trusts and Foundation. Now HMG Law, still at 126 High Street, the company holds no archives associated with Walsh or Nuffield; telephonic confirmation to the author 10.03.14. University of Oxford archives in relation to Lord Nuffield's trusts and foundation begin in 1936, after the completion of the Maternity and Residence projects; information from Dr Simon Bailey, Keeper of the Archives, University of Oxford.
19 19 July, 18 September, 13 November 1929; as note 15, ff.150, 157, 164.
20 F. Honigsbaum, 'Buzzard, Sir (Edward) Farquhar (1871–1945)', ODNB, 2004.
21 20 November 1929; OHA, as note 15, f.166.

buildings range from Thames House (1911–12), Upper Thames Street, in a Beaux-Arts manner, encrusted with architectural sculpture,[13] to the New Adelphi building, Robert Street (1936–38), an Art Deco office block described by Pevsner as 'savagely ungraceful',[14] similarly enhanced by sculpture. He was appointed President of the Architectural Association in 1922, and Vice-President of the R.I.B.A from 1934 to 1937. Like other versatile architects of the period who may not have left signature buildings, Hamp's name does not survive in general surveys of twentieth-century British architecture.

Internal dissent at the Radcliffe Infirmary, led by the maverick Dr Ernest Mallam (1870–1946), continued to delay matters.[15] In May, Morris offered £38,000 towards the building of the Maternity Department, to which he would add a further £40,000 if the public appeal raised £75,000.[16] On 9 May 1928, with Morris in the chair and a full complement of governors, the proposal was carried unanimously.[17] However, by autumn 1928, the Radcliffe Trustees had still not reached a settlement over the Observatory and its future, and Morris decided to deal with them personally. All correspondence with the Trustees was handed over to his solicitor, Andrew Walsh, who became the link between Morris and the Infirmary and, later, the University.[18] In November 1929 the Radcliffe Trustees finally agreed to the sale of the site, and Hamp was able to proceed.[19] Morris (now Sir William) was to buy the site for £100,000. At the same time, and impossible to refuse, the deal was now to include a Chair of Medicine, for another new knight, Sir Farquhar Buzzard,[20] and a Medical School for the University.[21]

Once all the decisions had been taken the building was swiftly completed, for in the early 1930s labour was cheap, and investing in building was seen as a way out of the Depression. Construction of the forty-bed Maternity Department began in

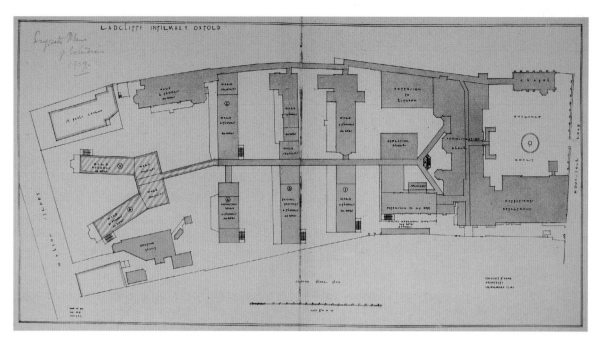

3.   Collcutt & Hamp, *Ground Plan of the Radcliffe Infirmary* showing proposed extensions in red. The Maternity Department is to the left in red cross-hatching. Pencil and wash, 1927. Radcliffe Infirmary Honorary Medical Staff Record of Meetings, July 1910 – July 1933, ff. 1–2. Oxfordshire History Centre (OHA, RI IL 1/2) (photo: the author; courtesy and © Oxfordshire Health Authority Archive).

4.   Collcutt & Hamp, architects' office photograph, 1931. The Walton Street façade of the new Maternity Department, showing *Maternity*, apparently treated in the same way as the coping stones of the parapet and wings. Oxfordshire History Centre, St Luke's, Cowley Road, (OHA RGN 6) (photo: courtesy and © Oxfordshire Health Authority Archive).

August 1930 and the first mothers were admitted the following July. A distinctly modernist Art Deco building as seen from Walton Street, it had the streamlined look associated with Cunard ship design, enhanced by the latest medical fashion for solaria, or sun platforms, accessed from the wards (fig. 4). It was opened on 22 October 1931 by the Duchess of York, the future Queen Elizabeth.

Coverage in the local press was extensive and inclusive. All local suppliers were credited, and advertised prominently in the *Oxford Times*.[22] The Duchess's dress, the variety of flowers and even Messrs. Elliston and Cavell's 'extra-thick brown "Battleship" lino' received attention.[23] The 'simplicity of line' and 'the aesthetic of modern ideas' were emphasised, yet nowhere was *Maternity*, the sculpture over the entrance to the building, referred to or commented upon. Illustrations showed the interiors and the 'impressive looking gate provided by Sir William Morris'.[24] Even the Radcliffe Infirmary Annual Report for 1931, despite declaring the opening of the 'new Maternity Home' the 'outstanding event of the year', omitted all mention of it, although the frontispiece illustration of the Walton Street façade clearly showed the pediment-cum-keystone, high-relief figure of *Maternity*.[25]

The completion of the second phase, the Nurses' Residence, was announced with much less fanfare in the *Oxford Times*, in March 1933.[26] The Residence abutted the original mid-eighteenth-century Infirmary building, and its façade gave onto the Woodstock Road (fig. 5). Unlike the quietly modernist Maternity Home, the

22 Under headings: 'A Notable Development/ Description of the New Buildings/Fine Achievement by Local Contractors'; *Oxford Times*, 23 October 1931, p. 17.
23 *Oxford Times*, 23 October 1931, pp. 12, 13, 17.
24 Ibid., p. 13.
25 Annual Report, *Radcliffe Infirmary and County Hospital*, Oxford, 1932, p. 7, and frontispiece; OHA RI/ A25.
26 *Oxford Times*, 24 March 1933, p. 16.

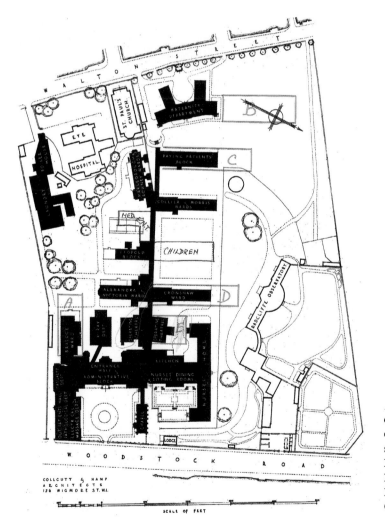

5. Collcutt & Hamp, *Ground Plan of the Radcliffe Infirmary*, c. 1935. Pen and ink. The Maternity Department is centre right top, the Nurses' Residence or Home is the solid black block centre right bottom. Oxfordshire History Centre (OHA, Honorary Medical Staff Hospital Extension and Development Sub Committee 1935–37; RI IL 2/ 1) (photo: the author; courtesy and © Oxfordshire Health Authority Archive).

27 Graham Varney, Director, Benfield and Loxley Ltd, Cowley, in conversation with the author, March 2013.

28 Quarterly General Court, 14 September 1932; OHC, OHA, Register No. 23, RI 1 C1/23, f. 16; Committee of Management, 25 April 1934; OHC, OHA, Register No.23, RI I C1/23, f. 71.

29 12 July 1931, Radcliffe Infirmary Honorary Medical Staff Record of Meetings; Oxfordshire History Centre, OHA RI IL 1/2, f. 306.

30 'Central feature' sounds like some form of sculptural element. Building Committee, 15 May 1931, 19 June 1931, 26 June 1931, ff. 47, 53; in Executive Committee, September 1930 – January 1933 OHC, OHA, RI I E 1/3.

31 26 June 1931; OHA RI I E 1/3, f. 58 ; A primary source of documents sent to the City Council or the City Engineers Department for approval or comment, were not available at the time of writing; email exchange with Debbie Taylor, Technical Team leader (Planning & Building Control, City Development, Oxford City Council), April 2014.

32 'An Oxford Sculpture by Laurence Bradshaw', Architectural Review, March 1932, vol. LXXI, No. 424, p. 94; cutting, HMI, as note 3, (BR/M12/14); paraphrased by P. Atterbury in P. Curtis (ed.), Sculpture in 20th-century Britain, a guide to sculptors in the Leeds Collections, HMI, 2003, vol. II, pp. 26–27.

33 Ibid.

34 R. Cork, Art Beyond the Gallery in early 20th Century England, Yale, 1985. Coincidentally Leeds' Collections hold three stone maquettes for the 'North Wind' for London Transport Headquarters, by Alfred Gerrard (1899–1998); acc. nos 2003.0029.0001–3; P. Curtis, as note 32, pp. 127–28.

35 R. Cork in E. Silber and T. Friedman, et al., Jacob Epstein Sculpture and Drawings, (exh. cat.), Leeds, 1987, p. 106.

36 Conversations between the author and Polly Holbrook, and Timothy Wilson, Keeper of Western Art, Ashmolean Museum, Oxford.

Residence was traditional, an essentially utilitarian brick building in 'Post Office Georgian'. As such it would have appealed to the funder, Sir William Morris, who was reportedly impatient of architects, preferring to work directly with builders.[27] The relief figures installed upon it may well have been a nod to Oxford's own architectural tradition, and an acknowledgement of its frontage onto one of the main roads into the city. More prosaically, the gables, which provided *exedrae* for the figures, were also discreet housings for water tanks (fig. 6). The residence was in operation by September 1932, and in April 1934, when Hamp's alterations to the entrance to the old Infirmary were complete, the Management Committee passed a vote of thanks 'for the very satisfactory and economical way in which he carried out the work'.[28]

A tantalising agenda note, '? Origin of Statue over Maternity Dept.', appears among a number of minor matters under Building Plans for the Maternity Department on 12 July 1931.[29] The query may have been answered in conversation, telephonically, or in the meeting, but appears not to have been minuted. This, the only reference to the sculpture discovered from surviving documentation in Oxford, suggests curiosity, but also doubt and covert antipathy. Lurking hostility may also be hinted at in the queries about the north elevation of the Nurses' Residence, and in the evident confusion between the two projects: the Building Committee had requested that Hamp submit 'an alternative design for the central feature of the northern face of the new Maternity [crossed out] Nurses [inserted] Department'.[30] Hamp produced an amended elevation and was instructed to forward it to the City Council for approval.[31] The deep silence that prevailed around the commissioning of the four pieces of sculpture may well have stemmed from anxiety about public reaction. *Maternity* would undoubtedly have been perceived as stylistically *avant garde* as the *Architectural Review* noted,[32] particularly in Oxford at the time. After philosophising on the nature and purpose of architectural sculpture, 'fundamentals the lay mind, which looks for sentiment or decoration in the manner of superimposed motives, fails to grasp':

[Maternity] has been vetoed as ugly, too powerful, too sad, or lacking in grace, and the artist himself interrupted by a variety of suggestions from butcher and baker, not to mention the bombastic colonel who bounced forward to exclaim: 'Good gracious me, what have we here? Huh! We'll soon have that down!' And conspire they did. Fortunately, a body of experts, including a prominent member of the Society for the Preservation of Oxford, and the architect himself, stepped in, and the group remains.[33]

Much of this is a stereotypical public response in the face of Modernism, reignited no doubt by the polilithic relief sculpture for Charles Holden's London Underground headquarters at St James's Park in 1929,[34] and the renewed furore over Epstein's figures on the British Medical Association (BMA) building in the Strand in 1931.[35]

The name that often springs to mind when considering low relief sculpture of this period, so pervasive was his influence, is that of Eric Gill. Indeed the campaign to preserve and restore the figures to the site after the completion of the recent redevelopment, stemmed from a popular misconception that the four relief figures were in some way associated with Gill.[36] In reality there is little to associate either *Maternity* or the three low relief figures on the Nurses' Residence with Gill, even stylistically. Perhaps it was the subject matter of the former, or its perceived 'modernity' — the simplification of form and the technique of direct carving —

Wards

THE
RADCLIFFE
INFIRMARY

Maternity Home

Nurses' Home

6. A page from Benfield and Loxley's *A Pictorial Record of Fifty Years of Building and Restoration*, 1953 (photo: the author; courtesy Messrs. Benfield and Loxley Ltd, Cowley Road, Oxford).

that suggested the possibility. There are collective memories that Gill carved the lettering for a commemorative plaque that hung above the fireplace in the dining room of the Radcliffe Infirmary, and that the (surviving) foundation stone inscription was lettered in Gill's workshop.[37] Certainly, in the interwar years, Gill's name would have been familiar in Oxford: his association started as early as 1905, and encompassed a dozen commissions for colleges and others commemorating famous men, and he was working on the *Stations of the Cross* for St Albans, Charles Street, Cowley, when he died.

The simplification of form and the scale of Bradshaw's *Maternity* (fig. 7) resonate more with the work of Epstein and Moore than with that of Gill. The bulky limbs and hammer toes, which are no more than a series of striated lines, are reminiscent of the block feet of African carving which had so strong an influence on

37 It has disappeared, and no documentation exists to substantiate this. The current catalogue does not refer to work at the Radcliffe Infirmary, but the list is by no means complete; D. Peace, *Eric Gill: The Inscriptions A descriptive catalogue*, London, 1994.

7.   Laurence Bradshaw, photographs of *Maternity*: a (left) may show a close up of the finished work with what looks like a unifying treatment, and b (right) shows the work being carved *in situ* (photo: courtesy Henry Moore Institute, Leeds (Bradshaw archive, acc. no. 53/ 1994)).

38 T. Friedman, 'The Hyde Park Atrocity' Epstein's Rima Creation and Controversy, Leeds, 1988; and E. Silber and T. Friedman, *et al.*, *Jacob Epstein Sculpture and Drawings* (exhib. cat.), Leeds, 1987, pp. 210–22, col. pls 62, 63.
39 *Maternity* (1924, Leeds City Art Galley), *Suckling Child* in cast concrete (whereabouts unknown, once owned by Jacob Epstein, 1927), and *Mother and Child* (Hirshhorn Museum of Art, Washington DC, 1931); see D. Mitchinson, '1930–1940', in A. Garrould, T. Friedman and D. Mitchinson, *Henry Moore Early Carvings 1920–1940* (exhib.cat.) Leeds City Art Galleries, 1982, p. 31.

contemporary sculptors. Maternity themes had been prominent in both Gill's and Epstein's oeuvre from 1910 to 1912 when they had worked closely together, and Epstein continued to work on them. Almost without exception Epstein's work before the Second World War attracted notoriety and obloquy.[38] At the London Underground Headquarters, 55 Broadway, it was Epstein's massive keystones — *Day* in particular — over the entrances that became the cause of public outrage, probably because they were literally in the public eye, while the others by Gill and Moore were far overhead. Henry Moore, a generation younger, was, like Gill and Epstein, a proponent of direct carving, and his similar subject matter was no less controversial.[39]

It seems unlikely that either William Morris, who made no pretence to artistic taste or interest, but had a vested interest in his own social advancement, or the Infirmary Committees would court controversy by approaching such figures.

Hamp, however, was experienced at employing sculptors on his buildings, and may have proposed the choice of Bradshaw.[40] Yet the mystery surrounding the Radcliffe Infirmary commission, and the almost complete silence at the time, may have stemmed from a collective desire not to provoke public opposition.

Laurence Bradshaw might have seemed unlikely to provoke controversy, as his work to date had been traditional, figuratively safe pieces, or light-hearted theatre designs. Of Irish extraction and trained at Liverpool School of Art, Bradshaw had become an assistant to Sir Frank Brangwyn (1867–1956). This association introduced Bradshaw to the aesthetic and social thinking of that other, earlier, William Morris, and may have led to his first commission, in a style described by the *Manchester Guardian* as 'Modern Baroque', for the Brompton Oratory in 1926–27.[41] Other commissions followed, but, when Bradshaw joined the Communist Party in the early 1930s, ecclesiastic commissions dried up.[42] He remained a card-carrying member of the Party until his death.[43] This allegiance forfeited him the American commission for the screen for the Time-Life Building in New Bond Street to Henry Moore in 1952–53,[44] when, at the height of Macarthyism, Bradshaw was blacklisted.[45] Ironically, his best-known work is the colossal head of *Karl Marx* (1956) in Highgate Cemetery, London. He contributed architectural ornament to many civic buildings, such as the Guildhall, Cambridge (1935–37), Watford and Winchester Town Halls (1933–40 and 1957), and Worthing Assembly Hall (1935–36),[46] often in composition materials, such as 'Empire stone' and concrete.[47] Interest in the possibilities of composites may have been part of his relationship with Stanley Hamp,[48] along with his apparent compatibility, for Bradshaw was described as 'a lucid and amusing raconteur'.[49] The Radcliffe Infirmary commission probably came directly from Stanley Hamp at a time when Bradshaw appeared to be on the threshold of success. Described by the *Daily News* as 'the brilliant young artist and sculptor', one of his theatre designs for a harlequin had been purchased by the Victoria and Albert Museum in 1928.[50] Hamp and Bradshaw were clearly agreed on the importance of architectural sculpture, for, as Bradshaw put it:

I belong to that group of artists who assert that the creative arts must be brought out of the art gallery and dealers' showrooms and again become a part of the environment of the city dweller and countryman alike, and that art in all its forms should have a close relationship to architecture.[51]

Maternity is composed of four worked blocks and, judging from the photographic evidence, was finished in situ (fig. 7b). In terms of architectural function and ornament, the work is an enlarged keystone. This is in keeping with Bradshaw's own assessment that 'my early work as a sculptor and mural decorator was a structural part of the building',[52] and bears out the observations made in the *Architectural Review*.[53] The technique of polilithic or 'polistone' pieces was deployed by other modernist sculptors such as Frank Dobson R.A. (1888–1963) and Siegfried Charoux (1896–1967).[54] The now weathered Portland stone may, from the evidence of contemporary photographs (figs 4 and 7), have been treated with a plaster or cement render that bound it visually into the similarly-treated coping stones of the parapet, which, given its original, expensive Portland stone medium, may indeed have been intended to reduce its impact on passers-by in Walton Street.[55] This gave it and the building a distinctive modernist appearance. The coating may have been

40 In conversation with Philip Ward Jackson, March 2013.

41 27 September 1928; Bradshaw archive, as note 3, (Cuttings, BR/M12).

42 *Ibid.*, (BR/P1/2,3, P3/A, BR/M10).

43 J. Seddon, 'From Worthing to Highgate and back: the career of Laurence Henderson Bradshaw (1899-1978)', *Sculpture Journal*, vol. 19.2 [2010], pp. 234–40. The commission is listed here as 'Oxford Redcliffe [sic] Maternity Home, 1935 (*Mother and Child* sculptures)'; Seddon, p. 238, n. 5.

44 *Ibid.*

45 Eileen Bradshaw in answer to Henry Moore Institute (HMI) archivist Helen Upton's questions, 27.07.1995; HMI, acquisitions file. Drawings for Time/Life Competition, HMI, 53/1994 (BR/D I.1–4)

46 As note 43.

47 'Empire' stone was a cast concrete which took colour and a hand-finished surface appearance. Made by the Empire Stone Works at Narborough, Leicestershire, which traded from 1900 to 1994; its last project was Terry Farrell's MI6 building at Vauxhall Cross, London.

48 Hamp was a promoter of pre-cast concrete construction, notably for wartime civil defence; *The Times*, 28 January 1939, p. 8, 4 February 1939, p. 8, 18 February 1939, pp. 13, 18, Monday, 6 May 1940, p. 4, *Builder*, 24 February 1939; (on-line access March 2013).

49 *The Times*, 18 March 1978, obituary, p. 16.

50 *Daily News*, 27 October 1928; Victoria and Albert Museum, 'design for harlequin' signed and dated 1926; acc.no. E.625-1928.

51 Bradshaw archive, as note 3; quoted in Seddon, as note 43, p. 239.

52 *Ibid.*

53 *Architectural Review*, as note 32.

54 For Dobson's 'polistone' groupings see *Architectural Review*, February 1932, vol. LXXI, no. 423, p. 49. for Charoux's contribution to the Festival of Britain (1951) see M. Banham and B. Hillier, *A Tonic to the Nation, The Festival of Britain 1951*, London, 1976, illus. pp. 94–95.

55 Advertisements, *Oxford Times*, 23.10.31, p. 17. The Concrete Stone Co. Ltd, Ranelagh Gardens, Fulham, 'Veronese cast stone and white stucco', and Messrs Constone Co. Ltd of Leicester, supplied materials for the RI site; the latter was in business at South Wigston until *c*. 2010; author checked via telephone directory and web.

removed in the renovation and reorganisation of the building in the mid-1970s,[56] revealing or perhaps being replaced by the ashlared stone surfaces of the quoins (fig. 1).

Bradshaw's three low-relief figures from the Nurses' Residence (fig. 2) are stylistically much more conventional than *Maternity*. The treatment of the three is identical, and recalls the distinctive and highly stylised cinema decoration of the period.[57] Their facture is sand-cast rather than carved, which implies an altogether cheaper and quicker approach to commission. Fig. 2a appears to be a visual conflation of the Greek god of medicine, Aesculapius, and of Hippocrates, the Ancient Greek 'Father of Western Medicine'. The snake was an early symbol of fertility, of rebirth and healing. Fig. 2b seems to be another conflated image: the goat-horned lyre is associated with Asteria who, fleeing Zeus, escaped by metamorphosing into the Island of Delos, where Leto gave birth to Apollo, the god of healing. Apollo in turn was the father of Aesculapius, whom he had torn from his mother's womb and given to the centaur Chiron to rear. Lyres are associated with the finding of the infant Moses who, later, with the help of a brazen serpent, cured his people of a pestilence. The third figure, *Hygieia*, was one of the five daughters of Aesculapius, all of whom had medical attributes (figs. 2c, 8). Specifically associated with health, cleanliness, and sanitation, hence 'hygiene', Hygieia's attribute is a snake drinking

56 Benfield and Loxley were responsible for the work, which cost £249,999, but apparently no documentation survives. Graham Varney, Director of Messrs Benfield and Loxley Ltd, in conversation with the author, March 2013.

57 See J. Alexander, designs for a cinema interior, probably Newcastle, 1930s. Watercolour; RIBA (4030, 4004); www.ribapix.com/index; accessed 11.03.13.

8. Laurence Bradshaw, photograph of the three reliefs for the Nurses' Residence, Radcliffe Infirmary, Oxford, 1931–32, possibly at maquette stage (photo: courtesy Henry Moore Institute, Leeds (Bradshaw archive, acc. no.53/1994)).

9. Collcutt & Hamp, architects' office photograph, Entrance to the Maternity Department, showing relief panels with bird and foliage ornament, 1931. (photo: courtesy Henry Moore Institute, Leeds (Bradshaw archive acc.no. 53/1994)).

from a vessel. These attributes can also identify the virtue of Prudence, as expressed in the New Testament.[58] There may even be in the leafing tree a subliminal reference to Eve, the mythical mother of all mothers. These possible layers of meaning suggest a none too sophisticated acknowledgement of context for a maternity department in a university city.

The only references to Bradshaw's work at the Radcliffe Infirmary appear to be in the *Architects' Journal*, where he is named in a caption, and the *Architectural Review* for March 1932.[59] The Review concludes a short editorial by saying that Bradshaw is 'now engaged upon 3 more figures for a new section of the Infirmary'.[60] It was the archival material at the Henry Moore Institute which definitively confirmed the Oxford Radcliffe Infirmary reliefs as his work through contemporary photographs (figs 7a, 7b, 8).[61]

The silence surrounding the commission may in part have been the result of Morris's overweening desire for social recognition. Throughout this period he was making connections via his private golf club at Huntercombe with men such as Farquhar Buzzard, who was also physician to the King, the Prince of Wales, the Duchess of York, and several Prime Ministers.[62] The control exercised by Morris over the development of the Radcliffe Infirmary affected every aspect of it, when 'in the difficult days ... the Professors descended upon the Infirmary', as Morris put it in a letter to Arthur Sanctuary, the Radcliffe Infirmary Administrator from 1921, who had clearly supported Nuffield throughout, on the latter's retirement in 1951.[63] It is significant that press photography avoids any image of the architectural

58 '... be ye as wise as serpents ...' Matthew 10: 16; See Alfred Waterhouse's Prudential Building, Holburn (1879) for two cast terracotta figures by William Birnie Rhind RSA (1853–1933).

59 *Architects' Journal*, December 1931, vol. 74, No. 1925, pp. 763–66.

60 *Architectural Review*, as note 32.

61 Inscribed on the back of a photograph of the Main Entrance to the Maternity Department, Radcliffe Infirmary Oxford: 'Oxford. Radcliffe Maternity Home main doorway. Carved and designed by Lawrence Bradshaw in Stone'; Collcutt and Hamp, Architects Office Photograph; HMI, as note 3.

62 Nuffield College Archive, inter alia Ms Nuffield N7/9/1, N7/11, N/7/20/1, N/7/21.

63 Nuffield to Sanctuary, 27 November 1951; see note 6, printed in OHA (pam. 920 NUFF).

ornament, preferring to concentrate on the personalities and the crowds attending the opening ceremony of the Maternity Wing, the cornerstone to Morris's ensuing social, political and philanthropic success.

After the war stone was in short supply as quarries were closed under nationalisation plans, and demand was high for the rebuilding programmes of the period. Economics and style converged, and casting methods were preferred in the era of Portland cement and Brutalist architecture. For Bradshaw, who had lost the entire contents of his studio, and with it almost all previous documentation, in a direct hit in 1940,[64] the post-war years saw a change in practice when, as did Epstein, Moore and a younger generation, he adopted modelling and bronze casting. Like Epstein, Bradshaw made a second, socially successful career in portrait sculpture. Ironically, Bradshaw's portrait style, specifically his memorial to Karl Marx and his portrait bust of George Pitt-Rivers, appealed to social realists across the political spectrum, both right and left. His cuttings albums in the Henry Moore Institute Archive are full of such contradictions,[65] but then extremes of political left and right are never far apart in socio-anthropological terms.

Postscript

The buildings were demolished in 2008 but the sculpture was salvaged after a public outcry and will be conserved and re-sited by the University in the vicinity of the Jericho Medical Centre, Walton Street, in autumn 2015.

Acknowledgements

I would like to thank Philip Ward-Jackson; Simon Bailey, Keeper of the Archives University of Oxford; Jackie Howson and Claire Mayoh, Henry Moore Institute, Leeds; Elizabeth Boardman, Archivist, Oxfordshire Health Archives, and Rachel Hancock and colleagues at the Oxfordshire History Centre, St Luke's, Cowley; Stella Wentworth and colleagues in the Local History Library, Central Library, Westgate, Oxford; Sara Murray and Graham Varney, Directors of Benfield and Loxley Ltd, Cowley; Clare Kavanagh and colleagues in the Nuffield College Library; Mark Norman, Head of Conservation, Ashmolean Museum, Oxford; Michael O'Leary of Collcutt & Hamp, Chesham, Bucks; Meghan Dickenson, Oxford University Estates Department; Debbie Taylor, Planning & Building Control, Oxford City Council; Anna Buruma, Central Saint Martin's College of Arts and Design Museum and Study Collection; Polly Holbrook and Ann Compton, Andrew Moss, Peter Howell, Ian Leith, Mark Stocker, Giles Woodforde, and my husband James Hamilton.

64 Inscription in Blue Book Press Cuttings; HMI, BR/M12.
65 Correspondence; HMI 53.1994/BR/C1/7; drawings (BR/D/H); press cuttings, (BR/M/10, and 11/45).

Philip Hendy and the South Wing Bedrooms at Temple Newsam: villain or hero?

Anthony Wells-Cole

There can be little argument that Philip Hendy (1900–1980) has been the most significant Director of the City Art Gallery in Leeds since its foundation in the 1880s. He was appointed to the post in 1934, having already worked at the Wallace Collection in London and the Museum of Fine Arts in Boston. For eight years — from 1937 until he left Leeds in December 1945 for a prestigious job in London — he was also responsible for Temple Newsam, the great house bought with its landscaped park from the Hon. Edward Wood in 1922. This article concentrates on Hendy's adaptation of South Wing bedrooms 'which have never contained anything of serious historical or artistic interest' for art exhibitions during the Second World War;[1] and the evidence for their former appearance which has emerged during their restoration in 1983 and 2004–05.

These rooms came into existence as a result of alterations during the half-century from the 1740s to the 1790s designed to modernise Temple Newsam and make it more appropriate for contemporary life. Until then the South Wing had remained virtually unchanged from its completion by Thomas Lord Darcy in about 1520: parlour, great hall, buttery and pantry on the ground floor, with cellars and kitchens below (and staircase in the angle of the South and West Wings); Great Chamber above, with some private accommodation over the kitchen. Sir Arthur Ingram had substantially remodelled much of the house in the twenty years from 1622 until his death, adding a larger parlour to the west and introducing a newel staircase (with a door out onto the terrace overlooking the formal parterre) between this and the hall. The original Great Chamber, regularly enriched and still listed in an inventory dated 1740, may shortly afterwards have been divided in two, to provide a new first-floor dining room and drawing room with plasterwork by Thomas Perritt who had been responsible for the plasterwork of the Library and Picture Gallery in the North Wing. But it was not until Charles, last Viscount Irwin, had James Wyatt move the main staircase away from the south front in 1777, and his widow, Frances, commissioned a Wyatt pupil, William Johnson, to move the kitchen and larders to the basement of the North Wing across the courtyard in the 1790s, that the South Wing could finally be properly south-facing, looking out over Capability Brown's landscaped park: five ground-floor reception rooms and bedroom accommodation above for some of Frances's daughters and grand-daughters, all behind a facade which mixes Classical and gothick detail in a curious amalgam (fig. 1).[2]

1 Annual Report [AR] of the Sub-Libraries and Arts Temple Newsam Mansion Committee for the year ended 31st March, 1939. These Annual Reports, together with Hendy's monthly Director's Reports [DR] to committee, and his informal notes on interiors in the house [HN] are in the files at Temple Newsam. So too are notes made by the present author [AWC] on discoveries made during the restoration of the house: those dealing with the South Wing are particularly extensive.

2 This passage made it impossible for the fireplace in the State Bedroom to share the chimney serving the great hall, which is on the north wall, so its fireplace was placed on the east wall, more or less over the middle of the great hall ceiling. To prevent the weight of a tall brick chimney bearing on the middle of a floor joist supporting the ceiling of the Hall, Johnson introduced a pair of subsidiary trusses — independent of, but parallel to the roof trusses — to take the weight of this chimney from a point above the ceiling to the chimney pot. Similarly, the south wall of the passage is a light-weight timber stud partition, and even this is trussed so that its weight is transferred to the cross-walls that divide the rooms below. All this is rather ingenious but its structural integrity was severely compromised in 1940–42 when the 'chimney-trusses' were severed in order to improve access around the underdrawings in case of fire-bombing: noticeable deflection to the floors of the bedrooms and dressing rooms resulted, and the ceiling of the Great Hall developed cracks.

1. The South Wing of Temple Newsam at the time of the visit of the Duke and Duchess of York in 1894.

Johnson divided the space further, a State Bedroom in the centre, dressing rooms either side, and a connecting passage overlooking the courtyard. So, from east to west, these first-floor rooms are now known as the Prince's Room (after the Prince of Wales who visited in 1868), lobby from a service stair, South Bedroom and Dressing Room, State Bedroom (with the bay window) and Dressing Room, French Bedroom (otherwise known as Lady William Gordon's Room) and Darnley Room at the west end — with the Grey Room immediately north of it. Although recorded in inventories in 1808, 1869, 1871 and 1904, there is no indication of how they were first decorated apart from the implication that, as no silk wall-hangings were mentioned, all must have had wallpapers.[3] The seven-day auction that followed the transfer of the house to Leeds Corporation in 1922 virtually emptied the interiors of their contents so that five years later, when a guidebook was published in 1927, their principal interest must have been in their spectacular Victorian wallpapers: the Prince's Room was said to contain only the double portrait of Henry 7th Viscount Irwin and his wife Anne, and eight other portraits; the South Bedroom only a portrait of Willem II, Prince of Orange, a bedstead and a seventeenth-century wardrobe; the South Dressing Room 'a number of Arundel prints'. The State Bedroom seems to have had just the Benjamin Wilson portrait of the five sisters, daughters of the last Viscount and Viscountess, while the State Dressing Room 'is hung with reproductions of well-known pictures. The French Room … contains some unimportant pictures'.[4]

3 In 1808 these rooms, again from east to west, were described as: 'Right Wing Attic — 1st Room at the End …
2d. Room Mrs Meynell's [third daughter of Lady Irwin, married Hugo Meynell 1782] …
3d. Room unfinished …
4th. Room Miss Meynell's [Elizabeth, younger daughter of Mrs Meynell] …
5th. Room, Miss Gordon's [Frances Isabella Keir Gordon, only daughter of Lord and Lady William Gordon] …
6th. Room Lady William Gordon's [Frances Ingram-Shepheard, second daughter of Lady Irwin, married Lord William Gordon 1781] …
7th. Room or Crimson Damask Bed room [so named from the silk bed furniture].'
4 S. D. Kitson and E. D. Pawson, *Temple Newsam* (Leeds, 1927), 39–40.

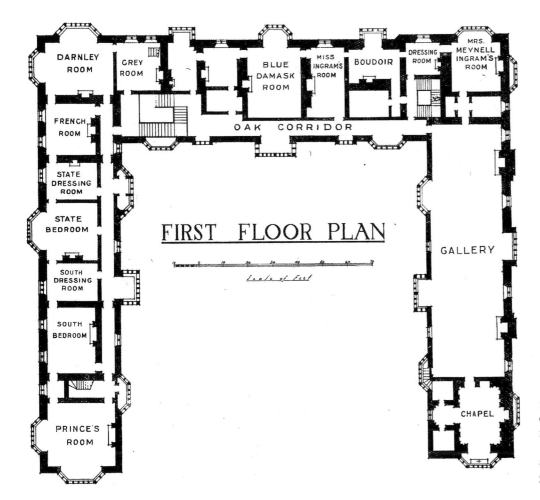

FIRST FLOOR PLAN

Scale of feet

2. Plan of the first floor of Temple Newsam. Taken from the seventh edition (1936) of Sydney Kitson's and Edmund Pawson's guide book.

No wonder Philip Hendy, after he had taken Temple Newsam under his wing on 8 April 1937, felt that these rooms '... have never contained anything of serious historical or artistic interest'. Reporting on the opening of his ground-breaking exhibition *Pictures and Furniture from Yorkshire Houses* in May 1938, Hendy noted: 'I have had to give most of my time to Temple Newsam during the month; but I think that the interests of the Mansion and the Gallery, if not identical, are quite complementary. Together they cover a very large field of interests, and the stimulation of that enlargement reacts beneficially upon each of them.' But the Munich crisis later that year turned his mind to preparations for possible war, in particular the use of the house for the storage and display of works of art from the Art Gallery. In an undated report, *In Case of War*, he suggested that 'The functions of the Gallery would be carried on sufficiently well in a building without a glass roof situated towards the edge of the town, where the chances of a direct hit would be less ... Temple Newsam would seem to be the ideal building.'

As early as May 1939 Hendy had identified four of the bedrooms and dressing rooms in the South Wing as ideal for display and by March 1940 had adapted three of them 'as galleries for modern paintings' — all this while redecorating the Great Hall below and the Picture Gallery in the North Wing, as well as making preparations for the possible invasion of Britain which included establishing a 'shooting-range in the cellar'.[5] By the end of June 1941 he had redecorated the Grey Room, also the South Passage and two rooms in readiness for the exhibition of work by

5 Hendy's undated 1940 report, *The Defence of Temple Newsam*.

3. The State Bedroom in 1941, during the Moore, Piper, Sutherland exhibition, with the South Dressing Room beyond.

4. The South Dressing Room during the First World War: this is the only record of the Victorian wallpaper removed in 1940.

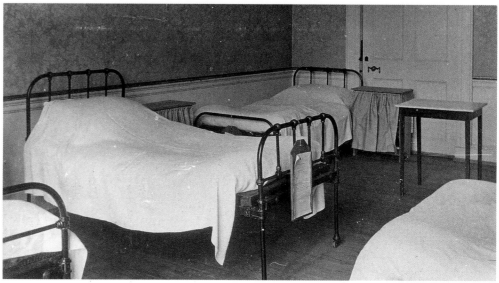

Graham Sutherland, John Piper and Henry Moore. Reporting on his temporary exhibitions of modern art at Temple Newsam in March 1941, Hendy noted that the exhibitions 'could not have been held if it had not been possible to continue to some extent the work of restoring the interior of the building. This has been confined however to the stairs and First Floor of the South Wing, where the repairs have made this part of the house a unit well fitted for exhibitions'.[6] Inexplicably he believed that they 'have also given back to it something of its architectural dignity.' The effect of the transformations can be seen in one of only three contemporary photographs, showing the former State Bedroom — and South Dressing Room beyond — during the 1941 exhibition of the work of Henry Moore, John Piper and Graham Sutherland (fig. 3): all the doors were taken off their hinges (but fortunately stored) and emulsion paint was used in place of the Victorian wallpapers (fig. 4). Picture rails reduced the apparent height of the walls and facilitated the hanging of pictures. By these means he contrived to make rooms look more like 'galleries'. Just out of the photograph of what had been the State Bedroom, the chimney piece was removed which (as Hendy later said of another room) 'made the hanging [of an exhibition, The Life Work of Richard Sickert, shared with the National Gallery in London] much easier.' As I wrote in 2005, 'Most damaging of the wartime alterations was the removal of chimneypieces from three of the seven rooms [on the first floor of the South Wing] and walling up the openings ... In the 1950s two more chimneypieces were replaced with ones from other houses.'[7] Equally damaging was his walling-across of two of the door openings. Unblocking one of these in 2004–05 revealed that this had been achieved with timber cannibalised from the historic runs of servants' bell-wires above the ceilings, a measure that Hendy specifically mentioned in his revealing account of work on the Domestic Passage on the ground floor of the North Wing where 'a great many obsolete pipes and wires and bells have been removed and have yielded a quantity of scrap. I have kept the chief row of bells, with their room titles, for sentimental reasons. The architecture is being simplified so that cleaning and decorating will be easier in future.' These words are equally applicable to his treatment of the South Wing: 'In the office [the former South Bedroom, last but one at the east end] the wall-papers, which were seven deep, were threatening to come down altogether and were harbouring a great deal of dirt and smoke.'[8] It was probably at this time that the celebrated Storks and Thrushes wallpaper which had been hung for a visit by the Prince of Wales in 1868 was finally removed (fig. 5), and Hendy's method of transforming the room into a 'gallery' was followed by one of his successors (fig. 6).

Hendy's intentions for Temple Newsam were absolutely clear and fully justified by the prevailing circumstances:

The main policy which has been pursued from the beginning has been twofold: the furnishing of the house, and the holding of loan exhibitions of modern art. The furnishing of an old house with furniture of the same period as the interior decoration is not in itself an idea of which the results can often escape the charge of deadness. There can be too much uniformity of style; there can be too carefully spontaneous an arrangement. These are inclined to suggest the habitation of ghosts ... A historical harmony may be a dead harmony, while an aesthetic harmony is always a living one ... The Art Gallery has yet to be built which is as beautiful as the English country house ...[9]

Aesthetics were paramount for Hendy. His alterations elsewhere in the house were the product not of wartime necessity — as were those in the South Wing

6 AR 1942. Hendy's exhibitions at Temple Newsam included Pictures and Furniture (1938), Chinese Art (1940), French Paintings of the 18th and 19th Centuries (1940), Drawings and Watercolours by Augustus John and other British Artists (1941), Henry Moore, John Piper, Graham Sutherland (1941), Jacob Epstein, Matthew Smith (1942), Paul Nash, Barbara Hepworth (1943), Roy de Maistre, Henri Gaudier Brzeska (1943), Philip Wilson Steer O.M. 1860–1942 (1944), Paintings by Ben Nicholson (1944), Ivon Hitchens, Henry Moore (1945). Among the hundreds of thousands of people who sought solace and inspiration at Temple Newsam during the war was the celebrated ceramicist Hans Coper, some of whose work is in the collection at Lotherton Hall.
7 Restoration! The Rebirth of a House (notes to an exhibition at Temple Newsam in 2005). Actually, Hendy removed the one in the Darnley Room in 1945: under the heading 'Restorations' he wrote in May that year that 'the modern stone mouldings [in the Darnley Room] have been removed from the fireplace and hearth, and the oak panelling and the pine floor have been made up over the gaps.'
8 DR 23 March 1942: no historic wallpapers were found during the restoration of this room in 1983.
9 AR 1942/3

bedrooms — but of improving, as he saw it, what the eighteenth- and nineteenth-century owners had left imperfect. This is not the place to discuss Hendy's impact on the rest of the fabric of Temple Newsam.[10] Many — most, even — of the results were frankly disastrous so that, from a country house perspective, perhaps it was as well that in December 1945 he left to succeed his near contemporary Sir Kenneth Clark (1903–1983) as Director of the National Gallery in London. His legacy at Temple Newsam was so strong, however, and his personality so magnetic that his policy of holding temporary exhibitions — now of decorative art rather than of modern art, as these collections had returned to the Art Gallery after the war — in the bedrooms and dressing rooms of the South Wing, allied to a cavalier attitude to a great historic house continued under two subsequent directors, right up until July 1983.[11] By then, the fashion for presenting the visiting public with a great country house shown simply as a backdrop for displays of the decorative arts, irrespective of its historic role as a place where family and servants lived and worked, had long had its day.

That year, 1983, in preparation for the exhibition *Historic Paper Hangings* [wallpapers] *from Temple Newsam and other English Houses*, five of the eight rooms were redecorated with wallpapers made in collaboration with the company that became Zoffany (three of these are still in place) and display cases that had been inserted into 'redundant' doorways began to be removed so that doors could be re-hung, and opened to provide vistas from the South Passage into the bedrooms and dressing rooms beyond. Together, the two phases of restoration, in 1983 and 2004–05, revealed not only the extent of Hendy's (and others') interventions but also some precious evidence of the original 1790s alterations by Frances, dowager Viscountess Irwin, and successive programmes of decoration at intervals of thirty or forty years. Thus a fragmentary wallpaper discovered still *in situ* on one wall of the lobby to the Prince's Room may also have hung in the Prince's Room next door and may date from the 1790s. Otherwise the earliest survivals must belong to the late 1820s alterations by her eldest daughter Isabella, the widowed Marchioness of Hertford, which seem to have affected every room in the South Wing. On the ground floor she remodelled the Great Hall and the two rooms either side to provide withdrawing rooms for the ladies — with a Chinese wallpaper given by her former *confidant* the Prince of Wales — and the gentlemen, to the east, with a breakfast room (hung with a pair of Brussels tapestries from the same source) and dining room to the west. This work may or may not have been occasioned by a disastrous fire mentioned in a single early twentieth-century reference.[12] The Regency survivals upstairs include a characteristic striped wallpaper uncovered in the State Bedroom and Dressing Room which had been decorated ensuite — a facsimile reproduction made by Allyson McDermott in 2005 has been hung in both these interiors — and a handsome set of cast iron fire-bars in the South Dressing Room, concealed (along with some gilt metal curtain rings and bits of gilded *papier-mâché*) when Hendy walled up the fireplace: this was married up when the room was restored in 2004–05 with a bright steel register surround which Hendy had banished to the cellars, and a genuine Regency chimneypiece bought in London.[13]

After Isabella's death in 1834 the next phase of redecoration was probably done in preparation for the visit of the Prince of Wales in 1868 when a blue-ground wallpaper printed with a damask-type pattern was hung in two of the rooms: reprinted by Allyson McDermott, this has been hung in the South Dressing Room

10 Ana Baeza Ruiz, a PhD Candidate in History of Art and Museum Studies at the University of Leeds/National Gallery, London, is writing her dissertation on Philip Hendy as a case study for the history of curatorship and its political, social and cultural contexts.

11 These exhibitions included *Chippendale Furniture* (1951), *Yorkshire Church Plate* (1958), *Glass* (1961), *Oriental Carpets* (1964).

12 Charles, 2nd Lord Halifax, in his speech when the house opened to the public in 1923; there are certainly charred structural timbers in the roof space over the Darnley Room at the west end of the wing, which have (probably mistakenly) been associated with the disastrous fire in 1636.

13 A window seat made in the 1940s and discovered on the joists above the ceiling has also been rebuilt here. The 2004–05 restoration reversed all Hendy's interventions in turning these rooms into 'galleries' in the 1940s. Besides obliterating chimney pieces and hearths, he had blocked the door from the State Bedroom to the South Passage and removed the jib-door (a concealed door decorated with the room) from the State Dressing to the bedroom beyond, Lady William Gordon's; as no historic wallpapers have been found here, another Regency stripe wallpaper, from her husband's dressing room elsewhere in the house, was reprinted and hung in 2005.

x

5.   The South Bedroom in 1868, hung with the 'storks and thrushes' wallpaper in preparation for the visit of the Prince of Wales in 1868.

6.   The South Bedroom during the Chippendale exhibition in 1952: the Victorian wallpaper has been removed and the chimneypiece concealed behind the bed.

7. The Darnley Room as decorated for the visit of the Duke and Duchess of York in October 1894.

8. The Darnley Room as transformed c. 1897.

172 PHILIP HENDY AND TEMPLE NEWSAM

where no historic wallpapers have been found.[14] The South Bedroom next door had what has become a celebrated wallpaper pattern incorporating storks (or cranes) and thrushes, visible (along with the handsome contemporary fossiliferous chimneypiece and fire-grate) in a single photograph of these first-floor rooms taken at the time of the 1868 visit (see fig. 5). Another 1860s damask-type wallpaper was found in the lobby between this room and the Prince's Room. Its pattern is identical to the crimson flock wallpaper hung in the Picture Gallery in 1826 but here it was simply printed in blue on a yellow ground. Both these spectacular Victorian wallpapers were reprinted by Zoffany and returned to the rooms in 1983.[15]

Emily Meynell Ingram had these bedrooms and dressing rooms redecorated in 1894 for another royal visit, this time by the Duke and Duchess of York. The easternmost room, which bears his name, received a wallpaper by Woollams and Co. in a pattern named *The Birkdale*.[16] After a chimney fire on New Year's Night in 1903 it was replaced by an even grander wallpaper which her brother also had in his great house at Hickleton near Doncaster. The most radical alterations were in the rooms at the west end of the South Wing. Here, the so-called Darnley Room — a complete misnomer for the room didn't come into existence until sixty years after Darnley's death — was first of all provided with a bed alcove by panelling across the windows of the south-facing bay, and hanging the walls with another version of the Storks and Thrushes wallpaper (fig. 7).[17] No more than three years after the royal visit, Mrs Meynell Ingram had the room completely panelled out in the early-English manner, with plaster ceiling and frieze copied from genuine examples elsewhere in the house and a fireplace to match (fig. 8). Hendy obliterated this in 1945 to provide space for the display of a tapestry (fig. 9) and redecorated the Grey Room next door which Mrs Meynell Ingram had hung with a polychrome French wallpaper with a pattern originating in an English printed cotton; the wallpaper was reprinted by Zoffany's and hung in 1983. The current Temple Newsam guide-book illustrates the present-day appearance of all but one of these South Wing bedrooms and dressing rooms (numbered 24–31), restored — after the depredations wrought by Hendy and his successors — with reinstated doors and chimneypieces where necessary, and wallpapers reprinted from originals dating from the late 1820s, 1868 and 1894. In the State Dressing Room restoration revealed the extent and ingenuity of Hendy's wartime intervention. When he removed the chimney-piece he blocked the opening with timber won from the bedroom next door, and from another room in the North Wing, with fragments of its Regency crimson flock wallpaper still adhering. A historic jib door was another victim of his determination to convert the room into a picture gallery: its reinstatement in 2004 led to the discovery of the moulded stone jamb of the early-Tudor entrance to the Great Chamber — proving incidentally that the Great Hall below had always been single-storeyed.[18]

So, the verdict on Philip Hendy at Temple Newsam? Villain or hero? For going beyond what was necessary in wartime to convert bedrooms and dressing rooms into galleries for pictures, undoubtedly a villain. But for his transformation of an empty house into a living museum of art, celebrated nationally, the writer of the Annual Report for 1945–46 was near the mark: 'In the last six years ... there has been full concentration on the development of Temple Newsam, the restoration of which stands as a monument to Mr Hendy's foresight and outstanding capabilities.

14 Apart from two tiny fragments of uncertain date.
15 The storks and thrushes paper was wrongly thought to be eighteenth century, possibly by the Eckhardt family of Chelsea in London (see Sugden and Edmondson, *A History of English Wallpaper*, London, 1926, p. 65); Emily Meynell Ingram also hung the damask-type wallpaper in her bathroom in the North Wing, and in the Drawing Room of her Staffordshire country house, Hoar Cross, which was built from 1862 onwards.
16 At the same time, the State Bedroom and Dressing Room received matching yellowish wallpapers, in a pattern based on silk damask. The Prince's Room was restored in 1983 with a facsimile of the wallpaper probably hung there in 1868; subsequently a photograph taken in 1894 was found, which enabled the *Birkdale* wallpaper design to be identified.
17 This work is mentioned in a letter from F. L. Wood to Mrs Meynell Ingram dated 6 July 1894: 'The window in Darnley Room is covered with very nice panels and when painted white will need no covering' (Hoar Cross MS, BB. Letters to E.C.M.I. 44a). Hendy (following Sugden and Edmondson, see note 15, Pl. 65) thought the storks and thrushes wallpaper here was probably of 1796.
18 The sixteenth-century jamb has traces of painted decoration, probably the marbling done by Henry Long in 1687–88.

9.   The Darnley Room after Hendy's removal of the chimneypiece *c. 1945*.

Under his direction it has become one of the most famous art museums in the country.' In the seventy years that have elapsed since Hendy's time, the decoration and furnishing of the house under successive directors and curators have been immeasurably enriched and accompanied by dynamic programmes of exhibitions, cataloguing, publication and education. Terry Friedman, who began his distinguished career in Leeds at Temple Newsam, would rightly have hoped that the place — after the present period of atrophy without curators — will somehow regain its place as the leading country house museum in Britain.

Chamberlin, Powell and Bon in Leeds:
a contextual reading

Penelope Curtis

Introduction

Nothing much has been published on Chamberlin, Powell and Bon (CPB) since 1974, when its huge extension for the University of Leeds was described as 'university-as-ideal-city' with its 'indoor streets' and 'linear places', 'great flights of steps, the high bridges and their tall propylaea-like piers'. It was also assessed as 'one of the most convincing outdoor spaces that British post-war architecture has to show'.[1] The work of CPB for the university embodies (as well as, if not better than, their work in the Barbican) a number of key aspects associated with contemporary architectural discourse on the collective heart of the city (fig. 1).

1 Lance Wright, 'University of Leeds: Criticism', *Architectural Review*, January 1974, p. 21.

1. Chamberlin, Powell and Bon, University of Leeds. The Mathematics, Earth Sciences and Physics block in on the left, with the Roger Stevens Lecture Theatre block on the right. The photograph shows this part of the campus shortly after completion, c. 1970 (photo: John Maltby, reproduced with the permission of University of Leeds Archive).

Gradually over the years, the monumental project which is the 1958–68 Leeds campus suggested itself to me both as a point of departure and as a point of return. The Leeds scheme has helped me clarify the material expression of the post-war relationship between sculpture and architecture. The 'New Monumentality' by which this relationship may be known is more conventionally associated with the sculptural importance of the buildings of Louis Kahn, Oscar Niemeyer, or Pier Luigi Nervi, but in Leeds we have a site closer to home, and closer to our everyday actuality.

I lived in Leeds for sixteen years and walked through the University Campus twice a day following my appointment as Terry Friedman's successor as Head of the Centre for the Study of Sculpture.[2] In that time I not only came to appreciate its tremendous audacity, I also began to see how that audacity was being eroded through superficial but deleterious efforts to make it prettier, clearer, or more 'up-to-date'. Contemporary artists had perhaps been the chief way in which my eyes were opened to the contemporaneity of this site: their work elsewhere in the world gradually situated for me the exceptional resource which we had here amongst us, a site that was both a building and a stage, a set of objects with their own backdrop. The more I came to know about it, the more I feared for its future, and I enlisted the help of artists and others in an exercise to get the campus listed by English Heritage. This was eventually effected, in June 2010, and the research outlined below began in my enthusiasm to understand its context.[3]

The New Monumentalty

During the Second World War, and immediately after it, some architects became preoccupied with the absence of architectural schemes that went beyond the merely functional. Nevertheless, given their familiarity with the recent building projects of Fascist regimes, they were equally nervous about promoting an architecture that was overtly aspirational. This search for a balance — between symbolism on the one hand and democracy on the other — was explored by a number of architects at this time, and it came to merge with the concern to find a way of integrating fine artists into the work of architects.

Perhaps the best known 'manifesto' of the New Monumentality is that compiled by the architect J. L. Sert, the artist Fernand Léger and the critic Sigfried Giedion. Their 'Nine Points on Monumentality' was produced as early as 1943, and though it was overtaken by Giedion's essay 'The Need for a New Monumentality', published the following year, it is still one of the clearest expressions of the debate.[4] The three authors stressed that monuments are 'intended to outlive the period which originated them', that they 'express the collective force' and are only possible when there is a 'unifying consciousness'. They noted that monumentality had been devalued since the mid-nineteenth century, and that 'so-called monuments of recent date have become empty shells'. They accepted that modern architects had to begin by tackling utilitarian buildings, but suggested that now they must address urban schemes in which 'monuments should constitute the most powerful accents'.

Sites for monuments must be planned. This will be possible once re-planning is undertaken on a large scale which will create vast open spaces in the now decaying areas of our cities. In these open spaces, monumental architecture will find its appropriate setting ...

Monumental architecture will be something more than strictly functional. It will have regained its lyrical value. In such monumental layouts, architecture and city planning could attain a new freedom and develop new creative possibilities ...[5]

2 I was at first appointed as Terry Friedman's successor as Head of the Centre for the Study of Sculpture but later was instrumental in amalgamating this within the larger Henry Moore Institute.

3 Seven buildings, including the Stoner, Manton and Garstang; the Computer Science, Mathematics and Earth Science Buildings, the SCR and the Edward Boyle Library were Grade II listed on 10 June 2010, ref. 1393835. This research was undertaken in tandem with commissions for new works made for exhibition at the Henry Moore Institute in Leeds, and published in part at that time.

4 Giedion's text was published in Paul Zucker's New Architecture and City Planning, New York, 1944. In September 1946 Giedion gave a lecture at London's RIBA which later led to a debate entitled 'In Search of a New Monumentality' published in the Architectural Review of September 1948, and to Lewis Mumford's 'Monumentalism, Symbolism and Style' in the same journal in 1949, in which he identified a necessary 'spaciousness and "aristocratic" ease'.

5 The full text is given by Joan Ockman in her invaluable Architecture Culture 1943–68. A Documentary Anthology, New York, 1993, pp. 29–30.

Though Sert, Léger and Giedion are more than open to the work of fine artists, it is clear that for them the monument is created by an amassing of shared skills and beliefs rather than by the isolated author, however brilliant he or she may be. The monument is seen as part of the city, as the expression of a collective will, and to lie as much in architecture as in art. The monument is also 'intended to outlive' its originating period and, as such, to 'form a link between the past and the future'. The work of the fine artist, moreover, is expressed within the work of the architect, and in something which goes well beyond the individual. These buildings did not require sculpture to be added, for they were already sculptural, at least in their points of significant punctuation. The architects' interest in embedding the fine arts in a wider work of social interpretation becomes clear and might be summarised as follows:

▪ **Factual analysis and its expression**: detailed statistics gathered by interview and questionnaire were expressed in innovative diagrams, and compiled into printed reports which then serve like manuals or pattern books.[6]

▪ **Pedestrianisation**: creating 'islands' free of traffic, either by raising them on platforms or by sinking the roads around them, allowed for pedestrian streets, protected rest- and play-areas, and modern city-squares.

▪ **Hierarchy**: offsetting a linear framework of flexible, modular 'serving' blocks of residential or administrative accommodation by one-off buildings of distinctive sculptural mass allowed the 'streets' to grow while retaining the significant buildings.

▪ **Truth to materials**: using concrete to its full extent as both a 'noble' and a versatile 'sculptural' material, suited to traditional handcarving and to modern mechanised techniques.[7] The use of materials links both to the concrete monumentality of Reyner Banham's 'New Brutalism' (1966) and to the post-war interest in English 'Townscape', which embraced the 'picturesque' admixture of shapes and materials, and the surface textures of vernacular cobblestones, bricks and other 'as found' mixtures.[8]

Chamberlin, Powell and Bon

In an age of powerful polemicists, the practice comprising Chamberlin, Powell and Bon was unusually silent. They published no statements or manifestos and apparently never spoke at conferences.[9] However, and in a post-war period when huge areas of urban Britain were lying destroyed by enemy action, or were slated to be demolished for reasons of social improvement, Chamberlin, Powell and Bon were involved in planning two of the largest cleared areas, in the heart of the City of London, and in the centre of the city of Leeds.

How should we interpret the work of such silent architects? In the words they chose to use in the meticulously prepared reports for the City of London Corporation or for the Court of the University of Leeds? In the words of others? There were reviews enough in the 1950s and '60s on their newly published projects and realised schemes, even if there has been almost nothing published since. Or should we interpret their work through the language of the forms themselves?

6 Research by Bullock, Dickens and Steadman on 'The use of models' and 'The Modelling of Day to Day Activities' was presented by Leslie Martin in his books (1969, 1972) and in the *Architectural Review* (April 1970).

7 Their colleagues recall foreign trips to see fine examples of cast concrete and of experimental off-site casting.

8 Gordon Cullen – also used by CPB – is the draughtsman most associated with the 'townscape' look promulgated in the *Architectural Review*. Cullen was also used by the Smithsons.

9 CPB were not public architects in the sense that the Smithsons were; they published almost nothing and made few statements. Nevertheless Chamberlin was a member of a number of important post-war planning committees. Key friends were the architects J. M. Richards, Jim Cadbury Brown and Theo Crosby. Conversation with John Honer, Cambridge, February 2008.

The Partnership

It was Geoffry Powell's winning of the Golden Lane Estate Competition which brought Peter (Joe) Chamberlin, Geoffry Powell and Christoph Bon — who were then teaching at Kingston — into being as a practice. Chamberlin, Powell and Bon was founded in 1952, when all three, who were born between 1919 and 1921, were around the age of thirty. (Chamberlin died in 1978, Powell and Bon in 1999.)

Aside from schools (two in London and one in Shipley), a seed warehouse and two housing developments in London, the practice was dominated by three projects: Golden Lane and the Barbican (1952 onwards), New Hall, Cambridge (1958 onwards), and the University of Leeds (1958 onwards). While the Barbican stretched on into the 1970s and '80s, New Hall and Leeds were substantially finished by around 1966 and 1974 respectively. It is arguable however that the practice was at the 'top of its game' in the early 1960s, when it was most often in the news.[10]

Geoffry Powell studied at the Architectural Association in London where he was a contemporary of Powell and Moya. A family man, who was to a degree separate from his two partners, he nevertheless shared their interest in Roman antiquity. Chamberlin studied at Kingston; Bon in Zurich, but from c. 1952 they lived together in London, with Chamberlin's wife, whom Bon married after Chamberlin's death in 1978. This close-knit group, with a background of considerable financial ease and education (Chamberlin had firstly studied Politics, Philosophy and Economics at Oxford; Bon had studied in Zurich and worked with BBPR in Milan), travelled extensively round Europe, and also in India. They visited new projects by Le Corbusier — they certainly went to La Tourette and were hugely enthusiastic about Ronchamp — as well as old urban centres. Their photographs of Milan, Venice and Rome illustrate the reports which they compiled for the Barbican and for Leeds and insert the architects into a humanistic, classical lineage. These reports, designed by the typographer Herbert Spencer (who also did the signage at Leeds and at New Hall),[11] equally link the practice to the tradition of Le Corbusier and of CIAM, in terms of the reports' graphic layout and horizontal format.

The Barbican

Following the wish of the Minister of Housing and Local Government to create in the Barbican area a 'genuine residential neighbourhood', the Corporation of London set up a Special Committee to take forward a plan for mixed housing types for different income levels. CPB had first put forward plans to the Corporation's Court of the Common Council in June 1955, and a year later their report, with sketches by Gordon Cullen, revealed what was to be their characteristic combination of concentration and grouping, with a strategic and pluralistic use of space,[12] where, for example, school playgrounds by day became residential open spaces in the evenings and at weekends. Already these drawings show the monumental and idealistic quality of their thinking: an amphitheatre, ornamental ponds, canal and cascades, loggia and sculpture were overhung with dense foliage.[13]

CPB were appointed by the Barbican Committee in November 1957 to prepare in detail and obtain planning approval before the following summer. In June 1958 they reported:

10 Between 1956 and 1965 the *Architectural Review* carried reports on four of their projects.
11 Herbert Spencer (1924–2002), English champion of the continental New Typography, was known for *Typographica*, the *Penrose Annual*, *The Visible World* and as Art Director of Lund Humphries.
12 They aimed for 300 persons per acre.
13 London Metropolitan Archives (LMA): COL/cc/07/01/A/89.

The basic form of the layout follows the historical precedent to be found in urban planning of grouping buildings flanking the sides of clearly defined open spaces dating from the Greek agora and repeated in Roman forums, the piazzas, plazas and places of Renaissance Europe up to the squares which are still such a familiar feature of London.[14]

In November 1958 CPB were given leave to proceed to the final report.[15] This was published in 1959, designed by Herbert Spencer, printed by Tillotsons and prepared by thirty-two people. Kenneth Browne did the sketches. Its hardback format precedes that which was to be used for Leeds, and makes similar use of photographs of historic sites — such as the Inns of Court, the Albany apartments in Piccadilly and Carlton House Terrace — to indicate its precedents. The scheme was described as having 'three stages from the modest and often intimate layer at ground level, through the larger scale of the higher layer ... reminiscent of the London squares, to the strong vertical dimension expressed by the towers'.[16] A 'cardinal principle' was the 'segregation of pedestrians from wheeled traffic' in order to 'preserve the precinctual quality of the new neighbourhood'.[17]

New Hall, Cambridge

In 1958 the competition for an entirely new college in Cambridge heralded the way for an era of adventurous university planning in the UK.[18] CPB were shortlisted for this new Churchill College[19] in 1959 and their plan linked Churchill to two other new colleges, New Hall and Fitzwilliam. Although this scheme came to nothing for the practice (Churchill was won by Sheppard; Fitzwilliam by Denys Lasdun),[20] it is interesting to see how their plan highlights some distinctive characteristics. Their link path from Fitzwilliam and New Hall (which shared a site) down to Churchill and a further nameless college might be read as a kind of processional way, complete with significant spaces marked by features such as pools, an obelisk, an amphitheatre and a plinth for sculpture.[21] However, CPB were then commissioned to design and execute the building for New Hall (now called Murray Edwards College), a college for women, much less financially well endowed than Churchill.

This important entry into collegiate architecture clearly helped CPB consolidate their ideas around the notion of community; in the Leeds plans they also look back to the Oxbridge ideal, in which communities of scholars are housed around a quadrangle, with private spaces set in proper relation to the communal spaces of the Dining Hall, the Library and the Chapel. (In this respect it may be relevant that Bon was born in St Gall, home to a famous monastic site and library.) In New Hall each of these three features was modelled in a manner quite different to that of the residential and administrative blocks; they were higher, rounder and more monumental. They might well be seen, indeed, as sculptural, and also as symbolic. In their intermediate report of November 1959 CPB describe the Dining Hall as a 'sculptural building' which needed the right shadows on its 'modelling'.[22]

In the intermediate report offered to the Council of New Hall CPB propose that this Dining Hall should have eight 'petals', each one shaped like a horseshoe. This was partly to allow the high table to be placed at the centre, thus avoiding some of the traditional formality, but also helping the Hall to feel used even when only a few members were dining. CPB's interest in community should be understood less in the sense of equality and more in that of hierarchy, i.e. the proper relation of the parts to the whole. (Certainly associate architect John Honer sees hierarchy as key to the practice's understanding of the urban centre.) Many different

14 LMA, C/90F Barbican Redevelopment, BR/15/PC/MP.
15 LMA, Barbican Committee Minutes 1957–63.
16 LMA, CLA/072/01/016, 'Barbican Redevelopment 1959', p. 56.
17 LMA, C/65D 21 September 1959, p. 2. Almost a decade elapsed before the next report was published, again in hardback. It took into account the continually evolving objectives as regards the desirability of incorporating the Guildhall, an art gallery and a lending library, and included drawings by Norah Glover for a much expanded cultural complex, including the theatre and concert hall. In 1963 CPB were advised to plan for a larger complex and to incorporate a library.
18 This first major post-war university architectural competition attracted a high quality of submissions, including entries by CPB, Lasdun and Stirling and Gowan, and set a blueprint for the renaissance in British University building thereafter. The winners were Sheppard, Robson and Partners. CPB and Lasdun both went on to gain related commissions as a result.
19 Two firms other than CPB were also short-listed: Howell, Killick, Partridge and Amis, and Stirling and Gowan.
20 There is also a drawing by Lasdun for New Hall (in their archives) which is dated 1958.
21 From plans held in the New Hall archive.
22 New Hall archive, NHAR 4/4/9.

arrangements of tables and chairs (from the round to the cruciform) illustrate the attention CPB gave to this functional and ceremonial aspect of college life. In April 1960 the Hall was shown as cruciform, with an apse, but by July the architects were again essaying the flower-like plan, with four apses interspersed by four smaller 'petals'. A block plan from October 1958 combines the Hall and the Library and provides a grand entry into the college between two pools and with the Chapel matched by an equivalent block. Between 1959 and 1960 CPB prepared four different ways of using the site and of relating the three key buildings to each other.[23]

By October 1960 the plans for the Hall show its current configuration: a dome supported by four spiral staircases, each built into a cubic space abutting the dome. Thus New Hall acquired its distinctive profiles: the huge white dome of its Hall and the basilica-like roof and arcades of its Library. The finishes are consistent throughout: the walls are of a pale concrete (limestone and white cement) which is either polished (for rails and pillars), cast against plywood or hammered (for beams and ceilings);[24] walkways are paved in brick or stone or cobbled; interior floors are in cork or quarry tiles; interior spaces are in Iroko wood and Sevenoaks bricks.[25]

University of Leeds

In advance of their existing architect's retirement, and in anticipation of rising student numbers, the University of Leeds set out to find a new architect.[26] As J. M. Richards was then the Hoffman Woods Professor, he was asked for advice. He first suggested Leslie Martin, but as Martin was too busy Richards proposed the same architects as those who had made the Churchill shortlist: Howell, Killick, Partridge and Amis, Dick Sheppard and CPB.[27] It is known however that Denys Lasdun, James Stirling and Bill Howell were those who were interviewed alongside CPB.[28] In 1958 the University, impressed at Chamberlin's willingness to consider the case from the point of view of its fundamentals, offered him the solo appointment, but he insisted on working with his practice.

A key part of the project was to sink the Inner Ring Road so as to allow the University to be joined to the city rather than cut off from it. The City and the University reached agreement on this major engineering project, and on the substantial demolition that was required in order to make the CPB plan a reality (fig. 2). If CPB's work in Leeds was obviously influenced by other contemporary architects such as the Smithsons, it was also clearly affected by educational theory which stressed a greater 'connectivity' in terms of shared functions and links between departments. The Leeds plan was the first to quantify contacts and movements across the campus, and CPB's complex diagram became a touchstone of this approach. The impressive surveys which are a key feature of the first report were inspired by Chamberlin and effected by a team of architects and researchers, working with the university. The diagram, published in the University of Leeds Development Plan, compiled by Chamberlin, Powell and Bon in 1960, shows the results of the architects' researches into the connexions and crossovers between students and departments (fig. 3). This attempt to visualise the way the buildings would be used ten years into the future has become a famous object of fascination.

By planning for a ten-minute changeover interval for lectures, and by establishing who needed lectures on what scale and how often, CPB reduced the number of lecture theatres by one third. Much of this 'synoptic timetabling' was prepared

23 Whereas the earlier plans space out the key buildings to the margins of the residential accommodation, the later plans cluster them in the centre, using the residential blocks more as a frame. Plans from July 1959 offer two alternatives: a round chapel spaced at some distance from an oblong hall which was again separate from an oblong library or a round chapel within a pool set at right angles to the library and on an axis with the hall. By November the chapel has become oblong and is set on an axis with the library, intersected by a quadrangle with an eight-petalled hall at its end. By April 1960 the plan has assumed its present shape (partly because of a necessary change in access) with a sunken court separating the hall from the cruciform library. (The oblong chapel was never built.)
24 In the interview with Elain Harwood the visual source for the pick-hammered concrete is given as the Hall of Coal at the Exhibition of Industrial Power in the 1951 Festival of Britain.
25 Reviewing New Hall in the *Architectural Review*, July 1966, p. 17, Nicholas Taylor praised its 'beautiful' fabrication, its 'social layout' and its 'spatial fluidity' but disliked its sacrificial pomp.
26 Lanchester and Lodge acted as the University's master architects until 1958; Lanchester had died previously, Lodge retired in 1958. The CPB master plan at first catered for 7,000 students − 3,000 of whom were to be housed on campus − but this figure was later revised to 10,000. Student accommodation was provided by Christopher Bon with The Henry Price Building (1963–64) and the Charles Morris Hall (1964–66).
27 Harwood interview, 6 January 1999 with Powell, Bon and Woods. In Leeds Lawrence Gowing and Alexander Gohr were supportive of CPB.
28 Notes held in the English Heritage files; apparently supplied by Chris Hammond of the University of Leeds.

2.   Chamberlin, Powell and Bon, University of Leeds, the part-cleared site in June 1967, showing the campus's relationship with the city. The Town Hall tower is on the skyline, the new Earth Sciences and Physics block is on the extreme left, with the Department of Physical Training in the centre (photo: reproduced with the permission of University of Leeds Archive).

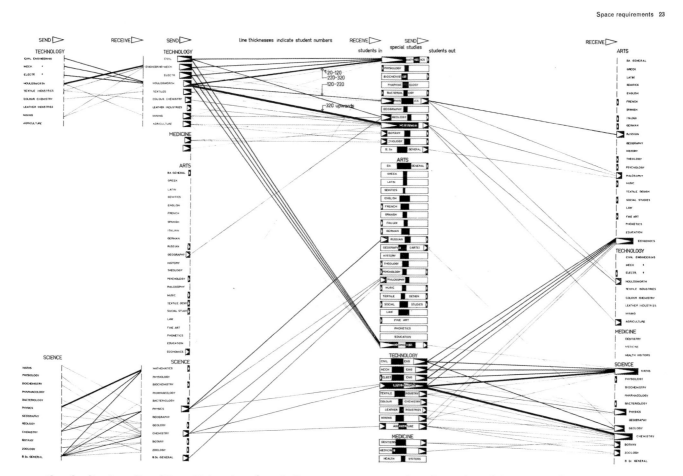

3.   Chamberlin, Powell and Bon, University of Leeds. 'Space requirements: the relationship of departments'. From the University of Leeds Development Plan, 1960 (photo: reproduced with the permission of University of Leeds Archive).

4.   Chamberlin, Powell and Bon, University of Leeds. Roger Stevens Building (1968–70) (photo: John Maltby, reproduced with the permission of University of Leeds Archive).

by Frank Woods; he recalls that economising in this way meant that they could still do something interesting with the rigid 96 shillings allowed per student by the Universities Grants Committee.[29] As the *Architects Journal* reported:

To the social brief and cost limits of the UGC has been added the stamp of the Chamberlin, Powell and Bon stable — positive, rational, yet sometimes curiously wilful and even overbearing in its mannerisms. Clearly and impressively they are creating a new order, correct as a stand against the surrounding chaos of Leeds ...[30]

As in London, CPB developed in Leeds a scheme involving a number of different levels, made more logical here by the relatively steep incline of the University's site, which rose over 216 feet, or the equivalent of eighteen storeys. The published plans[31] show the architects adhering throughout to a colour coding indicating altitude. This resulted in the attempt to link different levels across the site by horizontal walkways with individual colour codes.

The original plans for Leeds were graphically described in 1960; each of the so-called 'one-off' shapes is distinctive. The lecture halls like an 'upended concertina' (fig. 4); the sports centre with 'two truncated semi-cones on each side of a tent-like roof'; a 'sickle-shaped working library'.[32] The models which showed these shapes were white, although the building was always intended to be unpainted concrete.

29 Frank Woods in conversation with the author, Wimbledon, 28 February 2008. Woods had already executed a university plan for Stevenage when he joined CPB in 1959, and was heavily involved in the surveys and diagrams for the Leeds report. He suggests that the Bochum university plan picked up on these diagrams.
30 'M.R.' in the *Architects Journal*, July 1966, p. 12.
31 The drawings in the first report were by Norah Glover; highly impressionistic and somewhat overblown, they nevertheless gave some sense of volume to plans that were barely developed. In the next report she was replaced by a member of the CPB practice, Australian architect Darryl Jackson.
32 *Architects Journal*, May 1960, p. 787.

There were four building types:

- Spine
- Deck
- One-off
- Residential[33]

The Chancellor's Court complex was at first based on the shell domes as used by CPB at New Hall, Cambridge, and the form eventually used owed much to Louis Kahn. The first buildings were Mathematics, Earth Sciences and Computer Sciences (1966) (fig. 5), the Senior Common Room (1964–67) and the immensely long E. C. Stoner building (fig. 6). The core of the campus is the Roger Stevens Building (1968–70), with sixteen small lecture theatres and nine larger ones: these were the prototypes for the Barbican Theatre with their individual exits on every row.

By the mid-60s it is clear from correspondence that Chamberlin and Powell were not getting on well. With the failure of the University's bid to get permission to demolish the late eighteenth-century Springfield House in 1971 (and again in 1975), and with the decimation of the UGC budget in 1973 as a result of the oil crisis, the vitality seems to have gone out of the plan. In 1975 Chamberlin felt the 'cold light of reality has "frozen out" the aspiration of that period'[34] and he died only three years later. Building on the scheme continued nonetheless, with the Edward Boyle Library completed that year (extended 1994), and Economics and Social Sciences (Block 19) in 1978. However, the remainder of Blocks 19 and 38, intended in their modular design to be readily extendable, was never constructed.

5. (below) Chamberlin, Powell and Bon, University of Leeds. Departments of Mathematics, Earth Sciences and Physics (mid-1960s). View from the Senior Common Room, June 1967 (photo: reproduced with the permission of University of Leeds Archive).

33 *Architect & Builder*, February 1979, pp. 1–7.
34 Quoted by Robert Sladdin in his 'personal account' of 2003; English Heritage files.

In the comparative photographs which the architects chose for the Leeds plan (from Venice, Milan etc.) it is notable that they chose peopled spaces, and they later sought out the photographer John Donat for his skill in using people in architecture. There is a strong contrast between photographs which show the campus empty, and those which show it with students.

In the 1970s press coverage remained mainly positive: 'Human life in the city centre of the future could well be something like this, we feel ... The place is man-centred, yet has the grandeur and amplitude needed where people in quantity consort.'[35] '... you are in no doubt that you are in one of the most convincing outdoor spaces that British architecture has to show.'[36]

The major feature of 1974 from the *Architectural Review* highlights the following aspects of the scheme:

- 'an urban university'
- open to the city
- the parallels with an ordinary city centre

35 *Architectural Review*, Jan 1974, p. 3.
36 Ibid., p. 21.

6. Chamberlin, Powell and Bon, University of Leeds. E. C. Stoner Building (late 1960s) (John Maltby, reproduced with the permission of University of Leeds Archive).

- the horizontal indoor street

- the university as an ideal city

- the linear or extended 'place' (or square)

In 1977 a Spanish architectural review considered Leeds outstanding because it offered an '"ideal" city, perfectly integrated in the "real" city.'[37]

Coda

The Barbican and the Leeds schemes share a number of distinctive features. Their materials were basically the same, although the larger budget at the Barbican allowed for more expensive techniques. Both building projects lasted a long time (over fifteen years in Leeds, twenty-five in London) and were thus subject to changing trends in their interpretation. Both began in wholesale demolition but emerged into an era that was much more conservationist or conservative. CPB's relationship to old buildings is ambiguous; while in the Barbican they embraced historic traces such as city walls and monuments, in Leeds the listing of a single

37 *Informes de la Construcion*, November 1977, p. 33.

house effectively brought the scheme to an end. CPB were never afraid of 'history' and used it to make their case, both in their schemes and in the reports which were so carefully compiled to present their plans.[38]

A study of their schemes reveals CPB's deep affiliation with architectural precedents which allowed for a well-organised communal life. Italian piazzas, London terraces or Oxbridge colleges expressed the life of the individual as part of the community. It is those forms and the protected areas which they enclose — quadrangles, squares or gardens — which underlie the seemingly radical architecture of the Barbican or Leeds. This was an architecture of repetition — its potential for expansion and connectivity is clearly expressed by the diagrams — but also of distinctive 'one-off' forms. These were not just high, or circular, but extended to other more unusual shapes, such as a sickle, a fan or a concertina. These are the forms which (if equally vulnerable to criticism for their pseudo-religiosity or to budget restraints) bring us most obviously to the sculptural aspect of the New Monumentality. What this essay hopes to do is not only look back at a significant but little studied (and little loved) site in Leeds, but also to think about its inherent resonance for the future. This is more than the pious hope that this campus will soon be appreciated in the way that the Barbican is now appreciated, or that the University will start to preserve it rather than to destroy it, but rather that its formal power will inform our understanding about the relationship between social and visual aesthetics, and remind us of what can be achieved given the circumstances, even in Britain.

Acknowledgement

I am grateful to Gill Armstrong who has undertaken the picture research for this essay.

38 All the reports (two for Leeds and three for the Barbican) were designed by Herbert Spencer, who also did the lettering and signage for their buildings, including Leeds.

'We're split. The city's split, the committee's split, I even feel split myself':[1] Antony Gormley's *Brickman* and the Holbeck Triangle, Leeds

James Hamilton

On 7 November 1988 Leeds City Council turned down the final planning application that would have enabled the construction of Antony Gormley's *Brickman*, a public sculpture of international stature for a prominent site. The decision, taken by the South Division Plans Sub-Committee, on the recommendation of the Director of Planning, was a monumental loss of opportunity in the light of the subsequent success of Gormley's *Angel of the North* at Gateshead and other large-scale public sculpture projects. This paper is a first-hand account which sets out the pioneering nature and scale of the scheme, its chronology and local impact, and assesses the length of the shadow that the *Brickman* has cast.

A conversation about public sculpture opportunities in Leeds with Terry Friedman, then Principal Keeper at the City Art Gallery and head of the Henry Moore Centre for the Study of Sculpture, was an obvious first step when, in 1984, I became director of the Yorkshire Contemporary Art Group (YCAG). This was a publicly-funded organisation, comprising St Paul's Gallery in Leeds, Yorkshire Printmakers and Leeds Art Space Society, dedicated to the encouragement, funding and fostering of the visual arts in Yorkshire, with a further duty to devise and forward public art activities which might be controversial. One potential public sculpture site discussed between us was the Holbeck Triangle, two acres of disused land behind Leeds City Station. The subject had first been raised by my predecessor, Gerald Deslandes, and so the idea had been in the air some time.

The Triangle (fig. 1) is a former industrial site locked by rail lines since the mid-nineteenth century. Within it are the remains of Holbeck Lodge (1804), or 'Steam Hall', the former home of the engineer and inventor Matthew Murray (1765–1826), and reputedly the first private house in Britain to be heated by steam since the Romans.[2] Though there was no public access, except by trespass through an iron gate on Water Lane, it was the most highly visible and least regarded piece of wasteland in central Leeds, seen and yet not seen by many thousands of rail passengers every day. The site is now in active use for a purpose which, from a passing train, remains unclear.

However, the site was not seen then as having any purpose, but its promise as a site for public sculpture was clear to us. Its potential audience was large, but transitory and not always attentive, travellers preparing to get off the train at Leeds City

1 Cllr Bryan Walker, quoted in Martin Wainwright, 'Northern Brickmanship', *Guardian*, 17 October 1988.

2 Gillian Cookson, 'Murray, Matthew (1765–1826)', *Oxford Dictionary of National Biography*, Oxford University Press, 2004 [http://www.oxforddnb.com/view/article/19641, accessed 11 June 2014].

1.   Holbeck Triangle,
20 May 1988. Leeds
Museums and Galleries,
Henry Moore Institute
Archive (photograph:
British Rail).

3 BR Area Manager: Mike
Hodson; BR Community Unit
head: David Perry; Arts Council
Art for Public Places scheme:
Rory Coonan; Yorkshire Arts
Association Visual Arts Officer,
Yvonne Deane; Director of
Public Arts, Graham Roberts.
4 Peter Coles, *The Holbeck
Triangle, A Feasibility Study of Proposals
by Yorkshire Contemporary Art Group to
site Permanent Sculpture on an Inner
City Site Owned by British Rail*,
August 1985. Report
Commissioned by Yorkshire Arts
Association and the Arts Council
of Great Britain.
5 Quoted in Director of
Planning's Report, 7 November
1988, ref 88/20/00177, para
1.00, Planning Background.

Station, or to settle down for a journey. A sculptural solution for the Triangle would
need to be a work of simple lines, strong silhouette, and *gravitas* — a work that
would herald Leeds and reflect its strength, heritage, sense of self, cultural ambition
and imagination. So, with some sense of idealism, we believed that a sculpture on
the Triangle could be the prelude to the re-imagining of Leeds.

YCAG considered its approach, drawing on Terry's procedural advice. The land-
owner, British Rail, was immediately supportive. The BR Area Manager gave encouragement, and an initial grant of £35,000 came from the BR Community Unit.
Within months a further £5,500 was awarded from Business Sponsorship in the
Arts, adding to funds from the Arts Council's 'Art for Public Places' scheme, Public
Arts, and the Yorkshire Arts Association.[3] These monies paid for twenty artists to
be invited to submit proposals and for a feasibility study.[4] The project was rapidly
gaining momentum.

Planning permission for the use of the Holbeck Triangle as a 'modern sculpture
display area' was granted in October 1985, subject to conditions including the
control of access to the site and its landscaping.[5] Fifteen proposals were eventually
submitted, from Hilary Cartmel, Neil Conroy, Judith Cowan, Andrew Darke, Rachel
Fenner, Antony Gormley, Nicola Hicks, Andrew Logan, John Maine, Dhruva Mistry,

Joanna Mowbray, Charles Quick, Colin Rose, Keir Smith and Colin Wilbourn (fig. 2).

To keep the scheme in the public eye, and as an end in itself, Andy Goldsworthy was engaged for ten days as Artist-in-Residence on the Holbeck Triangle. There he produced a group of structures made from indigenous dandelions, bindweed and rosebay willow herb. These were displayed for as long as they survived on the Triangle itself in what the artist called 'a natural exhibition'. Photographs of Goldsworthy's Triangle works were subsequently shown in the exhibition *Between Trains* at St Paul's Gallery (September 1986). Goldsworthy wrote:

2. Martin Arnold (backview) with Colin Wilbourn on the Holbeck Triangle, during the artists' site visit, May 1986. Leeds Museums and Galleries, Henry Moore Institute Archive (photographer unknown).

In the ten days or so that I worked [on the Triangle] I discovered a wilderness in the city, a richness in its materials, a strong sense of its location — and an almost constant wind/breeze ... I have used the stalks, flowers and leaves to explore the nature, space and surface of the triangle — willow-herb stalks joined end to end — weaving in the direction of Leeds — constructions/scaffolding — dark lines against the sky — the same stalks split open, exposed white — hung against the internal dark space of a tunnel/entrance/hole. For me the triangle is a place of movement, growth, trains, wind — against the backdrop of Leeds.[6]

In 1989 Goldsworthy's Holbeck works were acquired by Terry Friedman for the Henry Moore Institute.[7]

Between Trains was accompanied by a public exhibition of maquettes, plans and drawings in Leeds' Bond Street Centre in September and October 1986 (fig. 3). Visitors were invited to vote on the proposals to guide the selection panel, composed of representatives of the Arts Council, British Rail, Yorkshire Arts Association, YCAG, the Henry Moore Centre and Leeds City Council.[8] The exhibits included Darke's *Holbeck Pyramid* of reflecting rainbow laser foil, Gormley's *Brickman*, Hicks's *Buffaloes*, Logan's *Reclining Nude of Leeds*, Mistry's *Reclining Nude*, Quick's *Light Line* and Wilbourn's *Water Table*, an anamorphic form of a table laid out for tea, which would appear in three-dimensions from a moving train.

One thousand and thirty-six votes were cast, with Colin Wilbourn (257) and Andrew Darke (205) emerging as the first and second choice. Antony Gormley's *Brickman*, projected to be 120 feet high, was the third choice (103). In the event, the first two had to be discounted, Wilbourn's because of the water-feature's maintenance costs, and Darke's on safety grounds, as BR feared it would flash in train drivers' eyes.

Gormley's two-metre-high maquette, *Brickman*, has a presence of overwhelming simplicity; its arms are fused to its sides, eyes blank, mouth closed, navel blind, genitalia unspecified, ankles stepped down to a brick plinth, ears formed as simple windows. The patina and layering of the bricks in the maquette, however, were peculiar to its scale. With mortar smeared here and there over the surface, and the occasional uneven brick course, the maquette had an instant antiquity, as if it were a miraculous survival from Ur, or an Ozymandian oversight. Through Terry Friedman's advocacy, the maquette was immediately bought by Leeds City Art Gallery (figs 6 and 7) where it is a popular exhibit and a reminder of what might have been.[9] However, it was clear that such rough and ready finish would not be achievable in the final work, given the pride of modern bricklayers, building regulations, and the professional guidelines of the House Builders' Federation.

The iconography of the *Brickman* is clearly recognizable as Gormley's, the form derived from a body cast of the artist. At once gentle and assertive, the *Brickman* radiates humanity and purpose, both as symbol and sentinel. In the mid-1980s, however, his was a relatively new voice, yet to resonate with the public in Britain, and not so familiar a visual language as it has since become. It followed critically acclaimed pieces such as the artist's *Bed* (1980–81) and *Still Falling* (Portland, 1983), and his 1984 exhibition at the Riverside Studios, but preceded widely known pieces *Field for the British Isles* (1993), *Another Place* (1997) and *Angel of the North* (1995–98).

Surrounding the Holbeck Triangle are three Victorian brick towers, each originally a chimney for the former pin factory, Tower Works. Modelled on Giotto's Campanile in Florence, the tower of Verona Town Hall, and the square-sectioned

6 St Paul's Gallery wall text.
7 HMI Archive, 2006.49. 'Photographs and drawings of proposals for a sculpture at Holbeck Triangle, Leeds, by Andy Goldsworthy'. See also, Terry Friedman and Andy Goldsworthy (eds), *Hand to Earth: Andy Goldsworthy Sculpture 1976–1990*, 1990, p. 63.
8 Selection panel: Cllr Pat Fathers, Leeds City Council; Dr Terry Friedman, Henry Moore Centre; Lesley Greene, Public Arts Development Trust, representing British Rail; James Hamilton, Yorkshire Contemporary Art Group; James Hurford, Arts Council; and Graham Roberts, Yorkshire Arts Association.
9 Accession number 1987.0036.

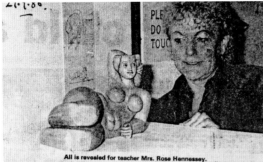

All is revealed for teacher Mrs. Rose Hennessey.

'Sculptures are off the rails for us!'

A statue of Liberty for Leeds would be the ideal sight to greet passengers arriving in the city by train, say visitors to a sculpture exhibition.

They gave the thumbs down to more intricate sculptures competing for a place on the Holbeck Triangle — a piece of waste land near the tracks leading into Leeds City Station.

The public are invited to give their views on 15 model sculptures in the Bond Street Centre, Leeds — and British Rail is giving away two first-class return tickets to London for "the most constructive comment".

Public opinion is to be taken into account when a judging panel chooses one of the works for the Holbeck Triangle.

The panel includes representatives of the Yorkshire Contemporary Art Group, British Rail, Leeds City Coun-

Story: JANET PARKIN

Pictures: TIM CLAYTON

cil, the Yorkshire Arts Association, the Arts Council of Great Britain and the Henry Moore Centre, Leeds.

A huge Leeds owl would be a better idea than most of the model sculptures, believes Mrs. Rose Hennessey, a teacher of Chapel-Allerton, Leeds.

She said: "I would like to see a figure of some kind associated with Leeds, because that would have more impact.

"I think that abstract art is not a thing most people are fond of."

She said that a huge owl might also be more vandal-

proof than more intricate sculptures.

Mrs. Hennessey added that the aim should be to create a "Statue of Liberty for Leeds".

Mrs. Pamela Krzyworaczka, 24, a civil servant, of Sandhurst Grove, Harehills, Leeds, said: "I think a lot of these sculptures need to make more of a statement. They don't stand out enough."

Retired painter and decorator Mr. Joseph Allerton — "not a Henry Moore fan" — was worried that some of the more intricate sculptures would attract vandals.

"I think this water sculpture is really nice, but you would get people climbing on it and dropping in litter."

Mr. Allerton, Whincover Drive, Old Farnley, Leeds, added: "I would like to see a figure that is recognisable as such."

Joseph Allerton, who is not too sure what to make of the work pictured on

3. 'Sculptures are off the rails for us!'.
Press cutting from Yorkshire Evening Post,
29 September 1986. Leeds Museums and
Galleries, Henry Moore Institute Archive.
Published with the permission of Yorkshire
Post Newspapers.

4. 'What a Liberty!' Press cutting from
Leeds Weekly News, 9 October 1986. Leeds
Museums and Galleries, Henry Moore
Institute Archive. Published with the
permission of Yorkshire Post Newspapers.

WHAT A LIBERTY!

100ft. man is 'sexless . . . like a Dr. Who monster'

LIBERTY STATUE FOR CITY

What's 100 feet tall, made of brick and would put the fear of God into King Kong and Godzilla put together?

You probably don't know the answer yet, along with most of the people I asked in Leeds this week, but you soon will do.

"He" is set to be the city's very own Statue of Liberty, a figure as big as a tower block and twice as imposing which will stand in the Holbeck Triangle where railway routes converge on Leeds City Station.

COMMISSION

The statue has been designed by London sculptor Antony Gormley, 36, who won the commission in competition with 14 other artists nationwide.

Gormley says of his creation: "The image is a human being made by

 You're telling us....

MIKE HURST REPORTS

collective labour. It evokes the materials and manufacture at the heart of this island. I hope it will make a contribution to building the future."

The project was thought up by the Yorkshire Contemporary Art Group and will be funded by British Rail, the Arts Council, Yorkshire Arts Association and Leeds City Council. No budget has yet been set for the work.

Director of the contemporary Art group, James Hamilton, is clearly excited by the design, and says: "It is a thrilling and inspiring project."

But what do the

people of Leeds think to the statue? The answer seems to be: "Not a lot!"

In a mini survey I found that out of 20 interviewees just three were "for" and 17 were "against."

John Naylor from Wetherby said: "It's a bit uninteresting. It looks a bit silly really although the idea of having a statue isn't bad."

Linda Brownsword, of Horsforth, commented: "It's horrible. It's nothing is it? Its more frightening than anything, there's nothing nice about it. It wouldn't attract me to go and see it."

Horsforth teenager

Michelle Dickinson thought it wasn't a patch on the original Statue of Liberty.

"As an impression of Leeds it doesn't have much impact. Next to the railway seems to be a pretty strange place to have it. It would be better in the city centre where more local people can see it.

Gary Crofts, of Bardsey, was even less impressed. "It looks a complete waste of money to me and I'm sure I could think of better things to put there," he said.

BRIGHT

"It's a good idea to have things to brighten up the city, especially when coming into Leeds, but I don't think this will do anything. I can't see anyone coming to Leeds to see it."

Two Leeds students in town planning — John Grant and Duncan Shaw — said the design

How we revealed plans for the statue in our September 25 issue.

wouldn't get their stamp of approval.

John said: "It looks like something from Dr. Who when they have some giant monster walking all over the place. It doesn't do anything for me though it's certainly unusual and people will remember it."

BLANK

Duncan added: "The Statue of Liberty has a lot more going for it. There doesn't seem to be a great deal to this. It's rather blank and sexless."

I asked a Leeds policeman what he thought, but he didn't think it was very arresting either.

"It's just a man with his arm at his sides. What it's supposed to be symbolic of I don't know. Nobody will see it apart from people on the trains travelling to Leeds."

Debbie Anderson, of Chapeltown, said: "It looks stupid, people probably won't come back again if they see that thing standing next to the railway!"

rtrait of the artist: London sculptor Antony Gormley with his winning brick statue of a man.

towers of San Gimignano respectively, the towers articulate the landscape, creating eloquent vertical accents with added exotic curiosity. As the artist had perceived, the *Brickman*, an equally eloquent and exotic intervention, would make a fourth vertical in this informal, quotidian urban neighbourhood, in tune not only with the local scale, but also with the local language of brick. The *Brickman* would further create an echo of the demolished factories and streets of back-to-back housing, all formerly built in brick, and bring a symbol of humanity back into dereliction.

News of the *Brickman*'s selection was immediately broadcast on the information board on Leeds station concourse. Letters soon appeared in the local papers, the *Yorkshire Post* and the *Yorkshire Evening Post*, some referring to the work as a 'monster', others as a waste of money, and another claiming that the vote was a sham. Immediate support, however, came from the *Yorkshire Post*, in a leader by their veteran art critic, Bill Oliver who, forty years earlier, had written the first article in a national paper supporting Henry Moore when he and his work were facing public misunderstanding at best, and vilification at worst.[10] Bill Oliver's *Brickman* article was echoed by reports in *The Times* and the *Daily Mail*.[11]

To build the *Brickman*, the Holbeck Triangle Trust, chaired by Martin Arnold, was formed as a dependent part of YCAG, with office accommodation supplied by BR above Leeds City Station.[12] We hoped that media comment would die down across this 'research and development' period, as indeed it did; but we were perhaps naively unaware of the opposition that was beginning to brew beneath the surface.

10 'Travelling Man', *Yorkshire Post*, 3 October 1986. Further Bill Oliver articles in the *Yorkshire Post* 17 September 1986 and 3 October 1986.
11 'A Liberty for Leeds', *Daily Mail*, 3 October 1986; *The Times*, 13 October 1986.
12 Trustees: Martin Arnold, Sir Hugh Casson, Lord Feversham, Richard Francis, Ernest Hall, Peter Hirschmann, Robert Hopper, David Perry.

5. Antony Gormley, early 1980s. Leeds Museums and Galleries, Henry Moore Institute Archive (photograph: Vicken Parsons).

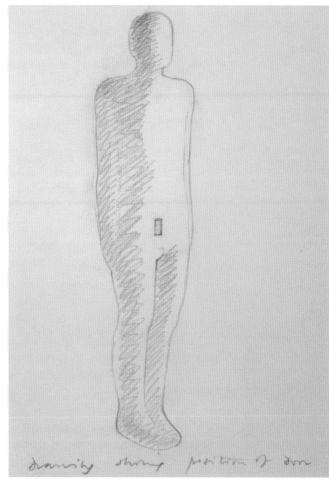

6.   Antony Gormley (b. 1950), Maquette for the Leeds *Brickman*. Fired clay, cement and fibreglass, 1986. 195 × 51 × 34 cm. Leeds Art Gallery, purchased with the aid of a grant from the MGC/V&A Purchase Grant Fund, 1987. 1987.0036. Leeds Museums and Galleries, Henry Moore Institute Archive (photographer unknown).

7.   Antony Gormley, Drawing for *Brickman*, showing position of door. Pencil on paper, 1988. 28 × 18.5 cm. Inscribed: [by artist, bottom] 'Drawing showing position of Door'; [by James Hamilton, top right, cropped], '2nd Revised Drawing/Received 26.2.88', Leeds Museums and Galleries, Henry Moore Institute Archive

In the meantime the Trust enjoyed the companionable and supportive collaboration of Antony Gormley, and the calm efficiency of the administrators Margi Husband, Dianne Cross and Joan West. My task was to raise more money for the project, publicise it, work with the artist and others to see it through its preparatory stages, and ensure it received planning permission. First, we consulted structural engineers, to ensure that the *Brickman* could actually make the transition from six-foot model to 120-foot-high colossus. Approached by Antony Gormley, Ove Arup and Partners, through the agency of their director Duncan Michael, appointed John Thornton to prepare a technical feasibility study. 'A project like the Brick Man', wrote Duncan Michael at the time, 'needs to develop a momentum, a critical mass ... and then to keep going through to completion. I hope that our support would help to ensure that success'.[13]

    The Arup report showed very clearly how the figure could be built, and that the most satisfactory way of constructing it was also the simplest.[14] Taking the artist's

13 Duncan Michael to J. Hamilton, 20 December 1986.
14 John Thornton, *Brickman by Antony Gormley, Holbeck Triangle. Report on Technical Feasibility Study*; Ove Arup, June 1987.

requirements fully into account, Thornton proposed a shell construction, three bricks thick, in Flemish bond and Quetta bond, to be laid 'overhand', from the inside the shell to the outside. It would be reinforced with stainless steel rods from the calves down into fifty-foot-deep foundations. Stainless steel bands would be set at critical points such as the thighs, chest and neck to strengthen the figure, and to function as bones and ribs do in the human body. The artist specified Saxon Antique Orange/Red clamp facing brick from Lancashire, as best meeting the structural and aesthetic problems posed by the *Brickman*. That it was to be Lancashire brick, despite an early announcement that local brick would be used, caused consternation in the Yorkshire press, and came to give the *Brickman*'s enemies additional ammunition.[15]

South Leeds is in the wide bowl of the Aire Valley stretching from the Woodhouse Ridge at the north to the M62 to the south. This is an exceptionally strong landscape, in which the sculpture, which would face south, would be but a dot, one tiny element among many, and no threat to the visual integrity of the whole. Planning permission was first sought in June 1988, when it was deferred 'to enable wider public discussion . . . and to enable more appropriate viewpoints of the statue to be prepared by the applicants'.[16] The *Independent*, reporting this, stressed that the Holbeck Triangle Trust was building for posterity, while the *Yorkshire Evening Post*, rightly in retrospect, claimed that with the deferral the *Brickman* project 'ran into trouble'.[17] With its implication that the decision might hang in the balance, this deferral prompted the Secretary-General of the Arts Council, Luke Rittner, to write to Leeds City Council expressing his concern at the delays to a project which 'marked an important step in inner city regeneration'.[18] Then the letters rolled in to the press again: 'Brick Monstrosity'; 'The Man's a Brick'; 'Brick Man a Landmark' and so on. The Leeds Urban Development Corporation weighed into the issue, but soon weighed out again by passing the decision on to the planning committee.[19]

As advocate for the *Brickman*, the Holbeck Triangle Trust organised an exhibition at Leeds City Art Gallery (29 September to 23 October 1988) to further raise public consciousness and encourage support for the plan (fig. 8). The show, which transferred subsequently to St Matthew's Community Centre in Holbeck, comprised the maquette, a large model of the Holbeck Triangle, a history of the project, photographs of the site with the *Brickman* montaged onto it, and further supporting material. Antony Gormley contributed his statement about the work:

The sculpture is a brick building in the form of a standing man. It is an object not a representation, which by using architecture as a metaphor suggests that the body is a site for the spirit. The sculpture is a powerful, enduring and universal image made of traditional local materials with the aid of modern technology. Its significance rests as much in its relationship to the surrounding industrial landscape of south Leeds and to Leeds' geographical position as central to the main island of Britain as it does to the space contained within the work.

The Trust's press release echoed Gormley's words, and enlarged upon how the *Brickman* would be built. It also made clear that the funding had by now been guaranteed from a local business source:

It is a breathtaking concept that will create a landmark for Leeds for centuries to come . . . It is a sculpture that will capture the imagination, challenge, excite and stimulate . . . The money used to build the Holbeck Sculpture — approximately £600,000 — will be new money tapped from new sources. It is not our desire to direct funds from other projects in the city, on the contrary it is envisaged that the investment will act as a 'pump primer', stimulating the flow of capital into the urban environment.[20]

15 For example *Yorkshire Evening Post*, 26 September 1988.
16 Director of Planning's Report, as in note 5, para 3.06.
17 Ian Williams, 'Permission to stand', *Independent*, 4 July 1988; *Yorkshire Evening Post*, 29 June 1988.
18 Luke Rittner to Councillor Walker, 9 July 1988.
19 Cllr Walker to J. Hamilton, 17 September 1988.
20 Exhibition Press Release, Sept–Oct 1988.

Outside the gallery a large banner advertised the show, and, driving around Leeds, was a decorated bus advertising the Art Gallery, with the Brickman shown walking down the stairs (fig. 9).[21] While the bus decoration lasted some months, the rapid removal of the banner (reportedly on the instructions of the Leader of the Council) revealed conflict within the city.[22] Councillor Bryan Walker, Chair of the Planning Committee, commented: 'We're split. The city's split, the committee's split, I even feel split myself'.[23]

Conflict over the *Brickman*, which appeared to spread across the Council and among its members and officers, was hinted at by Denis Healey, the former Chancellor of the Exchequer, Deputy Leader of the Labour Party, and MP for Leeds East. In conversation, Healey was equivocal

I'm not against your scheme. In fact I think it could be a very good thing. But it might be a disaster. That's the worry. It could either be a great triumph or a disaster. And then the people of Leeds would have to live with it ... It wouldn't affect me because I only come up once a month, and live in London ... Something also that worries me is its effect on children. It might frighten them, seeing it in the dusk and rising up in the morning.[24]

The views of other political figures reflected still more caution. Keith Hampson MP (Leeds North West) wrote:

I have been somewhat agnostic about a 120' brick man. It is not to me at least the best symbol for the regeneration of Leeds. What I favour would be a symbol that pulls the community together rather than one which produces such hostility in large measure.[25]

8. *The Holbeck Sculpture Exhibition*, Leeds City Art Gallery, September–October 1988. Installation view, with maquette. Leeds Museums and Galleries, Henry Moore Institute Archive (photographer unknown).

21 *Yorkshire Evening Post*, 21 January 1988.
22 William Packer, *Financial Times*, 11 October 1988.
23 Martin Wainwright, as in note 1.
24 From J. Hamilton memorandum of meeting with Denis Healey, 7 October 1988, Scarcroft Labour Rooms, Leeds.
25 Keith Hampson MP to J. Hamilton, 28 July 1988.

9. *First Stop for Brickman.*
Press cuttings from
Yorkshire Evening Post,
21 January 1988. Henry
Moore Institute Archive
2010.135. Published with
the permission of
Yorkshire Post
Newspapers.

First stop for brick man

THE controversial brick man of Holbeck, a 120ft Colossus planned for South Leeds, is about to make his first appearance in the city — on the side of a bus.

The huge structure, which is being planned next to the railway line south of Leeds City Station, is shown on a bus which has been specially decorated to mark the 100th anniversary of Leeds City Art Gallery.

The brainchild of Wakefield-based graphic designer Steve Denham, the design on the side of the bus appears to peel back to reveal its contents.

A day of children's events is being held at the Art Gallery in The Headrow on Saturday when the special guest will be Bob Holness, host of TV quiz show *Blockbusters*.

Starting from 10 am, there will be morris dancers, sculpture and print workshops, exhibitions, a steel band, a pipe and drum band, quizzes, prizes and free gifts.

The bus will be given an official send-off and a giant birthday cake will also be on show. YEP. 21·1·88

Giant step for the big brickie

The incredible brick hulk is just a step — though admittedly a very large one considering his size — away from becoming Leeds' most prominent citizen.

A couple of weeks ago City Beat promised to bring you news, as soon as it was available, of the progress of the scheme to build a 100ft statue of a man on a piece of land in the middle of railway lines near Leeds City Station.

Mr James Hamilton, director of the Leeds-based Yorkshire Contemporary Art Group, has now returned from London where artist Anthony Gormley briefed him on the latest situation.

Mr Hamilton told me structural engineers are currently putting the last touches to their final report and an application for planning permission is likely to go before Leeds City Council in July.

"We would hope to start on site in April and the statue will probably take about a year to build," he said.

"The cost is still not totally clear but it won't be as large as I thought at first. The engineers feel there are no real problems, as it is a simple structure like a chimney and only a small number of men will be working on it."

The group plans to start a public appeal to help to finance the world's funniest-shaped "chimney" as soon as planning permission is granted. Large sums have already been pledged by the city council, British Rail and others.

Mr Hamilton said most Leeds people were behind the project, despite the statue's controversial design.

"I've had great support from people wanting us to get on with it. Yes it is controversial, but all good things are."

196   ANTONY GORMLEY'S BRICKMAN

The former Home Secretary Merlyn Rees MP (Morley and Leeds South) wrote in favour of the *Brickman*, while adding that he 'wouldn't go to the stake for it'.[26] However, Derek Fatchett MP (Leeds Central, the constituency in which the Holbeck Triangle stands) emphasised, in his letter of support, that the sculpture 'would play a significant part in putting Leeds on the national and international artistic map'.[27]

Further strong support came from within the arts community. Lord Harewood, local grandee, art collector and former Director of the Edinburgh Festival and Chair of Covent Garden, described the proposal as

a really strong, imaginative concept ... The way into great cities by train can often have a depressing look about them, as if everything nearby had wanted to turn its back on the railway, but Leeds already provides a rather better 'first view' than many other cities. What an achievement it would be to have a landmark of this kind in the Holbeck Triangle![28]

Yorkshire-born novelist Margaret Drabble thought the design was

wonderful, and would add greatly to the Leeds landscape. It is most imaginative, and I am sure people would travel miles to see it — I know I would ... There are so few large scale, grand, exciting structures of this sort, and I think they raise the spirits enormously.[29]

Patrick Nuttgens, architect, academic and champion of Leeds, wrote of the 'spectacular' *Brickman*. He expressed his 'unhesitating support':

Gormley's Brickman ... will make a stunning contribution to the life of a great city, already celebrated for its supreme artistic and architectural innovations. I believe the sculpture will be entirely appropriate and add a new dimension to a celebrated city.[30]

The President of the Royal Academy, Sir Roger de Grey, added his voice:

I support the whole scheme with enormous and unbounded enthusiasm. Antony Gormley is a fine sculptor and the city of Leeds will gain enormously in prestige by this highly imaginative brick sculpture ... I have no doubt this sculpture will become a popular landmark and in due course a popular place for pilgrims to visit.[31]

In the *Daily Mail* Keith Waterhouse asserted staunch support:

The Colossus of Leeds will be a tonic not only for the city but for the nation, and the Brickman has my blessing with but one cavil — rather than be constructed of new brick, he should be built of old bricks from the acres of terrace homes laid waste by that same planning committee which is now humming and hawing over making a constructively outrageous decision for a change ... He isn't for anything, save for the cause of cheering us all up.[32]

On the other hand, Kevin Grady, director of the Leeds Civic Trust, expressed reservations. While broadly welcoming the proposal, Dr Grady pointed out that the sculpture's 'value would be much enhanced if access to the site could be opened up, so that people could quite literally visit the Brickman'; and that the adjacent towers should be 'cleaned and restored and the immediate vicinity laid out as a small park or square'. 'Generally', he added, 'Trust members were unimpressed with the sculpture on aesthetic grounds, but if the other deficiencies can be remedied perhaps it is a feature of the city which will grow on them.'[33]

The visitor's book in the exhibition recorded 1060 comments, of which 699 were in favour of the project, and 189 against:[34] 'The most impressive and awe-inspiring endeavour I have come across. Unequalled'; 'Yes, Yes, Yes. Leeds (and the nation) will be thankful in years to come'; 'I've travelled past that derelict patch for 20 years: I do enjoin, plead, that this imaginative scheme goes ahead'.[35]

26 Letter not in file, J. Hamilton recollection.
27 Quoted in Director of Planning's report, as in note 3, para 4.02.
28 Lord Harewood to J. Hamilton, 30 August 1988.
29 Margaret Drabble to J. Hamilton, 5 September 1988.
30 Patrick Nuttgens to J. Hamilton, 17 September 1988.
31 Roger de Grey to J. Hamilton, 20 September 1988.
32 Keith Waterhouse, 'The Brick Colossus', Daily Mail, 1 September 1988.
33 Kevin Grady to Cllr Brian Walker, 12 October 1988.
34 282 were 'no comment' and other impartial entries.
35 Comments from, respectively, D. MacGregor, Leeds; Leon Collins, Leeds; and Garth Pratt, Huddersfield.

As the exhibition ended, Joan Bakewell drew attention to the matter nationally in advance of the planning meeting. In the *Sunday Times* she summed up the history of the scheme and added:

Nobody has attempted it before. Structural engineers, bricklayers, builders have all been involved in solving the huge technical problems. How did they build the Sphinx? How did Eiffel erect his tower? That's the scale of the problem that has been set and solved. The excitement surrounding the project itself is keen. And there's a sense that Brickman could become the city's symbol. They once poured scorn on Sydney Opera House. Now it's on every postcard . . . Leeds has a great opportunity. Members of the planning committee should stride into their meeting proud and excited by the challenge. And make the right decision.[36]

However, in the days running up to the planning meeting the *Yorkshire Evening Post* organised a telephone poll on the proposal, one that appears to have been heavily influenced by the impression given by the paper that the £600,000 required to construct the sculpture would come from public funds. As a result, of the 3,114 votes registered, 2,284 were against the proposal and 830 in favour.[37] In response, the Leader of Leeds Council, Councillor George Mudie, expressed the view prevailing in Leeds' political circles: 'I am delighted but not surprised with the formidable common sense of the Leeds public. The result demonstrates that the scheme should not go ahead. Their common sense contrasts sharply with the airy-fairy views of celebrities who don't live within 100 miles of the city'.[38]

That effectively sealed the project's fate (fig. 10). In setting out his recommendations to the South Divisional Plans Sub-Committee to aid its decision, the Council's Director of Planning recommended that permission be refused firstly because it would be, 'alien in form and out of scale and character with its surroundings and with the buildings in the immediate vicinity . . . [and] seen to dominate by reason of its height, bulk and overall appearance the listed buildings in Globe Road (Tower Works) and Marshall Street.'

Secondly, there was no evidence from the business or development community that the *Brickman* would assist in the regeneration of Holbeck currently underway: 'in the opinion of the Local Planning Authority the proposed sculpture will detract from the overall character and appearance of this regeneration area to the detriment of future investment.'

Thirdly, no adequate measures have been put forward to serve the public interest; there was no public parking indicated, no means for pedestrian access or public viewing, and no proposals that would positively link this site to other regeneration and redevelopment sites in the vicinity.

Planning permission was refused by seven votes to one. YCAG's response described it as

a sad and disappointing decision by Leeds Planning Committee. They have been offered a monument of world significance, in unique surroundings, and they refused it in the face of worries about access, car parking, and fears that it might dominate its surroundings. The Committee's advisers make no positive effort to see the value of the sculpture in terms of its potential as a unique attraction and embellishment for Leeds. Far from dominating listed buildings, the sculpture blends with and complements them, and would surely be a prime candidate for listed building status itself in time . . . The Committee fears that the work would be too popular . . . and this has prevented the officers from looking at ways around the site access and parking problem which a bit of lateral thinking and rational discussion would solve.

36 Joan Bakewell, 'Vote to cement history', *Sunday Times*, 30 October 1988.
37 *Yorkshire Evening Post*, 19.10.88 and 20.10.88. The validity of the poll was later castigated by MORI, Peter Hutton to J. Hamilton, 26 October 1988.
38 *Yorkshire Evening Post*, 20 October 1988.

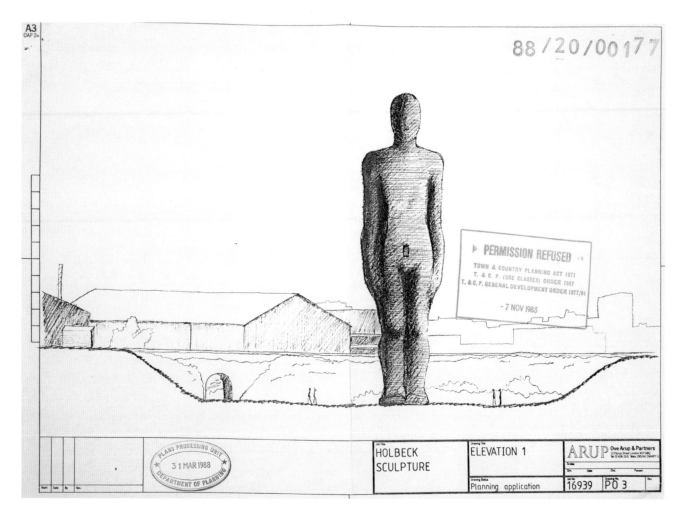

Fallout in the press split along predictable lines. Regretting the decision, the *Yorkshire Post* commented:

It seems a pity that the proposal for a 120-foot-high brick statue of a man has been tripped up by nothing more evocative and compelling than one city's local planning committee ... Could it be that policy makers shrank at the last moment from the risk of creating a brick folly? ... There never was much chance of the brick man becoming a civic monument. But he might have provided a marker of sorts, a kind of urban lighthouse which informed (forewarned?) visitors that the shapeless agglomeration of buildings arriving next to platform X or Y was in fact Leeds.[39]

The *Yorkshire Evening Post*, on the other hand, had no sympathy:

After messages of support from the great and the good, it has fallen to members of the local planning committee to scupper plans for the Brickman of Holbeck. Which is exactly as it should be. ... From the outset too little thought was given to environmental considerations. The Brickman's backers cannot now complain if, for that reason, it has failed.[40]

Antony Gormley criticised the planners for their 'lack of vision', and spoke eloquently about Leeds' perception of itself. The planners 'clearly have a more timid idea of the city's future than me. Leeds had a chance to make a public statement about its existence. It will regret this decision'.[41]

Twenty-seven years on, it is clear where some mistakes were made by the scheme's advocates. Councillors, opinion formers such as Leeds Civic Trust, and the press were not sufficiently lobbied to make it quite clear that the construction of

10. Ove Arup and Partners, Holbeck Sculpture: Elevation drawing within planning permission application documents: Permission Refused, 7 November 1988. Leeds Museums and Galleries, Henry Moore Institute Archive.

39 'Dreams and dust', *Yorkshire Post*, 8 November 1988.
40 'No home for Brick Man', *Yorkshire Evening Post*, 8 November 1988.
41 David Marsh, 'What next in the Brick Man saga?', *Yorkshire Evening Post*, 8 November 1988.

the *Brickman* would not have been a drain on public funds. In retrospect, Joan Bakewell's article, effectively telling the committee what to do, may have been counter-productive in the febrile Yorkshire-centric political mentality of the time. Further, the title of the work was probably a mistake, the more so in the years immediately following the Yorkshire Ripper murders in Leeds and Sheffield. Gender politics in Leeds were powerful in the late 1980s.

As Antony Gormley suggested, the Planning Committee appears to have found the pioneering role thrust upon them difficult to handle. The City Council, seemingly cowed by some parts of the press and a small but vocal public opinion, had allowed an issue that had city-wide and national significance to be determined by a sub-committee, rather than its main Planning Committee. A letter received some days after the fatal planning meeting expressed severe local disappointment: 'As a native of Leeds I find it deeply shaming to be associated by proxy with such a classic act of weary Northern nihilism ... There are more people on your side than may be apparent at the moment'.[42] Derek Fatchett MP astutely concluded, 'I feel it is partly an attempt by the City Council to avoid the ultimate decision. I sense that they would be very happy if you exercised your right to appeal and then they could say that the final decision was taken by the Secretary of State'.[43]

However, by then we felt knocked about and had other things to do, one being the ultimately mishandled attempt to find a site for the work in another city. Insularity and old-fashioned conservatism in Leeds, the kind that in the 1980s found unopposed objection to 'airy-fairy views of celebrities', and an unwillingness to foresee local benefits that have surely followed to the north east in the wake of the *Angel of the North*, all combined to kill the *Brickman* in Leeds.[44]

It is tempting to wonder whether the outcome would have been the same a few years later, once the Albert Dock initiative in Liverpool had proved itself and Birmingham's Symphony Hall and its associated public art had revitalized cultural life in the Midlands. Now, towns and cities from St Ives and Margate to Wakefield and Dundee all exploit art and culture as part of their strategies for regeneration. But bold art and architecture in public places have always aroused strong passions. Dare we believe that the evidence of visitor figures and economic benefits as well as evident public enjoyment have made such a case as the Leeds' *Brickman* a thing of the past?[45]

Acknowledgements

Thanks to Claire Mayoh and Jackie Howson, Henry Moore Institute, Leeds; Martin Arnold; Sir Antony Gormley.

Unless otherwise noted all material referred to here can be found in the Henry Moore Institute Archive, Holbeck Triangle Trust papers given by Martin Arnold (2009.115) and James Hamilton (2010.135)

42 Graham Barker to J. Hamilton, 24 November 1988.
43 Derek Fatchett MP to J. Hamilton, 17 November 1988.
44 See also Doug Sandle, 'Public Art and City Identity – political and cultural issues in the development of public art in the UK city of Leeds', in A. Remesar (ed.), *Waterfronts of Art 2. Art for Social Facilitation.* Monografies socio-ambientals, 30, Barcelona, Universitat de Barcelona, 2000; Miles, M., *Art for Public Places: Critical Essays*, Winchester School of Art, 1989.
45 The *Brickman* still remains controversial in Leeds, an absent but still a dominating presence more than 25 years on. In a letter to the *Guardian* (28 June 2014) Doug Sandle wrote, 'Pointing out that the Angel of the North is inappropriate to represent Leeds (Letters, June 26) only emphasises how the city lost out in rejecting Antony Gormley's proposal for the Leeds Brick Man – twelve years earlier and fifteen metres taller than the Angel'.

The published writings of Terry Friedman

Compiled by Christopher Webster

1970

T. Friedman, 'Romanticism and Neoclassicism for Parlington: The Tastes of Sir Thomas Gascoigne', *Leeds Arts Calendar*, 66, 1970, pp. 16–24.

1971

T. Friedman, 'Aspects of nineteenth century sculpture in Leeds: 1, the Northern Society exhibitions', *Leeds Art Calendar*, 69, 1971, pp. 22–28.

1972

T. Friedman, *Joseph Gott 1786–1860 Sculptor*, Leeds, 1972.
T. Friedman, 'Aspects of nineteenth century sculpture in Leeds: 2, patronage of the Benjamin Gott family', *Leeds Art Calendar*, 70, 1972, pp. 18–25.
T. Friedman, 'James Gibbs's Designs for Domestic Furniture', *Leeds Arts Calendar*, 71, 1972, pp. 19–25.

1973

T. Friedman, *Immortal fame: an anthology of drawings and models for English sculpture*, Leeds, 1973.
T. Friedman, 'John Cheere's busts and statuettes from Kirkleatham Hall', *City of York Art Gallery Quarterly*, 26, 1973, pp. 922–27.
T. Friedman, 'A noble magnificent statue', *Leeds Art Calendar*, 72, 1973, pp. 5–13.
T. Friedman and D. Linstrum, 'A Tour of Architectural Splendour', *Country Life*, 8 February 1973, pp. 334–36.
T. Friedman, *In Praise of James Gibbs*, Leeds, 1973.

1974

T. Friedman, *The Man at Hyde Park Corner: Sculpture by John Cheere 1709–1787*, Leeds, 1974.
T. Friedman, 'Turnerelli's bust of Queen Charlotte' in *Leeds Art Calendar*, 75, 1974, pp. 12–18.

1975

T. Friedman, 'The English Appreciation of Italian Decorations', *Burlington Magazine*, vol. 117, no 873, 1975, pp. 841–47.
T. Friedman and D. Linstrum, *The Artist and the Yorkshire Country House*, Harrogate, 1975.
T. Friedman, 'The Georgian Library', *Leeds Arts Calendar*, 76, 1975, pp. 10–17.
T. Friedman, *Leeds: an Exhibition Celebrating European Architectural Heritage Year*, Leeds, 1975.

1976

T. Friedman, 'Foggini's statue of Queen Anne' in *Kunst des Barock in der Toskana*, Munich, 1976, pp. 39–56.

T. Friedman, 'Sir Thomas Gascoigne and his Friends in Italy', *Leeds Art Calendar*, 78, 1976, pp. 16–23.

T. Friedman, 'A Temple Newsam Mystery Solved', *Leeds Arts Calendar*, 78, 1976, pp. 5–11.

T. Friedman, *Engraved Cards*, Leeds, 1976.

T. Friedman, 'The Ingenious Mr Lodge's View of Leeds', *Leeds Arts Calendar*, 79, 1976, pp. 25–6.

T. Friedman, 'Leeds in 1844', *Leeds Arts Calendar*, 79, 1976, pp. 27–32.

1977

T. Friedman, *The Lumley busts of Tudor sovereigns: from the collection of the Earl of Scarborough*, Rotherham, 1977.

T. Friedman, 'Allegory of Stomer's The Adoration of the Shepherds', *Leeds Arts Calendar*, 81, 1977, pp. 5–9.

1980

T. Friedman, 'Cavalier's Charles II on horseback', *Leeds Art Calendar*, 86, 1980, pp. 4–13.

T. Friedman, 'Samuel Joseph phrenologized', *Leeds Art Calendar*, 86, 1980, pp. 20–28.

T. Friedman, 'Sheemakers's Monument to the Best of sons' in *Burlington Magazine*, vol. 122, no. 922, 1980, pp. 61–67.

1981

T. Friedman, 'Cavalier's Charles II on Horsback', *Leeds Arts Calendar*, 88, 1981, pp. 4–13.
T. Friedman, 'A Convenient and Pleasant Habitation', *Leeds Arts Calendar*, 89, 1981, pp. 5–13.

1982

T. Friedman, *James Gibbs Architect 1682–1754: 'a man of great fame'*, London Borough of Richmond upon Thames, 1982.
A. Garrould, T. Friedman, D. Mitchinson, *Henry Moore: early carvings 1920–1940*, Leeds, 1982.
T. Friedman, 'The Henry Moore Centre for the Study of Sculpture', *Leeds City Art Gallery 1888–1982*, 1982, pp. 17.
T. Friedman, 'Introducing Caro and Paolozzi', *Leeds Art Calendar*, 91, 1982, pp. 21–27.
T. Friedman, 'Rysbrack and Gibbs', in K. Eustace, *Michael Rysbrack: sculptor 1694–1770*, Bristol, 1982, pp. 16–22.

1983

T. Friedman, *The sculpture of Lucy Lyons*, Leeds, 1983.
T. Friedman, *John Farnham: sculpture and drawing*, Leeds, 1983.

1984

T. Friedman, *James Gibbs*, New Haven and London, 1984.
T. Friedman, *Malcolm Woodward: sculpture and drawings*, Leeds, 1984.
T. Friedman, 'Rodin is dead' in T. Knipe (ed.), *Drawing in air: an exhibition of sculptor's drawings 1882–1982*, Sunderland, 1984.
T. Friedman, 'James Parmentier in Leeds: a Newly Discovered Drawing', *Leeds Arts Calendar*, 94, 1984, pp. 3–8.
T. Friedman, *George Meyrick: Six Sculptures*, Leeds, 1984.

1985

T. Friedman, 'A "Beautiful true genteel likeness"', *Leeds Art Calendar*, 97, 1985, pp. 15–22.
T. Friedman, 'Sculpture', in: Wilton-Ely, J, (ed.). *A tercentenary tribute to William Kent*, Hull, 1985.

1986

A. Robertson, M. Remy, M. Gooding, T. Friedman, *Surrealism in Britain in the thirties: angels of anarchy and machines for making clouds*, Leeds, 1986.
T. Friedman, 'Saito: a view from Britain' in, *Yoshishige Saito: Sisyphus*, Japan, 1986, pp. 7–8.
T. Friedman, 'A "Palace worthy of the grandeur of a King": Lord Mar's designs for the Old Pretender', *Architectural History*, 29, 1986, pp. 102–33.
T. Friedman, 'Sculpture in Britain Between the Wars. London', *Burlington Magazine*, vol. 128, no 1003, pp. 764–66.
T. Friedman, *Great Paintings of Victorian Daily Life*, Leeds, 1986.

1987

Friedman, T., Silber, E., et al, *Jacob Epstein: Sculpture and drawings*, Leeds, 1987.

T. Friedman, 'Nost at Rothwell' in *Church Monuments*, II, 1987, pp. 22–31.

1988

T. Friedman, *The Hyde Park atrocity: Epstein's Rima: creation and controversy*, Leeds, 1988.

T. Friedman, 'Elaine Kowalsky and the Henry Moore printmaking fellowship' in N. Walsh, (ed.). *Hearts and vessels: new work by Elaine Kowalsky*, Leeds, 1988.

T. Friedman, 'Journeys' in *Andy Goldsworthy: mountain and coast: autumn into winter: Japan 1987*, Nagoya, 1988, pp. 11–12.

T. Friedman, 'A modernist masterpiece by Maurice Lambert', *Leeds Art Calendar*, 102, 1988, pp. 20–26.

T. Friedman, 'Lord Harrold in Italy 1715–16: Four Frustrated Commissions to Leoni, Juvarra, Chiari and Soldani' in *Burlington Magazine*, vol. 130, no. 128, 1989, pp. 836–45.

1989

R. Ward, N. Walsh and T. Friedman, *Rob Ward: drawings 1977–87: epiphany drawings 1988–1989*, Leeds, 1989.

1990

T. Friedman and A. Goldsworthy (eds.), *Hand to earth: Andy Goldsworthy sculpture 1976–1990*, Leeds, 1990.

1991

T. Friedman, 'The architecture of the square', in *As above so below*, Leeds, 1991, pp. 61–72.

T. Friedman, 'Chronology of a low dishonest decade', in *David Smith: medals for dishonour 1937–1940*, Leeds, 1991, pp. 64–70.

T. Friedman, 'The young Henry Moore in London, Paris and Florence', *Leeds Art Calendar*, 109, 1991, pp. 12–18.

T. Friedman, '"High and Bold Structures": a Georgian Steeple Sampler', *Georgian Group Journal*, 1991, pp. 6–20.

1992

T. Friedman et al, *Eric Gill revealed*, London, 1992.

1993

T. Friedman, *Four centuries of sculptors' drawings from the collection of Leeds City Art Galleries*, Leeds, 1993.

T. Friedman, D. Linstrum, B. Read, D Rooke and D. Upton, *The alliance of sculpture and architecture: Hamo Thornycroft, John Belcher and the Institute of Chartered Accountants' building*, Leeds, 1993.

T. Friedman, 'Herbert Read on Sculpture' in B. Read and D. Thistlewood (eds.), *Herbert Read: a British vision of world art*, Leeds, 1993.

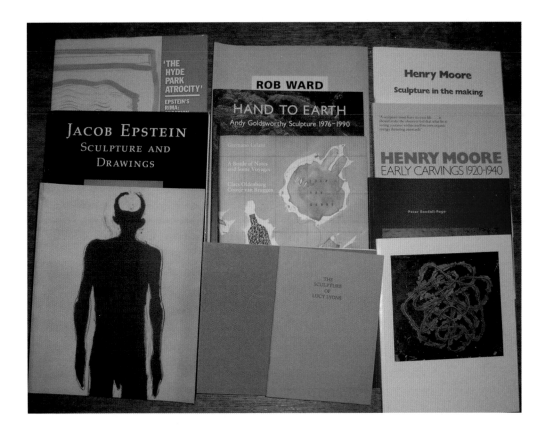

T. Friedman, '"Behold the Proud Stupendous Pile": Eighteenth-Century Reflections of St Paul's Cathedral' in J. Bold and E. Chaney (eds), *English Architecture Public and Private*, London, 1993.

1995

T. Friedman, 'The Transformation of York Minster, 1726–42' in *Architectural History*, 38, 1995, pp. 69–90.

1996

T. Friedman, *Wood: Andy Goldsworthy*, London, 1996.

T. Friedman, 'The Golden Age of Church Architecture in Shropshire' in *Shropshire History and Archaeology*, LXXI, 1996, pp. 83–134.

P. Curtis and T. Friedman (eds.), *Leeds' sculpture collections illustrated concise catalogue*. Leeds, 1996.

1997

T. Friedman, *Church Architecture in Leeds 1700–1799*, Leeds, 1997.

T. Friedman, 'James Wyatt's Earliest Classical Churches', *Georgian Group Journal*, VII, 1997, pp. 56–70.

T. Friedman, 'Oratorial Machines for Furniture Historians', *Furniture History*, 33, 1997, pp. 84–103.

T. Friedman, 'James Gibbs, Thomas Wagg and the Georgian Staircase at 16 Arlington Street', *Over Seas*, Sept.–Nov. 1997, p. 9.

T. Friedman, 'Baroque into Palladian: the designing of St Giles-in-the-Fields', *Architectural History*, 40, 1997, pp. 115–43.

1998

T. Friedman, 'Retrieving lost meanings in Hamo Thornycroft's 'The Mower'', in *Work and the image: the image of the worker in the work of the sculptor*, Leeds, 1998, pp. 2–3.
T. Friedman, 'Gibbs's Library at St Nicholas, Newcastle upon Tyne' in *Architectural History*, 41, 1998, pp. 261–77.
T. Friedman, 'Thomas Hardwick Jr's Early Churches' in *Georgian Group Journal*, VIII, 1998, pp. 43–55.

1999

T. Friedman, '"Demi-gods in Corduroy": Hamo Thornycroft's Statue of *The Mower*', *The Sculpture Journal*, III, 1999, pp. 74–86.

2000

A. Goldsworthy and T. Friedman, *Time: Andy Goldsworthy*, London, 2000.
T. Friedman, 'The Church of St Peter-le-Poer Reconsidered' in *Architectural History*, 43, 2000, pp. 162–71.

2001

T. Friedman, 'St Chad;'s Church, Stafford: A Young and Beautiful Virgin and her Decayed and Doting Husband' in *Architectural History*, 44, 2001, pp. 258–64.

2002

T. Friedman, 'Willey Reveley's All Saints', Southampton' in *Georgian Group Journal*, XII, 2002, pp. 74–93.

2003

T. Friedman, 'The Octagon Chapel, Norwich' in *Georgian Group Journal*, XIII, 2003, pp. 54–77.

2006

T. Friedman, '"The Fate of Sublunary Things": Lives of Medieval Churches in Georgian Times', *Georgian Group Journal*, XV, 2006, pp. 69–87.

2010

T. Friedman, '"An unbound prospect of a very rich country": James Gibbs and Wentworth Castle', in P. Eyres (ed.), *Wentworth castle and Georgian political gardening: Jacobites, Tories and dissident Whigs: the proceedings of the 2010 Wentworth Castle conference*, Northern Heritage Publications, 2010.

2011

T. Friedman, *The Eighteenth Century Church in Britain*, New Haven and London, 2011.
T. Friedman, 'The Progress of Professional Architects in Eighteenth Century Leeds' and 'Thomas Johnson (1762–1814) in C. Webster (ed), *Building a Great Victorian City: Leeds Architects and Architecture 1790–1914*, Huddersfield and London, 2011, pp. 31–42 and 43–60.
T. Friedman, 'John Carter (1748–1817) and the late Georgian struggle for Gothic authenticity' in C. Webster (ed.), *Episodes in the Gothic Revival*, Reading, 2011, pp. 13–44.

T. Friedman, 'Rivalry Between York and Lincoln, or the Art of Georgian Church Paving' in *Georgian Group Journal*, XIX, 2011, pp. 75–93.

2012

T. Friedman, '"an unbounded prospect of a very rich Country": James Gibbs at Wentworth Castle', in P. Eyres (ed.), *Wentworth Castle and Georgian Political Gardening: Jacobites, Tories and dissident Whigs*, Stainborough, 2012, pp. 71–90.

2013

T. Friedman, 'The Rossi Books and England', in A. Antinori (ed.) *Studio d'Architettura Civile*, Rome, 2013, pp. 213–31.

2014

T. Friedman, 'Here art shall reign: a Georgian Enlightenment extravaganza' in *Georgian Group Journal*, XXII, 2014, pp. 95–108.

Acknowledgement

In compiling this list, valuable assistance was provided by Jackie Howson.